THE YALE-HOOVER SERIES ON AUTHORITARIAN REGIMES

GULAG LETTERS

ARSENII FORMAKOV

EDITED, TRANSLATED, AND WITH AN
INTRODUCTION BY EMILY D. JOHNSON

Hoover Institution
Stanford University
Stanford, California

Yale UNIVERSITY PRESS
New Haven and London

Financial support was provided by the Office of the Vice President for Research, the Provost, and the College of Arts and Sciences of the University of Oklahoma.

Letters and photographs from the Arsenii Ivanovich Formakov Papers, Hoover Institution Archive, reprinted by permission of Ausma Polonska, for the estate of Arsenii Formakov.

Correspondence of Aleksandr Solzhenitsyn published with the permission of Natalia Solzhenitsyn.

Yale University Press books may be purchased in quantity for educational, business, or promotional use. For information, please e-mail sales.press@yale.edu (U.S. office) or sales@yaleup.co.uk (U.K. office).

Set in Sabon and Berthold City Bold type by Newgen North America.
Printed in the United States of America.

Library of Congress Control Number: 2016953815
ISBN 978-0-300-20931-0 (hardcover : alk. paper)

A catalogue record for this book is available from the British Library.

This paper meets the requirements of ANSI/NISO Z39.48-1992 (Permanence of Paper).

10 9 8 7 6 5 4 3 2 1

Contents

Acknowledgments

Many people, organizations, and institutions provided help and support as I worked on this project. I am grateful to Julie Cassiday, Alan Barenberg, Golfo Alexopoulos, Carol Ueland, Lazar Fleishman, Mark Harrison, Norman Naimark, and the anonymous readers who evaluated my manuscript for their suggestions for improving the text. Boris Ravdin provided a great deal of assistance in preparation for and during my research trip to Latvia. Dan Healey and Nikita Lomagin both helped when I had questions about archival materials. I am very grateful to have had the opportunity to participate in the Hoover Institution's Summer Research Workshop on Authoritarian Regimes on several occasions. Paul Gregory played a key role in encouraging my work on this project. I am very grateful to Lora Soroka, Carol Leadenham, Eric Wakin, and the staff at the Hoover Institution Archive and Library for their assistance. The staff of the Memorial Society in Moscow, the Scientific-Information Center of Memorial in St. Petersburg, the State Archive of the Russian Federation, the Museum of the Occupation of Latvia in Riga, and the State Archives of Latvia were generous with their time and assistance. Molly Murphy and the staff of the Inter-library Loan Department at the University of Oklahoma's library worked miracles. My parents, Phil and Kathie Johnson and Leith

Johnson and John Martinez, all helped facilitate the research travel required for this project by stepping in at key moments to provide childcare. My daughter Cerria was remarkably patient as I worked on the manuscript. Catharine Nepomnyashchy provided support and advice until her death and is sorely missed.

Funds provided by the National Council for Eurasian and East European Research (NCEEER) and American Councils, under authority of Title VIII grants from the U.S. Department of State, supported the work contained in the Introduction to this volume in part. The views contained in the Introduction are the author's own. Additional financial support for this project was provided by the Hoover Institution, the South Central Modern Language Association, the Oklahoma Humanities Council, and the College of Arts and Sciences, Vice President for Research, Research Council, Provost, and Faculty Senate of the University of Oklahoma. I am grateful to Natalia Solzhenitsyn for granting permission for the publication of the Aleksandr Solzhenitsyn correspondence contained in the Appendix to this volume, and to Ausma Polonska for allowing me to share her family's story.

Note on Transliteration, Punctuation, and Formatting

Although standard Library of Congress transliteration is employed in most places in this book, the spelling of some names (Evgenia, Dmitri, Ananievich, Vertinsky) has been simplified in the interest of accessibility or in keeping with established tradition. The first name Alexander is generally spelled in keeping with English-language norms. In the case of the author Solzhenitsyn, I use the transliteration Aleksandr because this is the name that he published under in English. Places in which the letters have been abridged are marked with a bracketed ellipsis; other ellipses reflect the punctuation used in the original Russian-language text. As a general rule, titles of books and films are provided in transliterated Russian followed by an English translation in brackets or parentheses when first used. In some instances, I have defaulted to the English when these titles reappear, with an eye to making the book more accessible to nonspecialists. Periodical titles (such as *Pravda* and *Izvestiia*) are generally provided in transliterated Russian, as is the norm in most publications. In rare instances where this seems likely to impede the understanding of nonspecialists, I default to English. In the case of some very well known works of literature (such as *One Day in the Life of Ivan Denisovich* and *Dead Souls*), I have opted to omit the transliterated Russian.

Introduction

Emily D. Johnson

ON DECEMBER 2, 1944, a fellow inmate who served as the head of the accounts department at the local outpost of the Krasnoiarskii Labor Camp (Kraslag) ran over to see Arsenii Formakov at the needle-making shop where he worked. "Let's see you dance," he teased, and handed Formakov the postal form that accompanied a wire transfer sent from Riga. Formakov recognized his wife's handwriting, and tears welled up in his eyes as he read the brief, tender note that she had written at the bottom of the form for him: this was the first communication that he had received from her in three and a half years.[1] Within days a real letter followed. For the next three years, until his release from the labor camp in December 1947, Formakov remained in regular communication with his wife and children. The letters that he sent them during this first term in the camps and, to a lesser extent, during a later period of confinement (1949–1955), which today form part of the Hoover Institution Archive's extensive holdings on the history of the Baltic states and the Soviet labor camp system, represent the subject of this volume. These documents offer an immediate eyewitness account of daily life in a typical Soviet labor camp and provide a sense of the difficult choices that inmates faced as they struggled to survive.

1. See Formakov's February 6, 1945, letter to his wife.

The notoriously brutal forced labor system in which Formakov was confined took shape gradually over the first decades of the Soviet period.[2] Although as early as 1918 the Bolshevik government in Moscow began confining those it deemed enemies in camps, initially these detention sites were organized on an ad hoc basis and regimes varied, depending on local circumstances and whether a particular camp was run by the criminal justice system or the secret police. For the most part, early Soviet detention sites aimed to isolate potentially dangerous elements from the rest of Soviet society and, when possible, rehabilitate them. Labor, to the extent that it happened at all amid the chaos of the Civil War (1918–1922) and the difficult period of reconstruction defined by the New Economic Policy (1921–1928), was primarily understood as a means of reforming the prisoners or reducing the expense of running the camp, rather than as a more substantial contribution to the national economy. Until the end of the 1920s, most Soviet labor camps were small and reported to local as opposed to national organs.[3]

A number of factors began to change this situation at the end of the 1920s, leading to the rise of the mass system of forced labor that Formakov would encounter in the 1940s. The crash industrialization campaign introduced with the First Five-Year Plan led to ambitious construction projects and efforts to extract natural resources in distant, forbidding locations that required vast reserves of unskilled labor just as new purges and the ruthless collectivization campaign were increasing the numbers of incarcerated exponentially.[4] Moreover, in the early 1930s, the consolidation of the labor camp system under a new structure within the Soviet People's Commissariat of Internal Affairs

2. For more detailed information on the history of the Soviet labor camp system, see Anne Applebaum, *Gulag: A History* (New York: Anchor Books, 2004); Steven A. Barnes, *Death and Redemption: The Gulag and the Shaping of Soviet Society* (Princeton, NJ: Princeton University Press, 2011); and Oleg V. Khlevniuk, *The History of the Gulag: From Collectivization to the Great Terror* (New Haven: Yale University Press, 2004).

3. *Sistema ispravitel'no-trudovykh lagerei v SSSR. 1923–1960. Spravochnik,* Obshchestvo "Memorial," Gosudarstvennyi Arkhiv Rossiiskoi Federatsii (hereafter GARF) (Moscow: Zven'ia, 1998), 17, 25.

4. Ibid., 27–28; Alan Barenberg, *Gulag Town, Company Town: Forced Labor and Its Legacy in Vorkuta,* The Yale–Hoover Series on Stalin, Stalinism, and the Cold War (New Haven: Yale University Press, 2014), 18; James R. Harris, "The Growth of the Gulag: Forced Labor in the Urals Region, 1929–31," *Russian Review* 56, no. 2 (1997): 265–80.

(NKVD), the Main Administration of Labor Camps (Glavnoe Upravlenie Lagerei, known by the acronym GULAG), allowed for more systematization of camp life and made it possible for the detention system to take on greater economic tasks. Prisoners logged, mined for gold, asbestos, and uranium, built factories, dug canals, and laid railroad tracks—sometimes along routes that later proved useless. Scholars today remain divided as to whether the GULAG's efforts to develop some of the Soviet Union's most forbidding landscapes, regardless of the cost in human lives, ever made economic sense.[5] In one respect, however, this drive clearly succeeded: it spread a model of camp organization and forced labor developed in the 1920s at secret police–run detention sites, including the notorious Solovetsky labor camp, across the length and breadth of the Soviet Union, allowing the penal system to expand and absorb the wave of victims sentenced during the great purges of the late 1930s. Over time, "Gulag" came to signify not just the administrative unit that governed the labor camp system beginning in the 1930s, but also the Soviet penal system as a whole.

By the start of World War II, when Formakov received his first sentence to hard labor, the population confined in Soviet labor camps and colonies stood at 2.3 million.[6] The release and conscription into the army of large numbers of inmates sentenced for petty crimes beginning in the first months of the war, however, soon reduced this total. Viewed as particularly dangerous and potentially traitorous, those left behind in the Soviet Union's camps during the war years faced increasing scrutiny and deteriorating conditions. The war exacerbated the supply problems that the labor camp system had always faced, leading to disastrous shortages of food, clothing, and medicine. Mortality rates soared: according to official Soviet statistics, one in every four inmates in Soviet labor camps and colonies died in 1942, and one in every five in 1943.[7] Nonetheless, inmates faced continual demands that they increase their work output and thereby aid in the war effort.

5. Paul R. Gregory and Valery Lazarev, eds., *The Economics of Forced Labor: The Soviet Gulag* (Stanford, CA: Hoover Institution Press, 2003).

6. "Gulag v gody voiny: Doklad nachal'nika GULAGa NKVD SSSR V. G. Nasedkina, avgust 1944 g.," *Istoricheskii arkhiv*, no. 3 (1994): 64, as cited in Barnes, *Death and Redemption*, 113.

7. GARF, f. 9414, op. 1, d. 328, l. 82, as cited in Barnes, *Death and Redemption*, 116.

Although mortality rates fell sharply after the war, in other respects life in the Gulag became even harder. At new strict-regime "special camps," prisoners sentenced for the most serious crimes endured particularly harsh and dehumanizing conditions, had little opportunity to communicate with the outside world, and worked even longer days.[8] Moreover, even at ordinary camp subdivisions like the ones in which Formakov was held, tensions remained high. The influx into the camp system of individuals hardened by years of war heightened the system's volatility. The career criminals, who had exploited and brutalized political prisoners with the tacit approval of the camp authorities in the prewar era, and even the camp authorities themselves now sometimes faced violent opposition: veterans straight from the front were not easily cowed. A bloody conflict also broke out between those professional thieves who refused to work in deference to the code of the criminal world and those more accommodating to the demands of the system. In part as a result of these tensions, the networks of informants operating within the camp system, which had grown exponentially during the war years, continued to expand: according to some estimates 8 percent of Soviet labor camp inmates were serving as informants by 1947.[9] Informing won inmates the kind of privileges that often meant survival, but it also came with risks: accounts of some survivors luridly describe reprisals against those suspected of reporting to the authorities.[10]

Kraslag, the camp in which Formakov was held from 1941 to 1947, in many respects represented a typical Soviet labor camp and reflected, over the course of its existence, these larger patterns of development. Founded in 1938 and based in the city of Kansk in the Krasnoiarsk region, it was primarily a forestry camp that held a heterogeneous population of about 15,000 inmates during most years of Formakov's internment, including men and women sentenced for a range of politi-

8. Introduced in 1948, special camps (*osobye lageria*) grew out of a harsh regime for priority offenders introduced in 1943 that was known by the old tsarist-era term for forced labor: *katorga*. For a discussion of both *katorga* regime subcamps and special camps of the postwar period, see Barenberg, *Gulag Town, Company Town*, 64–66, 96–104; and Barnes, *Death and Redemption*, 20–21, 164–73.

9. V. N. Zemskov, "GULAG (istoriko-sotsiologicheskii aspekt)," *Sotsiologicheskie issledovaniia*, no. 7 (1991): 3–17, as cited in Barnes, *Death and Redemption*, 182.

10. Aleksandr I. Solzhenitsyn, *The Gulag Archipelago, 1918–1956: An Experiment in Literary Investigation*, 3 vols., trans. Harry Willetts and Thomas P. Whitney (New York: Harper and Row, 1974–1978), 3: 233–48.

cal and criminal offenses, unfortunates condemned to multiyear terms for violating draconian labor laws, and representatives of most of the Soviet Union's major nationalities.[11] Conditions at the subcamps and work sites where these prisoners lived generally counted as average by Gulag standards. During the worst wartime shortages, the death rate rose to 7 or 8 percent a year, a significant figure but far lower than that recorded in detention places farther from supply lines.[12] Like many camps of its size, Kraslag had a Cultural-Educational Sector that organized theatrical performances and film screenings, a transportation depot, bath houses, infirmaries, cafeterias, a postal service, storehouses, and various small manufacturing enterprises and administrative offices. For prisoners who secured jobs indoors in one of these support sectors, life might seem almost bearable. For those out in the cold or heat cutting and hauling logs, it was very hard.

Today Kraslag is often remembered for one aspect of its history. In the 1940s, the camp served as a key detention site for prisoners from Latvia, Lithuania, and Estonia, which were forcibly annexed to the Soviet Union in summer 1940 and subjected to a terrible purge before falling to the Germans in summer 1941. Formakov's letters represent a valuable source of information on the experience of the victims of this reign of terror, particularly as it pertained to Latvia. Written by an ethnically Russian Latvian citizen, they remind us that the human rights abuses that took place in Latvia following Soviet occupation in 1940 and during Soviet efforts to repacify the area after World War II affected citizens from all major ethnic groups, including the large Russian minority that had existed in the area for hundreds of years.

THE CONTEXT OF FORMAKOV'S ARREST

During the interwar period, Formakov (1900–1983) was one of the most prominent cultural figures in the Latvian city of Daugavpils (known as Dvinsk from 1893 to 1920 and in many Russian-language

11. *Sistema ispravitel'no-trudovykh lagerei v SSSR*, 211–21; see also the page created by the Krasnoiarsk affiliate of the human rights society "Memorial": "Chto takoe Kraslag?" http://www.memorial.krsk.ru/FAQ/017.htm.

12. "Chto takoe Kraslag?" For general information on mortality in the camps during the war, see I. V. Bezborodova, Introduction to vol. 4 of *Istoriia Stalinskogo Gulaga: Konets 1920-kh—pervaia polovina 1950-kh godov. Sobranie dokumentov v semi tomakh* (Moscow: Rosspen, 2004), 51–56.

texts from later periods). Part of a community of ethnically Russian Old Believers that had migrated to the area in the seventeenth century, Formakov worked for close to a decade in his twenties as a classroom teacher before securing a post as one of two school inspectors appointed by the Latvian Ministry of Education to oversee the country's Russian-language schools.[13] He also edited and co-owned the city's Russian-language newspaper, *Dvinskii golos* (The Voice of Dvinsk), worked as a journalist for prominent Russian-émigré periodicals based in Latvia and other areas of Europe, and published three books of poetry and two novels. He was active in the Union of Old Believer Councils and Congresses in Latvia (Soveta staroobriadcheskikh soborov i s"ezdov v Latvii), an important political organization for Latvia's Russian minority community in the early 1930s, and participated in the Sokol movement, a network of sporting and social associations popular with Slavic youth in a variety of Eastern European countries that aimed, through regular gymnastic exercise and other cultural programming, to strengthen the whole individual and sustain national consciousness.[14] In Latvia, Sokol organizations sought to prepare young people to work for the future benefit of Mother Russia and tended to attract members with right-wing and even monarchist views.[15]

Formakov's high-profile involvement in the cultural and political life of Latvia's Russian community, the explicitly anti-Soviet character of some of the articles, essays, and fiction that he published in the 1920s and the 1930s, and his work with both the Sokol movement and the Union of Old Believer Councils and Congresses in Latvia made him an

13. Old Believers were schismatics who rejected the reforms that Patriarch Nikon introduced to the Russian Orthodox faith in the seventeenth century. On Latvia's Old Believer community, see Aleksij Žilko and Eduard Mekšs, "Staro-obriadchestvo v Latvii: Vchera i segodnia," *Revue des études slaves* 69, nos. 1–2 (1997): 73–88.

14. On the Union of Old Believer Councils and Congresses in Latvia and Sokol, see Tat'iana Feigmane, *Russkie v dovoennoi Latvii: Na puti k integratsii* (Riga: Baltiiskii russkii institut, 2000), 211, 249. For biographical information on Formakov, see E. B. Meksh, "A. I. Formakov (1900–1983): Biografiia (po vospominaniiam docheri E. Formakovoi," *Baltiiskii arkhiv: Russkaia kul'tura v pribaltike* 7 (2002): 350–60; F. P. Fedorov, "Lirika Arseniia Formakova kak iavlenie provintsial'noi kul'tury," *Russian Literature* 53 (2003): 150–52; and the biographical note in *Vestnik Soveta staroobriadcheskikh soborov i s"ezdov v Latvii*, no. 1 (1931): 19.

15. Feigmane, *Russkie v dovoennoi Latvii*, 215–18.

obvious target for repression when the Soviet Union invaded Latvia in June 1940. During the 1920s and 1930s, special agents of the NKVD kept close tabs on Russian émigré organizations abroad, focusing particular attention on entities operating in countries that bordered the Soviet Union, such as Latvia, and on groups, like Sokol and the Union of Old Believer Councils and Congresses in Latvia, that cultivated ties with similar organizations in other European countries.[16] The NKVD maintained records of individuals associated with each organization, which, once Soviet troops crossed the border, quickly morphed into lists of potential subjects for repressive measures. As recent work by Latvian historians has shown, members of Russian émigré organizations represented some of the earliest victims of the twelve-month-long Soviet reign of terror that followed the June 1940 invasion. Moreover, the Soviet state treated this subset of victims with unusual viciousness: almost a third of those arrested were sentenced to death, damned as members of the "White Guard opposition" for their work with groups that the NKVD deemed hostile and dangerous.[17]

Formakov was arrested on July 30, 1940, just six weeks after Soviet troops occupied Latvia and a few days before the formerly independent nation's incorporation into the Soviet Union. He was, by all accounts, one of the first individuals arrested in Daugavpils. Tossed into the city's investigative prison, he was held for six months in solitary confinement before his tormentors even bothered to call him for interrogation. When he did finally see an interrogator, he broke down quickly and signed the confession to anti-Soviet activities prepared for him: his investigator promised that if he signed, he would be allowed a visit with his wife, who had been pregnant with their second child at the time of his arrest, and, moreover, assured him that he could always recant his statement at trial anyway.[18] Desperate for news of his family's

16. Irēne Šneidere, "Padomju represijas pret Latvijas krieviem 1940. gada vasarā," *Latvijas vēstures institūta žurnāls*, no. 1 (2005): 112–14.

17. Ibid.; Dzintars Ērglis, Irēne Šneidere, Rudīte Vīksne, Arturs Žvinklis, "Padomju represijas Latvijā 1940. gada jūnijā–augustā: struktūranalīze," in *Totalitarian Occupation Regimes in Latvia, 1940–1964: Research of the Commission of the Historians of Latvia, 2003* (Riga: Latvijas Vēstures Institūta Apgāds, 2004), 114–16.

18. See the citation from Formakov's 1959 rehabilitation petition cited by Šneidere: "Padomju represijas pret Latvijas krieviem 1940. gada vasarā," 117–18.

condition, Formakov agreed. He got two brief visits with his wife, as the investigator had promised, and learned that she had given birth to a healthy child—a daughter rather than the son he had imagined based on what he perceived as color clues in a package he received in prison. Formakov never, however, had the chance to recant: there was no trial. Instead his case passed directly to the NKVD's Special Board (Osoboe Soveshchanie) for sentencing, as was common at the time.[19]

Altogether Formakov languished in prison in Daugavpils for eleven months, waiting first for his investigation to get under way and then to learn his sentence. Finally, on June 24, 1941, he was ordered to gather his things and, with a large group of other inmates, was herded onto a truck and moved to the city train station. German forces had invaded the Soviet Union two days before and were advancing on Daugavpils, necessitating a hasty Soviet retreat. In all the chaos, regulations regarding the transport of prisoners broke down; in some cases, prisoners were dispatched without their files and moved in open trucks that did not isolate them from the surrounding population.[20] As he passed through Daugavpils, Formakov was able to see the windows of his family's apartment and even exchanged words with an acquaintance.[21] He had heard the first German bombs explode while still in the Daugavpils prison. Moved east in a cattle car, he and the other prisoners peered through chinks in the hopes of glimpsing something that would provide information about the progress of the war. The train slowly traveled past Smolensk, Kulikovo Field, and Lev Tolstoy station, to Samara, Ufa, and then on to a transit prison in Krasnoiarsk, where Formakov spent a month before being dispatched by barge to Eniseisk. Several months later, he was transferred to Kraslag in Kansk.[22] He had, he learned at last, received an eight-year term at hard labor.

19. On the NKVD's Special Board, see J. Arch Getty and Oleg V. Naumov, *The Road to Terror: Stalin and the Self-Destruction of the Bolsheviks, 1932–1939*, trans. Benjamin Sher (New Haven: Yale University Press, 1999), 5, 122–24, 192, 547; and Solzhenitsyn, *Gulag Archipelago*, 1: 281–86.

20. On the chaos accompanying the last deportations prior to German occupation, see Irēne Šneidere, "The Fate of Latgale Civilians in the Camps and Prisons after the Arrest on 14 June 1941," *Deportation of 14 June 1941: Crimes against Humanity. Conference Reports. Abstracts* (Riga: State Archives of Latvia, 2001), 236–37.

21. See Formakov's letter to his wife dated November 9, 1944.

22. See Formakov's letter to his wife dated July 28, 1944.

From the moment he left Daugavpils, Formakov was frantic for news of his wife and children. Had the family been evacuated from the city before the Nazis seized it? Had they been arrested by the Soviet secret police and deported to some other part of the Soviet Union in the days before the German invasion, as the families of most political prisoners in Latvia were? Formakov wrote from Kansk to the Central Information Bureau on the Affairs of the Evacuated in Buguruslan and to other Soviet agencies in an effort to secure information but had no luck locating them.[23] Until summer 1944, when Soviet troops were on the verge of recapturing Daugavpils, he could not send mail directly to Latvia to make inquiries. As soon as this changed, he began writing to every address he could recall, hoping for some news of their fate. Thanks to blind luck, he managed to find them relatively quickly. An old acquaintance saw a letter that Formakov had addressed to general delivery in Daugavpils at the post office, and wrote back to tell him that his wife and children were in Riga, living with his in-laws. Within a few months he had reestablished regular communication.

LABOR CAMP LETTERS AS HISTORICAL AND LITERARY SOURCES

This book includes many of the letters that Formakov exchanged with his family between 1944 and 1947, while he was interned in Kraslag, and also a handful of communications from the early 1950s, when he was in a labor camp in Omsk following a second arrest in 1949. Some of the letters passed through the official camp postal system and bear stamps showing that they were inspected by the camp censorship office. Others were smuggled out of the camp by free laborers or "de-convoyed" inmates, who enjoyed the trust of the camp administration and could travel beyond the confines of the camp without an armed escort.[24] Predictably, in such illegal communications, Formakov is more frank in his descriptions of camp life and his account of the strategies that he relies upon for survival. He explains how he smuggles letters

23. See Formakov's letter to his wife dated January 1, 1945.
24. On the privileges that de-convoyed inmates enjoyed and their role as intermediaries between labor camps and the world outside, see Wilson T. Bell, "Was the Gulag an Archipelago? De-convoyed Prisoners and Porous Borders in the Camps of Western Siberia," *Russian Review* 72 (January 2013): 116–41.

out of camp, recounts near fatal accidents at work, details his efforts to recover his health following bouts of bloody diarrhea brought on by nutritional deprivation and overwork, and acknowledges hunger and shortages more explicitly. Even in illegal communications, however, Formakov does not convey the full horror of the camp world to his relations. He never mentions the physical abuse that represented a routine element of interrogations; the many inmates who died of hunger, thirst, and exposure in the cattle cars that slowly conveyed them to their places of internment; or the guards, dogs, and punishment cells that terrorized the camp population. From his letters, in fact, it might almost appear that Soviet labor camp inmates lived in conditions that differed little from those experienced by much of the country's free population during World War II and the famine of 1946–1947. After all, in these periods, Soviet citizens outside the camps also often starved to death, worked grueling shifts in dangerous conditions, and experienced desperate shortages of clothing, consumer goods, housing, and fuel.

Formakov's reticence in describing life in the Soviet Union's labor camps and prisons represents a standard feature of labor camp correspondence from the period. Even in letters that they sent illicitly, inmates rarely risked making even vague allusions to the culture of violence that represented the defining characteristic of the Soviet labor camp and prison system. Inmates knew that censors inspected the camp mail and that writing too frankly about conditions might lead not just to the confiscation of the letter but also to the loss of privileges, days spent in punishment cells, an abrupt transfer to a special camp for those who had violated regulations, or, in severe cases, new charges of anti-Soviet agitation. Moreover, even illegal communications were not necessarily private. In the Soviet Union during the Stalin period, all mail was subject to censorship. During World War II, special military censorship bureaus were supposed to inspect and stamp all regular correspondence sent to and from areas of the Soviet Union operating under martial law. Even in other periods, as at least some prisoners would have known, secret NKVD-run censorship offices within post offices read mail sent by and to individuals deemed of interest, and some portion of the mail sent by ordinary civilians.[25] This elaborate system of checks encour-

25. A. S. Smykalin, *Perliustratsiia korrespondentsii i pochtovaia voennaia tsenzura v Rossii i SSSR* (St. Petersburg: Iurid. Tsentr press, 2008); V. S. Izmozik, *Glaza*

aged self-censorship. Afraid of getting themselves or, worse yet, their relatives into more trouble, inmates wrote carefully and remained silent about many aspects of their experience.

Personal factors also encouraged both prisoners and their relations to refrain from revealing many hard truths. Often each correspondent hoped to ease the other's anxiety and, by focusing on the positive, shore up his or her morale. During the difficult war and postwar years that coincided with Formakov's first camp sentence, prisoners received enough information about events outside from Soviet propaganda and the first-hand accounts of new arrivals to know that their relatives might be living amid ruins and have little to eat themselves.[26] Did it really make sense to describe the full horror of your circumstances when there was probably nothing your family could do to help? Inmates were sometimes so alarmed by reports of Nazi atrocities, ruined cities, and food shortages that they tried to help their families. In his letters, Formakov offers to send money home to his wife several times, and this is by no means exceptional: many inmates wired small sums from their camp accounts at least once or twice; some even tried to smuggle clothing and food out of camp to their relations.[27]

Relatives outside the camps also often omitted facts about their own lives in the letters that they mailed to prisoners with the aim of alleviating anxiety or sparing grief. For instance, during Formakov's second term in the camps, his by-then-teenage son Dmitri drowned while swimming in a local river. Formakov's wife concealed this information from him for over a year out of concern that the news would destroy

---

i ushi rezhima: Gosudarstvennyi politicheskii kontrol' za naseleniem Sovetskoi Rossii v 1918–1928 godakh (St. Petersburg: Izdanie Sankt-Peterburgskogo Universiteta Ekonomiki i Finansov, 1995).

26. On living conditions in the Soviet Union during the war, see Mark Harrison, "The Soviet Union: The Defeated Victor," in *The Economies of World War II: Six Great Powers in International Comparison,* ed. Mark Harrison (Cambridge: Cambridge University Press, 1998), 290–92.

27. During the war, the camp system recognized inmates' desires to send support home as legitimate. An NKVD circular issued in January 1944 authorized inmates to send up to half the funds in their camp accounts home to their relations: "Tsirkuliar No. 6 ot 7 ianvaria 1944," GARF, f. 9401, op. 1a, d. 117, l. 12. For an instance in which an inmate tried to procure winter clothing for a loved one outside the camp, see letter from Petr Lazutin to Larisa Beskodarnaia dated October 29, 1945, Memorial Society Archive, Moscow, f. 1, op. 1, d. 2614, l. 70.

his morale.[28] Relatives routinely tried to reassure inmates that they were managing fine, even when they faced persecution for their association with an "enemy of the people" and struggled to retain employment or scarce housing space.

Given how guarded labor camp letters usually are, one might assume that these documents hold little promise as sources for historical inquiry. Such correspondence, it is true, will not provide substantial new evidence of the human rights abuses that occurred in the Soviet Union during the Stalin era; it contains nothing to equal the devastating scenes of horror described by Aleksandr Solzhenitsyn, Varlam Shalamov, Eugenia Ginzburg, and other survivors of the Soviet penal system who began to write memoirs and works of fiction chronicling their experiences during the brief period of liberalization following Stalin's death in 1953 known as the Khrushchev Thaw. In fact, read alone, outside the context of the larger canon of literature describing Soviet mechanisms of repression, private labor camp correspondence might reasonably count as misleading: because they systematically omit references to physical coercion and violence, these documents make the camp experience seem less awful than it was.

No source of information about Stalinist mechanisms of repression, however, is perfect. Works of fiction and, indeed, memoirs that describe Stalin-era labor camps rely so heavily on literary models that one cannot take them as an exact, factual account of past events and conditions. In writing about their experiences, the first great chroniclers of the Stalinist labor camp system, including Gustaw Herling, Solzhenitsyn, Shalamov, and Ginzburg, made use of descriptive and structural clichés drawn from earlier literary works set wholly or in part in prisons, including the most important prison text for Russian authors, *The House of the Dead*, the novel that Fyodor Dostoevsky wrote based on his experiences at hard labor in the 1850s. Similarly, later generations of Gulag chroniclers tended to hew closely to the models established by Herling, Solzhenitsyn, Shalamov, and Ginzburg: in memoirs and interviews produced during the late Soviet and post-Soviet periods, survivors often explicitly reference descriptions of the camp system by their best-known predecessors or unconsciously in-

28. Meksh, "A. I. Formakov (1900–1983)," 356.

terpolate sections of earlier accounts into their own memories.[29] Like Ginzburg, Olga Adamova-Sliozberg describes glancing in a mirror at a bath house during mandatory disinfection procedures following transport from a prison to a labor camp and failing to recognize herself at first: instead she finds her mother's face gazing back at her.[30] Similarly, Formakov himself, in a lightly fictionalized Gulag memoir that he began to write, most likely in the 1960s or 1970s, borrowed liberally from the best-known account of the camp system legally published in the Soviet Union during the Thaw period, Solzhenitsyn's *One Day in the Life of Ivan Denisovich*. Known to the Formakov family as "Byloe" (Bygone Days), this fragmentary, unpublished text survives today only in xeroxes of a hand-edited typescript.[31]

In reference to such cases, one can argue that over time the established canon of Gulag literature partly subsumed individual memories, leaving collective myth and literary constructs in the place of personal histories. Of course, in a larger sense, as Maurice Halbwachs notes, for all of us, "the framework of collective memory confines and binds our most intimate remembrances to each other."[32] Signs of this dependence, however, become more obvious when individuals understand

29. Leona Toker discusses the standard features of Gulag memoirs as a genre in *Return from the Archipelago: Narratives of Gulag Survivors* (Bloomington: Indiana University Press, 2000), 73–100.

30. Eugenia Ginzburg, *Journey into the Whirlwind* (San Diego: Harvest Books, 1995), 315; Olga Adamova-Sliozberg, *My Journey*, excerpted in Simeon Vilensky, ed., *Till My Tale Is Told: Women's Memoirs of the Gulag*, trans. John Crowfoot, Marjorie Farquharson, Catriona Kelly, Sally Laird, and Cathy Porter (Bloomington: Indiana University Press, 1999), 47.

31. The copy in the Hoover Institution Archive lacks a title page, so I list its traditional title provisionally: Arsenii Ivanovich Formakov Papers, Box 1, folder 14, pp. 18, 38. Compare with Alexander Solzhenitsyn, *One Day in the Life of Ivan Denisovich*, trans. Ralph Parker (New York: Signet Classics, 1998), 95, 109. Note also how Feliks Arkadievich Serebrov weaves literary references into his account of his labor camp terms: "Bridging Separate Worlds: Interview with Feliks Arkadievich Serebrov," conducted and introduced by Emily D. Johnson, trans. Elizabeth Stine and Katherine R. Jolluck, in *Gulag Voices: Oral Histories of Soviet Incarceration and Exile*, ed. Jehanne M. Gheith and Katherine R. Jolluck (New York: Palgrave Macmillan, 2011), 169–89.

32. Maurice Halbwachs, *On Collective Memory*, trans. and ed. Lewis A. Coser (Chicago: University of Chicago Press, 1992), 53.

themselves to be providing testimony on a large-scale cultural turning-point or tragedy. In such instances, the boundaries between personal and collective experience blur: authors feel compelled to speak for a larger community and may not want to confine themselves to describing what happened to them personally. Instead, consciously or unconsciously, they craft narratives that read as model illustrations of a shared past. Fragments of stories culled from the testimony of earlier witnesses that seem particularly expressive of the common lot blend with individual recollections; in the pursuit of a higher, symbolic truth, writers may sacrifice fidelity to the facts as such. Because of this process, Gulag memoirs and interviews, for all they move us and inspire ethical reflection, present problems when used as historical sources.

Similarly, the vast caches of official reports, decrees, and memos detailing the operations of the labor camp system released when Soviet secrecy laws loosened in the late 1980s, for all they have revolutionized research in Soviet history, also reflect clear biases. Bureaucrats working for the Soviet state faced pressures to falsify numbers so that specific institutions and individuals could claim success in meeting planning targets or responding to the latest directives. Orders and regulations issued in Moscow often proved impossible to implement in the provinces. In the correspondence of Soviet officials and institutions, the human factor is often lost. All sources have limitations; new sources merit attention if they, despite their shortcomings, offer a new perspective that complements the information we already possess.

As the sections of the Formakov correspondence published here will show, private labor camp letters meet this standard in several key respects. First, for all their seeming limitations, these documents hold promise as a subject for both literary and historical analysis because they preserve within themselves a time-stamped record of the communicative constraints that affected Soviet society as a whole in this period. By noting what inmates wrote home, we can, at least to some extent, retrace the flow of information through Soviet society. We see the extent to which official censorship rules governing prisoner mail and other regulations designed to ensure the isolation of the camp population were enforced in practice, and we get a sense of what real men and women felt that they could risk in mail sent through the regular camp postal system and in illicit communications. Moreover, even when the replies that a prisoner received do not survive, as is the case for the sections of the Formakov correspondence that date to the 1940s, intertextual evidence within a one-sided correspondence often allows us to determine, in at least general terms, how relatives outside the camps understood and reacted to the information that they received about detention sites. Inmates reply to the letters they received from home in their own communications: they answer questions, dispel misunderstandings, and respond to expressions of sympathy. These reactions offer valuable clues as to the content of missing communications.

The voids that mar Gulag correspondences are as evocative of the conditions that produced them as their messages. Occasional black marks left by censors; pages torn or rendered illegible as the result of water damage; everything that inmates and their relations do not say; interruptions in the flow of communication that drag on for weeks or months as the result of an inmate's transfer to a new detention site, the confiscation or loss of intervening letters, poor weather, the war, or any number of other factors: these absences and breaks in the texts reflect the limitations on the exchange of information that frustrated both Soviet labor camp inmates and their loved ones. Letters offered inmates an opportunity to communicate with those that they had left at home, but they also underscored the reality of their separation: geography, the time it took for a letter to reach its intended recipient, and the gulfs in understanding that resulted from disparate experiences all inhibited feelings of closeness. Families like the Formakovs had to work hard to remain connected in these circumstances.

Inmates often painstakingly crafted the letters that they sent home because these communications represented the only way in which they could show love to those they had left behind and participate in family life. The communications that Formakov mailed to his wife and children, for instance, include hand-made greeting cards for birthdays and holidays, poems composed for individual family members, short stories and comic strips written for his children, and one small note inscribed on birch bark with a stylus that represents a modern version of the birch-bark manuscripts produced in medieval Russia. Such lovingly crafted messages vividly evoke the pain and sense of loss that family members separated by arrests felt.

Labor camp correspondences also capture aspects of camp life that memoirs and other eyewitness accounts of camp life written after the fact generally do not reflect with real accuracy: the immediate impressions of prisoners and the particulars of day-to-day existence. As our perspective on events evolves over time, our memory of the past shifts: later insight overwhelms initial impressions; we ascribe to ourselves powers of foresight and analytical abilities that we did not in reality possess; we rationalize and regularize our experience with an eye to crafting a cohesive, sympathetic self-narrative. Like diaries, camp letters are valuable because of their immediacy: they enrich our understanding by offering a time-stamped window on a past that was still unfolding. They lead "us to those unpredictable shores where choices can still be made, where interpretation remains still possible," and deliver "a material that is blurred, disparate, discontinuous, [and] irreconcilable."[33] Moreover, because they tend to focus on current events, letters also capture particulars of camp life that rarely figure in other sources: the names of films screened in camp, information about what books and periodicals inmates had access to, references to when and how they received particular pieces of news, and the prices of specific items available in camp kiosks or through illicit channels. Such basic information about day-to-day life tends to fade from memories over time and, in any case, might not seem important enough to include in an account written years after the fact, but it can substantially enhance our understanding of the past. For example, the fact that inmates enjoyed screenings of the Sonja Henie film *Sun Valley Serenade* and John Ford's *The Hurricane* in 1944, as Formakov enthusiastically reports to his wife, underscores the perversity of Gulag life: for all their supposed isolation, Soviet labor camps were in many respects very closely integrated into the culture of the country as a whole.[34] Detention sites short on even the most basic foodstuffs could receive, through regular distribution channels, foreign films purchased by the Soviet state just that year, which, even in the Soviet Union's central cities, would have represented hot tickets and offered, in at least a limited way, a window on capitalist lifestyles.

33. Editors' introduction to *Intimacy and Terror: Soviet Diaries of the 1930s*, ed. Véronique Garros, Natalia Korenevskaya, and Thomas Lahusen (New York: New Press, 1995), xv.

34. For examples of studies that challenge old ideas concerning the Gulag's isolation, see Golfo Alexopoulos, "Amnesty 1945: The Revolving Door of Stalin's Gulag," *Slavic Review* 64, no. 2 (Summer 2005): 274–306; and Bell, "Was the Gulag an Archipelago?"

THE FORMAKOV LETTERS IN THE CONTEXT OF
LATVIAN HISTORY

The Formakov family correspondence is also important for what it tells us about mid-twentieth-century Latvian society. Although Forma-kov was Russian in nationality, he spoke Latvian well enough to translate serious works of literature and clearly saw himself both as spiritually connected to the Russian motherland that had given rise to his religious faith and cultural traditions, and as a part of the multi-ethnic Latvian state in which he had lived most of his adult life. The letters that Formakov sent home to his wife reflect this sometimes uneasy dual identity. Formakov maintained close ties with other pris-oners from Latvia in the camps. He celebrated private holidays with them, shared the Latvian newspapers that he received from his wife, and traded scarce goods with them. He also, however, clearly recog-nized that in the predominantly Russian-speaking environment of the camp, ethnic Latvians faced specific challenges that he did not share: Latvian-speakers sometimes needed help composing letters home be-cause camp censors either refused to accept or discouraged letters writ-ten in languages other than Russian; camp theatricals and other forms of cultural work, a sphere of activity that helped sustain Formakov, offered fewer attractions and opportunities for ethnic Latvians because they focused on Russian culture and used the Russian language. For-makov's unpublished camp narrative suggests that the war effort itself may have also represented a point of division: in this text, Latvian pris-oners react differently to war news than the Russians in camp and can-not muster the feelings of loyalty for Mother Russia that Formakov's ethnically Russian narrator regularly expresses.[35]

The story of the Formakov family, nonetheless, is in many respects a quintessentially Latvian story. The dates of Formakov's two arrests correspond to the two great waves of Stalinist repression that swept across Latvia in the 1940s, the mass arrests and deportations of 1940–1941, and the deportation of 1949. Each tore thousands of families from their homes, dispatching adult males, more often than not, to labor camps or firing squads, and sending women and children into internal exile in distant settlements in Siberia, Central Asia, and the

35. [Byloe], 5–6.

Urals, where conditions were only slightly less onerous than in the camps themselves. Many never made it back home to Latvia.[36] The war between Nazi Germany and the Soviet Union, of course, affected every family in Latvia. Many, like the Formakovs, found themselves separated by the front, military deployment, or labor conscription and lost their homes. Others, including virtually all of the Latvian state's large Jewish population, lost their lives to fascist extermination squads or in the Nazi regime's ghettos and death camps. These two midcentury historical traumas, the waves of repression associated with Soviet occupation and the suffering experienced during the Nazi period, represent the cornerstones of Latvian identity today and occupy a central place in the nation's dominant historical narrative, which casts Latvia as the victim of two horrific occupations.

The Formakov family exemplifies the fate of Latvia as a whole in the mid-twentieth century in terms of the horrors it faced. In their resilience and the ability of individual members to survive successive crises, however, the Formakovs count as unusually fortunate in the context of their own place and time. Before abandoning Daugavpils to the Germans, the Soviet secret police simply executed some inmates held in the Daugavpils investigative prison along with Formakov.[37] Formakov escaped this fate and went on to survive two terms of hard labor in the Soviet Union. In each case, after his release he was allowed to return home to his wife in Riga, although the Soviet state did not allow some of those deported from Latvia in the 1940s to go home until the 1960s. In both 1940–1941 and 1949, although the Soviet state often arrested or sent into internal exile the spouses of those it subjected to repressive measures, Formakov's wife managed to remain at liberty and found a way of supporting herself and the children. The entire Formakov family survived World War II. Although political pressure forced Anna Ivanovna to divorce Formakov following his arrest in 1949, the couple continued to correspond and remarried in 1957, two years after

36. Irēne Šneidere reports that no more than 25 percent of the inhabitants of Latgale who were arrested on June 14, 1941, survived imprisonment in Soviet labor camps. "The Fate of Latgale Civilians in the Camps and Prisons," 236.

37. S. G. Kuznetsov, "Slava i neschast'e Daugavpilsa (M. Kallistratov v obshchestvenno-politicheskoi zhizni goroda, kraia i Latvii 20–30-kh gg.)," *Pervye dobychinskie chteniia* (Daugavpils: Daugavpilsskii Pedagogicheskii Institut, 1999), 89.

Formakov returned to Riga from his second term in the camps. The family unit remained intact and individual members survived thanks both to their willingness to compromise and accommodate the political authorities in at least some situations, and also to the letters that they exchanged during periods of separation, which, even though written under constraints, helped preserve essential attachments.

THE CAMP MAIL SYSTEM AND CENSORSHIP

The official regulations that governed the operations of the Soviet Union's many labor camps and prisons theoretically allowed most inmates to correspond with their relations at least periodically following sentencing. The frequency with which prisoners could send and receive mail depended on the time and place in which they were held, the crime for which they had been sentenced, and their behavior. Generally, prisoners convicted of ordinary crimes enjoyed essentially unlimited mail privileges unless subject to special penalties in connection with some disciplinary infraction. Inmates sentenced for political reasons, like Formakov, often faced no limits on the amount of mail they could receive but could only send a few letters each month or, if they were confined in the notorious special camps (*osobye lageria*) of the late Stalin period, as few as two a year.[38] Officially, Formakov could write home only once every three months during much of his first sentence, as he reports in the letters he sent home.[39]

Camps consistently struggled to enforce such rules, however. In detention sites with a mixed inmate population, high turnover, overcrowding, and poor staffing made it difficult to differentiate among the incarcerated according to their sentences, as centrally issued instructions demanded: just keeping prisoners and their documents together represented a challenge, given frequent transfers.[40] In many places,

38. See, for instance, "Vremennaia instruktsiia o rezhime soderzhaniia zakliuchennykh v ITL NKVD SSSR. Prilozhenie k prikazu NKVD 00889 ot 2 avgusta 1939," GARF, f. 9401, op. 1a, d. 35, ll. 21-23.

39. See the letter to his family dated April 24, 1945. In Formakov's fictionalized memoir, the limit is described as even harsher, two letters per year: [Byloe], 124.

40. See, for instance, "Prikaz NKVD 021 ot 15 ianvaria 1940," GARF, f. 9401, op. 1a, d. 61, l. 25; "Prikaz NKVD 001408 ot 6 noiabria 1940," GARF, f. 9401,

prisoners in restricted categories managed to send mail out through the official mail system far more frequently than rules allowed; moreover, as mentioned earlier, many inmates, like Formakov, also found opportunities to dispatch additional correspondence covertly through free laborers or de-convoyed prisoners. Some political offenders managed to send hundreds of letters a year through a combination of legal and illegal channels.[41] Thousands of collections of prisoner correspondence have surfaced over the past twenty-five years in public and private archives around the world; more and more are gradually making their way into print.[42]

Although theoretically all correspondence sent by or to labor camp inmates through the official camp mail system passed through a careful censorship review, in reality these procedures, like so much of labor camp life, were often rushed and implemented chaotically. Salary lists issued by the NKVD in the late 1930s and the 1940s show that the post of censor paid relatively poorly: in Soviet labor camps, censors earned less than the accountants and stenographers, and only a little more than typists and cashiers.[43] As a result, such jobs held little prestige and did not attract workers who were particularly well educated or well

---

op. 1a, d. 564, l. 7; "Prikaz NKVD 0290 ot 24 iiuliia 1942," GARF, f. 9401, op. 1a, d. 118, l. 102; GARF, f-r 8131, op. 37, d. 361, l. 125. Sometimes inmates arrived in labor camps with files and sentencing documents in a language other than Russian, further complicating operations: GARF, f-r 8360, op. 1, d. 13, l. 235. On how inmate turnover affected record keeping in camp, see Alexopolous, "Amnesty 1945," 287–88.

41. See the following large examples of camp correspondence: Vasilii Evgen'evich Solomin Fund, NITs Memorial, St. Petersburg; and Nikolai Pavlovich Antsiferov Fund, OR RNB, f. 27, d. 139–43, 154, 232. Orlando Figes published a study of a large camp correspondence: *Just Send Me Word* (New York: Metropolitan Books, 2012).

42. The archives maintained by Moscow's Memorial Society and the Scientific-Information Center of the St. Petersburg branch of Memorial contain large collections of labor camp correspondence. For published examples of Gulag correspondence, see P. V. Florenskii, . . . *prebyvaet vechno: Pis'ma P. A. Florenskogo, R. N. Litvinova, N. Ia. Briantseva i A. F. Vangengeima iz SLONa v chetyrekh tomakh* (Moscow: Mehdunarodnyi Tsentr Rerikhov, 2011); A. F. Losev and V. M. Loseva, "*Radost' na veki: perepiska lagernykh vremen* (Moscow: Russkii put',' 2005); Z. B. Osipova, ed., *Sluzhili dva tovarishcha: Kniga o zhizni kinodramaturgov Dunskogo i Frida* (Moscow: Eksmo, 2003), 161–261; and Nadezhda Ulanovskaia and Maia Ulanovskaia, *Istoriia odnoi sem'i* (St. Petersburg: Inapress, 2003).

43. See, for instance, GARF, f. 9401s, op. 1a, d. 40, l. 95.

qualified; the acute labor shortages that affected the camp system during the war and the immediate postwar period only exacerbated this issue.[44] Passing references in official documents and accounts written by former inmates suggest that women often served as censors, including the wives of NKVD officers stationed at the camp. In locations that could not easily recruit free laborers, the camp administration sometimes appointed inmates, including in at least some instances political prisoners, despite the fact that official instructions on censorship work issued in 1947 banned the use of convicts in such positions, and the 1939 instruction stipulated only that free laborers, as opposed to security officers, "could" undertake such work in the colonies that held very low-level offenders.[45]

In addition to low pay, censors faced unrealistic workloads. In campsites with populations of 3,500 inmates in many periods, a single censor bore responsibility for inspecting all incoming and outgoing prisoner mail supposedly in a maximum of five days; as a result of staffing shortages, censors sometimes even had to handle much larger populations of inmates.[46] Backlogs of mail were a notorious issue and figure regularly in both camp inspection reports and prisoner complaints. A 1950 inspection report for Kraslag, for instance, notes that, on the day of inspection, the senior censor faced a backlog of 1,844 long-delayed letters, and that often inmates never received the mail sent by friends and relatives.[47] In camps with large numbers of inmates who spoke languages other than Russian, censors faced additional problems. Theoretically, Soviet minorities had the right to correspond in their native

44. On staffing shortages in the camp system, see Paul R. Gregory, *Lenin's Brain and Other Tales from the Secret Soviet Archives* (Stanford, CA: Hoover Institution Press, 2008), 92. Statistics on the educational level of camp employees for the Ministry of Internal Affairs' Northern-Ural Criminal Labor Camp for 1950 show that most had only a primary education. GARF, f-r 8380, op. 1, d. 29, ll. 141–42. Note also the discussion of difficulties recruiting free laborers with a reasonable literacy level contained in GARF, f-r 8360, op. 1, d. 27, l. 134.

45. GARF, f-r 9401s, op. 12, d. 225, l. 112; GARF, f. 9401, op. 1a, d. 37, l. 93; GARF, f-r 9407, op. 1, d. 1488, l. 168. Also see Jacques Rossi on the use of prisoners as censors: *Spravochnik po Gulagu, chast' 2*, 2nd ed., trans. Natal'ia Gorbanevskaia (Moscow: Prosvet, 1991), 2: 276–77.

46. GARF, f-r 9407, op. 1s, d. 1537, l. 16; GARF, f-r 9401s, op 1a, d. 113, l. 34, l. 40.

47. GARF, f-r 8360, op. 1, d. 9, ll. 95–98.

languages, and censors were supposed to find a free laborer or carefully vetted prisoner convicted under a nonpolitical statute to translate any letter that they could not read themselves.[48] However, given the number of languages in use in the Soviet Union and the isolation of some Gulag outposts, this requirement presented challenges: both evidence drawn from the correspondence of inmates such as Formakov and passing references in official memos suggest that, despite official regulations, in many camps inmates were either told they could not correspond in languages other than Russian or found, by dint of hard experience, that mail written in other languages simply never reached its addressee.[49] If they wanted to write home, they had to find another inmate to help them compose the letter in Russian.

Low pay, poor staffing, and pressure to meet processing targets all complicated efforts to implement centrally issued censorship instructions. Although regulations barred prisoners from writing home to their relatives about the location of the camp in which they were held, the work they were performing, camp regulations and procedures, unsatisfactory living conditions, epidemics, and production accidents, and also from providing the names of other inmates, such basic facts about camp life often appear in letters that clearly passed through the official mail system, suggesting that censors sometimes worked carelessly or turned a blind eye to what they considered small infractions.[50] In a sense, this is understandable. The system for censoring the camp mail was in many respects unworkable: instructions on labor camp censorship work issued in 1939 and 1947 demanded that censors compose a separate memorandum on any piece of mail that they considered at all

48. See, for instance, the 1947 censorship instruction attached to GARF, f. 9401, op. 1a, d. 225, l. 116.

49. For instance, a 1950 inspection report on Kraslag noted critically that, because of a lack of translators, letters that arrived in camp written in languages other than Russian were simply not distributed to inmates. GARF, f-r 8360, op. 1, d. 8, l. 81. See also GARF, f-r 9407, op. 1, d. 1488, l. 189.

50. For a more complete list of topics deemed off limits in prisoner correspondence, see the 1939 and 1947 instructions on censorship procedures issued as attachments to the following NKVD orders: "Prikaz 001418 ot 21 noiabria 1939," GARF, f. 9401, op. 1a, d. 37, ll. 92–101; "Prikaz 00634 ot 16 iiunia 1947," GARF, f. 9401, op. 1a, d. 225, ll. 111–24. Complaints about careless work by camp censors appear periodically in official inspection reports. See, for instance, GARF, f-r 9407, op. 1, d. 1488, l. 189.

suspicious or of operational interest, complete with an exact citation of the passage that had aroused their concerns. Eleven and fourteen separate forms for tracking prisoner mail accompanied the 1939 and 1947 instructions on censoring prisoner mail respectively.[51]

Practical constraints often limited the ability of prisoners to communicate with their relations at least as much as camp regulations. As Formakov's letters home show, prisoners in camps struggled to obtain paper and writing implements. Formakov could get writing supplies because he volunteered in the camp Cultural-Educational Sector and because he often held desk jobs as opposed to assignments involving outdoor physical labor. Other inmates, however, were less fortunate and struggled to find basic supplies and the spare time and physical energy to write.

For inmates who succeeded in overcoming these obstacles and establishing regular correspondence, letters could provide very significant survival advantages. Obviously, contact with loved ones at home helped boost morale and gave prisoners a reason to hang on, but it also conferred other benefits. The receipt of a letter from an inmate often inspired relatives to take action on his or her behalf. They might renew efforts to appeal a conviction, mail packages of warm clothing or food that could sustain the prisoner, or wire funds to a prisoner's account. Prisoners who even occasionally received funds and packages from home lived markedly better than other inmates in camps. They had a supplemental source of scarce fats, vitamins, and sugars vital for maintaining health, could potentially replace items of clothing worn thin, and also had things to trade and give as gifts to individuals of influence.[52] Even if some of a package's contents were stolen, its arrival

---

51. GARF, f. 9401, op. 1a, d. 37, ll. 95–101; GARF, f. 9401, op. 1a, d. 225, ll. 117ob.–124. On bureaucracy and arbitrariness in the camps, see Wilson T. Bell, "The Gulag and Soviet Society in Western Siberia, 1929–1953" (Ph.D. diss., University of Toronto, 2011).

52. Reciprocal favors (*blat*) and bribes played an important role in labor camps just as they did in the rest of Soviet society. Prisoners engaged in informal exchanges with other inmates who occupied positions associated with authority or access, free laborers, guards, and even officers. On the role of bribes and *blat* in Stalinist culture, see James Heinzen, "The Art of the Bribe: Corruption and Everyday Practice in the Late Stalinist USSR," *Slavic Review* 66, no. 3 (Fall 2007): 389–412; and Alena V. Ledeneva, *Russia's Economy of Favours: Blat, Networking and Informal Exchange* (Cambridge: Cambridge University Press, 1998).

still might lead to a better work assignment, a sleeping spot, and a measure of protection.

Formakov managed to secure decent work assignments even before he began to receive packages and funds from home in 1944 by ingratiating himself with the camp authorities through participation in propaganda and agitation work, but the support his wife sent still enhanced his life in significant ways.[53] Parcels from home brought newspapers that he could trade with smokers short of rolling papers for extra portions of food, hygiene supplies such as soap that helped stave off illness, and even formal clothing items such as ties and dress shirts that allowed him to costume himself appropriately for appearances on stage at camp theatricals and hence made him more valuable to the camp Cultural-Educational Sector. Like the character Tsezar in Solzhenitsyn's novella *One Day in the Life of Ivan Denisovich,* in the last three years of his first term at hard labor, Formakov would have counted as "well-off" in the context of his camp and attracted envy from his fellow prisoners: the support his family provided, in conjunction with his fortunate work assignments, insulated him from the worst hardships in Kraslag, helped him secure access to goods and services that were in short supply, and kept him relatively healthy.[54] Those without such advantages would have looked on hungrily and hoped, often in vain, for a small "share" of the extras he enjoyed. Although inmates such as Formakov often did give some of the rations and supplies that they received from home to their closest comrades, they could not share with everyone and still improve their own odds of survival. Making it through a labor camp term required both hard-nosed calculation and a strong instinct for self-preservation.

53. The terms "agitation" and "propaganda" were often linked in Soviet rhetoric and can seem synonymous from a Western perspective. "Agitation" means using political messages to raise consciousness and morale with the aim of inspiring people to contribute enthusiastically to the construction of socialism.

54. Solzhenitsyn, *One Day in the Life of Ivan Denisovich,* 38. In the novella, Solzhenitsyn contrasts Tsezar, an intellectual from Moscow with strong family support, with his main character, Ivan Denisovich, a peasant, who rarely sends or receives letters and discourages his family from sending packages because he knows they are destitute themselves (107). Although the book valorizes Ivan and seems critical of Tsezar, it also shows how Ivan and other inmates benefit from Tsezar's good fortune: Tsezar gives Ivan cigarette butts and food at key moments in the narrative (25, 123, 137). Such scenes highlight the way private packages benefited the economy of the camp system as a whole.

To some extent, even those who ran the Soviet labor camp system recognized the role that support from home could play in prisoner survival. During World War II and the postwar famine years, the NKVD and the Main Administration of Labor Camps in Moscow ordered camp bosses to encourage prisoners to write home and ask for packages, which they viewed as an important secondary line of support for the labor camp system in the campaign to reduce unacceptably high mortality rates. Throughout the rest of the Stalin period, the NKVD required prisons and camps to track the number of private packages that arrived, and also the amount of food and clothing that entered the penal system through this mechanism.[55] Such policies discouraged labor camps from restricting correspondence too severely: prisoners who could not write their families received few packages; letters constituted proof of life.

In summary, from a number of points of view, letters represented a key factor in the economy and social life of the Soviet labor camp system. For inmates such as Formakov, letters boosted morale and also helped, because they often led to assistance from home, enhance chances of survival. For the bosses who ran the Soviet Union's prisons and labor camps and for the Soviet state as a whole, prisoner correspondence brought other benefits. Letters, one can argue, helped keep both prisoners and their relations in line by reminding them that they still had something to lose. They also ensured that private packages continued to flow to the Soviet Union's detention sites, thereby providing a secondary line of supply in difficult periods, and they constituted a potentially valuable information source that made it possible for state agents to track the mood of both prisoners and their relations. The Soviet system itself, in a number of respects, had a vested interest in not completely circumscribing the ability of ordinary prisoners like Formakov to correspond with their families; imperfect enforcement of some regulations designed to ensure the isolation of the camp system and the secrecy of its operations may have functioned as a stabilizing factor, helping sustain repressive policies that were, from many points of view, fundamentally irrational.[56]

55. See, for instance, "Tsirkuliar No. 366 ot 1 sentiabria 1942," GARF, f. 9401, op. 1a, d. 118, l. 174.

56. Robert Conquest, Foreword to Gregory and Lazarev, *The Economics of Forced Labor,* vii–xi. Of course, poor enforcement of other regulations worsened

ARSENII FORMAKOV'S EARLY LIFE AND CAREER
AS AN EDUCATOR AND JOURNALIST

A few additional facts about Arsenii Formakov's biography provide a context for the letters that follow. Formakov was born in the year 1900 in the city of Libava (Liepaja), which at the time, like the rest of what is now Latvia, constituted part of the Russian Empire. His parents were more educated than most members of the area's generally insular, predominantly rural Russian Old Believer community.[57] Formakov's father, Ivan Vasilievich, excelled at school and worked as a clerk in the office of the military commandant of Dvinsk before going on to secure a job with the railway system in Libava. He also played a notable role in the Old Believer renaissance that took place in the first two decades of the twentieth century.[58] He loved books and had a personal library of 300 volumes, many of which he had rebound himself. Formakov's mother, Pelageia Kuzminichna (née Kapustina), was from a wealthy family in Dvinsk and had attended a German-language high school for girls. The resources provided by her family enabled the Formakovs to live comfortably: ultimately Arsenii Formakov would inherit two apartment buildings in Dvinsk from his mother.

During World War I, the Formakov family evacuated to Velikie Luki in the Pskov oblast (administrative district) of Russia proper where, in 1916, Formakov graduated from a secondary school (*real'noe uchilishche*) that offered a modern curriculum, including scientific disciplines, as opposed to a classical education. He then went on to study at the Institute of Railway Transportation Engineers in Petrograd, where he appears to have remained enrolled until at least May 1919.[59]

---

conditions for prisoners: they often received much less food than dietary norms required. Bell, "The Gulag and Society in Western Siberia," 143–47.

57. For demographic information on Latvia's Russian minority during the decade preceding World War II, see T. Feigmane, *Russkie obshchestva v Latvii (1920–1940 gg.). Uchebnoe posobie* (Riga: Latviiskii Universitet, 1992), 5–7, 23.

58. F. P. Fedorov, "O russkom soznanii Latgalii," in *Geopanorama russkoi kul'tury: Provintsiia i ee lokal'nye teksty,* ed. L. O. Zaionts, V. V. Abashev, A. F. Belousov, and T. V. Tsiv'ian (Moscow: Iazyk slavianskoi kul'tury, 2004), 84, 95; http://e-libra.ru/read/203823-geopanorama-russkoj-kultury-provinciya-i-ee-lokalnye-teksty.html.

59. On problems in dating when Formakov abandoned his studies, see Fedorov, "Lirika Arseniia Formakova," 151.

Although relatively little is known about the time Formakov spent in Petrograd, it seems likely that his enthusiasm for silver-age Russian literature and culture solidified in this period. In a brief, unpublished account of his student years, Formakov describes standing in line to get tickets to hear Feodor Chaliapin sing at the Mariinskii Theater, enthusiastically discusses student literary magazines, and also notes the responses of both avant-garde and conservative artists to the first anniversary of the October Revolution.[60] Other prose works by Formakov suggest that he attended major literary events while in Petrograd and perhaps had the chance to see the poets Sergei Esenin and Alexander Blok deliver readings.[61] On balance, however, Formakov's experience of the city seems to have been negative as a result of the disorder and privations associated with the Revolutionary and Civil War periods. In his unpublished memoir, he notes the slender rations served in the institute's cafeteria, recalls the terrible cold in its unheated classrooms, and also recounts with horror a scene of mob justice that he witnessed: the beating and summary execution of a twelve-year-old street urchin caught stealing.[62]

Such episodes of violence and the harsh living conditions he encountered in Petrograd may have played a role in Formakov's decision to abandon his studies and rejoin his family, which, by 1919, had returned from Velikie Luki to Dvinsk, but family crises also contributed. In 1919 Formakov's father died in a typhus epidemic, and several months later his fourteen-year-old brother Mikhail was arrested by the Bolsheviks for his supposed participation in a counter-revolutionary plot and shot.[63] Understandably, given his brother's fate, Formakov did not recall the period he spent under Bolshevik rule during the Civil War in positive terms. Negative appraisals of Soviet Russia surface regularly

60. "Pervyi oktiabr' v Petrograde: Po vospominaniiam," Arsenii Ivanovich Formakov Papers, Hoover Institution Archive, Box 1, folder 13.

61. Eduard Meksh, "Esenin v tvorcheskoi sud'be Arseniia Formakova (20–30-e gody)," *Literatura. Rusistica Vilensis. Nauchnye trudy* (Vilnius: Vilnius Izdat. Vilniusskogo Universiteta, 2004), 30; http://www.russianresources.lt/archive/Formak/Formak_7.html.

62. "Pervyi oktiabr' v Petrograde," 3.

63. See the interrogation records in Formakov's 1940–1941 and 1949 criminal files: State Archives of Latvia, f. 1986, op. 1, d. P-1545, ch. 1, l. 14, ll. 61–62; f. 1986, op. 1, d. P-1545, ch. 2, ll. 20–21.

in the journalistic pieces and fiction that Formakov wrote during the 1920s and the 1930s. For instance, in one 1928 article, Formakov remembered the mood in Petrograd a decade earlier as "crushed by the vice of the first year of Bolshevism, poised to fall into German arms, and inclined to view that fall as a deliverance."[64] Formakov's 1929 novel *Nasha iunost'* (Our Youth) contains a brief description of the main character's desperate attempts to flee famine-gripped Civil War Petrograd and notes atrocities and incidents of looting committed by the Red Army in the region surrounding Dvinsk in 1919, during the period of "Soviet slavery."[65] Similarly, in the 1938 novel *Faina,* which draws on impressions gathered during a 1927 trip to Russia that Formakov made on his Latvian passport as part of a group of educators, the main character emotionally proclaims himself a "loyal citizen" of Latvia, the country that "saved [him] from a red nightmare and created for [him] a peaceful life and normal living conditions."[66]

Formakov arrived in Dvinsk just as borders between Bolshevik Russia and the newly independent Latvian state were about to stabilize. In January 1920, after months of fighting, Latvian forces at last gained control of Dvinsk, which they promptly rechristened Daugavpils. As a result of evacuations, war deaths, and epidemics, the city had lost almost three-quarters of its population since the beginning of World War I, dropping from 112,837 to approximately 30,000 inhabitants. In the process, it had become more Latvian ethnically, as Russians and Jews had left in large numbers. It remained, however, one of the more diverse regions of the new Latvian state. Russians constituted 17 percent of the city's population in 1925, Jews 31 percent, Latvians 27 percent, and Poles 17 percent, with Belarusians and Germans making up most of the remainder.[67] Of these groups, Russians represented the least

64. "Desiat' let nazad," *Slovo,* no. 799 (1928): 5, as cited in Fedorov, "Lirika Arseniia Formakova,"151.

65. *Nasha iunost'* (Riga: Mir, 1929), 42, 47, 67, 97.

66. *Faina* (Riga: Logos, 1938), 88–89.

67. Z. I. Iakub, *Daugavpils v proshlom: Publikatsiia kraeveda* (Daugavpils: A.K.A., 1998), 99–100. For comparison, in 1897 Jews constituted 46 percent of the city's population, Russians 28 percent, Poles 16 percent, Germans 4 percent, and Latvians only 2 percent. The population of Daugavpils did not rebound to pre-1914 levels until the 1970s. The demographic statistics I cite follow contemporary convention and conflate Latvians and Latgalians, an ethnic subgroup associated with the Latgale region that surrounds Daugavpils. As Deniss Hanovs and Valdis

educationally and economically advantaged. They suffered from illiteracy rates of close to 60 percent in 1920 and primarily worked in agriculture. Few owned the land they farmed.[68] Moreover, once Latvia gained independence, its Russian minority faced a new barrier to advancement: very few, particularly in the Latgale region that surrounded Daugavpils, spoke the new state language of Latvian, which made participation in the national political process difficult and ultimately would limit access to even secondary school.[69]

Although some of the Russians residing in Daugavpils in the 1920s were true émigrés who had fled the Soviet Union for bourgeois Latvia, most, like Formakov's family, had long-standing ties to the area. They, in many cases, had not moved at all; the borders of Russian/Soviet territory had simply shifted east around them. As a result, as Iurii Abyzov points out, such individuals saw a familiar landscape outside their windows every morning and lived, in many cases, pretty much as they had before the Revolution, but, paradoxically, found themselves suddenly transformed from the leading ethnos of an empire into a minority within a new nation-state with an alien official language and unfamiliar symbols of state power.[70]

With his Russian technical degree incomplete and few specialized skills at his disposal, Formakov needed to find a way to support himself in this socially and politically complex environment. Soon after returning to Latvia, he enrolled in a short-term pedagogical course and, by April 1920, had secured a job teaching in a local Russian-language school. In this position, Formakov emerged as an influential advocate

Tēraudkalns note, however, prior to the Ulmanis era, these ethnicities were often viewed as distinctive. *Ultimate Freedom—No Choice: The Culture of Authoritarianism in Latvia, 1934–1940* (Leiden: Brill, 2013), 79–108.

68. T. Feigmane, "Russkaia shkola v Latvii (1918–1940 gg.)," in *Russkie Pribaltiki: Mekhanizm kul'turnoi integratsii (do 1940 g.),* ed. Tat'iana Iasinskaia (Vilnius: Russkii kul'turnyi tsentr, 1997), 134–35. See also E. Tikhonitskii, "Obrazovanie sredi russkikh v Latvii," in *Russkie v Latvii: Sbornik "Dnia russkoi kul'tury,"* ed. V. V. Preobrazhenskii (Riga: Izdanie Komiteta po ustroistvu "D.R.K." v gor. Rige, 1933), 83; and S. Trofimov and B. Engel'gardt, "Khoziastvennoe polozhenie russkogo men'shinstva v Latvii," ibid., 108–9.

69. Feigmane, *Russkie obshchestva v Latvii,* 5–10, 23; Feigmane, *Russkie v dovoennoi Latvii,* 241–42, 249–50.

70. Iurii Abyzov, "Latviiskaia vetv' rossiiskoi emigratsii," in *Blokovskii sbornik,* no. 13 (Tartu: Kafedra Russkoi Literatury Tartuskogo Universiteta, 1996), 282–86.

for the cultural advancement of Latvia's Russian minority and began to take on a variety of leadership roles. In addition to serving as a school inspector from 1929 to 1932, he helped organize the Daugavpils Teachers Union, acted as the representative for Russian teachers to the Daugavpils City School Board (Gorodskaia Shkol'naia Uprava), and won election to the City Council (Gorodskaia Duma), where he participated in the finance and schools commissions. In addition, in 1931 Formakov published a Russian grammar textbook designed to improve instruction in Latvia's Russian-language primary schools.[71] These varied forms of educational activism placed Formakov at the center of the fight to preserve the relatively liberal educational policies introduced by the new Latvian state in 1919 and to maintain at least some autonomy for minority schools. Even in the late 1920s, this position faced regular challenges in the Latvian parliament (Saeima), where many deputies felt that only a strong policy of Latvianization could help the country shake off the legacy of Russian cultural imperialism. By the early 1930s, when Formakov began to shift his focus from education to journalism, such views had led to policy changes that compromised the ability of minority schools to function.[72] Under the Latvian nationalist authoritarian regime of Kārlis Ulmanis, which held power from 1934 to 1940, many Russian-language schools simply closed. This dismayed community leaders such as Formakov who continued to see such institutions as key to improving the lives of Latvia's Russians and to preserving the Russian traditions that seemed so threatened within the Soviet Union itself.[73]

Like teaching and educational administrative work, journalism afforded Formakov opportunities to work for the advancement of Latvia's Russian community. Formakov dated the start of his career as a writer to 1922, the year in which he first published in Latvian newspapers and journals.[74] Initially he primarily wrote poetry, but by 1926

71. "Arsenii Ivanovich Formakov," *Vestnik Soveta staroobriadcheskikh soborov i s"ezdov v Latvii*, no. 1 (1931): 19.

72. E. Tikhonitskii, "K piatnadtsatiletiiu Russkoi shkol'noi avtonomii. (Po ofitsial'nym dannym)," in *Russkie v Latvii, chast' 2. Sbornik "Dnia russkoi kul'tury,"* ed. V. V. Preobrazhenskii (Riga: Komitet po Ustroistvu D.R.K v gor. Rige, 1934), 48–53.

73. Feigmane, *Russkie v dovoennoi Latvii*, 245–62.

74. Note the date of this item from a Riga newspaper: "15-letie literaturnoi deiatel'nosti A. I. Formakova," *Segodnia*, no. 98 (April 10, 1937). An article from

he was a regular correspondent for the *Dvinskii golos,* and soon after he began contributing articles to *Slovo* (The Word), a Russian national democratic paper based in Riga. Formakov wrote on a broad range of subjects in the 1920s and the early 1930s: reviews of contemporary novels, plays, and operas; pieces on language usage, pedagogy, and local personalities; childhood reminiscences focusing on life in Latvia's Old Believer communities; notes on atrocities committed by the Bolsheviks; and coverage of current events in Latvia and abroad. Many of Formakov's best-known pieces focused, however, on literature. He wrote moving tributes to Nikolai Gumilev, a Russian poet executed in 1920 by the Soviet secret police, and the poet Sergei Esenin, who committed suicide in Leningrad in 1925. He also published an essay describing a visit to the home of Igor Severianin, a Russian poet who emigrated to Estonia following the October Revolution. The travel sketches that Formakov wrote following his trip to the Soviet Union in 1927, which served as precursors to the novel *Faina,* also proved popular: Formakov published a whole series of such pieces in Latvian newspapers and then placed a long essay focusing on his visit to the graves of Blok and Esenin in the Parisian émigré journal *Chisla* (Numbers).[75]

Such successes encouraged Formakov to make journalism a full-time career. When the publisher of *Dvinskii golos* passed away in 1933, Formakov and M. Sviranskii acquired the paper, and Formakov became its primary editor and correspondent.[76] In the years that followed this acquisition, Formakov's literary career reached its apogee: he became the Daugavpils bureau chief for *Segodnia* (Today), the most important Russian-language newspaper in the Baltics, and emerged as one of the best-known Russian journalists in Latvia. This position allowed him

---

Nash daugavpilskii golos suggests, however, that Formakov published at least one article while in Petrograd during the Civil War in the newspaper of the Kadets (Constitutional-Democratic Party), *Nash vek* (Our Era). See A. F. [Formakov], "Nomer staroi gazety. (Pamiati M. I. Ganfman)," November 30, 1934.

75. Iurii Abyzov, *Russkoe pechatnoe slovo v Latvii, 1917–1944 gg. Bio-bibliograficheskii spravochnik,* 4 vols. (Stanford, CA: Stanford Slavic Studies, 1991), 4: 242–51.

76. The paper's name changed several times. In 1933 it became *Nash Dvinskii golos* (Our Voice of Dvinsk), then, in 1934, *Nash Daugavpilskii golos* (Our Voice of Daugavpils), and finally, in 1940, *Nash golos* (Our Voice). Iurii Abyzov notes that between 1933 and 1940, Formakov personally wrote much of the content of the paper. *A izdavalos' eto v Rige: 1918–1944. Istoriko-bibliograficheskii ocherk* (Moscow: Biblioteka-fond "Russkoe Zaberezh'e," 2006), 296, 310, 330, 338, 346.

to promote efforts to create an umbrella organization that would link together the Old Believer communities of the Baltic states so that they could advocate for themselves more effectively.[77]

During the Ulmanis years, Formakov had to exercise restraint in his work as a journalist and editor. Shortly after seizing power on May 15, 1934, the Ulmanis regime closed several dozen newspapers that it deemed guilty of partisan politicking and imposed strict new censorship regulations on the remaining periodical press that banned editorializing on controversial political and social issues. Henceforth all papers were expected to serve the common cause and "work toward the restoration of the twice-liberated [Latvian] state."[78] State officials urged journalists to "reflect the positive sides of life more" and refrain from "irresponsible criticism."[79] In order to remain open, the newspaper that Formakov co-owned and edited in Daugavpils, now renamed *Nash Daugavpilskii golos* (Our Voice of Daugavpils), had to avoid expressing concern about government policies and decrees. The paper could report on policies that doubtless distressed many of its readers, such as restrictions on the use of minority languages in both local and national government and requirements that teachers in Russian schools pass Latvian-language examinations to keep their jobs, but it could not question the wisdom or fairness of these new rules. Like other Latvian papers, *Nash Daugavpilskii golos* printed enthusiastic tributes to Ulmanis and celebrated the positive effects of his policies. Well before his 1940 arrest, Formakov had learned how to adapt to censorship restrictions and obsequiously parrot the slogans of the day, skills that ultimately contributed to his survival during his two terms in Soviet labor camps.

LITERARY REPUTATION AND LEGACY

Formakov also achieved at least limited success as a poet and novelist in the 1920s and the 1930s. While few of his contemporaries viewed him as a major European writer, his work did attract enough attention

77. Žilko and Mekšs, "Staroobriadchestvo v Latvii: Vchera i segodnia," 83.

78. "S"ezd v Rige redaktorov provintsial'nykh gazet," *Nash Daugavpilskii golos*, October 23, 1934.

79. "Pressa dolzhna pomogat' pravitel'stvu sluzhit' narodu," *Nash Daugavpilskii golos*, November 13, 1934.

to merit reviews in Russian émigré periodicals in both Latvia and Paris. Most notably, in 1930, the Russian writer Nikolai Otsup published a review of Formakov's 1926 book of verse, *V puti* (On the Way), in the Parisian journal *Chisla*. Although Otsup dismissed Formakov's poetry as "provincial," he noted in the review that the author's prose work was considerably more polished and might merit attention in a future issue.[80] More recent critiques of Formakov's work have largely echoed this assessment. Since the collapse of the Soviet Union, scholars working in both Latvia and Russia have rediscovered Formakov's writing, and articles on his life and career now appear regularly in a variety of venues. By and large, the most comprehensive pieces written on Formakov's verse have focused on obvious influences and have conceded that, when compared to the best Russian-language verse of the 1920s and 1930s, Formakov's poems appear both dated and derivative, although some individual works do represent exceptions.[81]

Formakov's best prose, however, continues to attract admirers. In the studies that he wrote of Formakov's work before his death, the literary scholar Eduard Meksh returned repeatedly to Formakov's *Faina* and to the shorter travel sketches about Soviet life that had preceded it, finding in these texts insightful meditations on the émigré condition and on the divided loyalties that men like Formakov experienced. Arkadii Petrovich, the autobiographical main character of *Faina*, Meksh notes, travels to Soviet Russia in search of his "spiritual homeland": he feels grateful and loyal to the Latvian state in which he lives but also longs "to reconnect with the Russian spirit" and to "show his reverence for all that remains holy in Russia."[82] Within Soviet borders, however, Formakov's main character finds only disappointment: drab living conditions, abysmal service, and a cultural life deformed by the mechanisms of political control repel him to such an extent that ultimately he disavows any connection with the country: "No, he did not feel that he was in his homeland. He was surrounded by hostile or, at best, indifferent elements, like a pilot as he crosses over the ocean. His land was over there, across the border."[83]

80. N.O., review of A. Formakov, *V puti*, *Chisla*, no. 4 (1930): 266.

81. See, for instance, Meksh, "Esenin v tvorcheskoi sud'be Arseniia Formakova"; and Fedorov, "Lirika Arseniia Formakova."

82. *Faina*, 89, as cited in "Esenin v tvorcheskoi sud'be Arseniia Formakova."

83. *Faina*, 90.

Arkadii feels out of place in Soviet Russia in part because he perceives it as a graveyard, important for the relics it contains rather than as the site of vital contemporary culture. He is "making a pilgrimage to grave sites. Dead churches, dead museums, because of summer vacation, even the schools are dead."[84] Indeed, many of the sites that Arkadii visits while in Moscow and Leningrad yield somber reflections: the grave of the poet Alexander Blok lies untended, adorned by a chipped cross, a small bronze icon partly spoiled by whitewash, and discarded watermelon seeds; plans are already under way to tear down both the Iverskaia Chapel and the Cathedral of Christ the Savior; at the Tretiakov Gallery, staff whisper about the valuable paintings that have "disappeared without a trace."[85] Moreover, the old friends with whom Arkadii meets in Russia live in cramped communal apartments, work twelve- to fifteen-hour shifts washing floors, and fantasize about escaping to the West. Even the book's title character, Faina, a sympathetic Communist Youth League member whom Arkadii meets by Blok's grave, seems "sickly and overwrought," and hence nothing like the healthy, optimistic new generation of young people that the Bolshevik state aspired to create. Given that, as one of Arkadii's travel companions notes, "Blok gave the name Faina in his verse to one of the aspects of Russia," this character's "sad eyes and nervously twitching brow that testify to hard years spent as an orphan in childhood and a shattered youth" presage nothing good for the country's future.[86]

In identifying the Soviet Union as the graveyard of Russian culture, Formakov, of course, followed a great tradition: the use of this trope represented one of the dominant trends in literary accounts and visual depictions of Petrograd following the Revolution.[87] Formakov, however, introduces something new by weaving these elegiac notes into a travel narrative that sends a group of "foreign" Russian-speaking tourists to explore Soviet reality, both on their own and with the help of solicitous official guides. *Faina* includes detailed descriptions of a whole series of key Soviet tourist sites, including the Pushkin Apartment Mu-

---

84. Ibid., 89.
85. Ibid., 107.
86. Ibid, 57.
87. Anna Lisa Crone and Jennifer Day, *My Petersburg/Myself: Mental Architecture and Imaginative Space in Modern Russian Letters* (Bloomington, IN: Slavica, 2004), 91–143.

seum in Leningrad, the wooden Lenin Mausoleum on Red Square, the Tretiakov Gallery, and the Tolstoy Museum in Moscow, in each case capturing the iteration on display in the late 1920s, just as the New Economic Policy was giving way to the First Five-Year Plan and the cultural revolution. Moreover, the reader also follows along as Arkadii and the other Russo-Latvian educators go on three model excursions designed to exemplify the kinds of structured educational tours that had emerged as an important pedagogical trend in the Soviet Union in the 1920s: "On the Streets of a Big City," "Around the Kremlin," and "Retracing the Events of October."[88] Questions and answers along the routes highlight the changes that have taken place in Moscow since the Revolution and also the cultural distance that has grown between those separated by the new Soviet border erected less than a decade before:

"By the way, what is that monument, professor?"

On a tall obelisk in the middle of the flowerbeds across from the entrance, they noticed the names of the "fathers" of socialism from Marx to Plekhanov. The shattered remains of shields [from a coat of arms] were visible on the pedestal.

"As you see, it is a monument to socialist leaders. It used to be a monument to the three-hundredth anniversary of the Romanov Dynasty."

"Economical!" noted Rozanov. The professor pretended that he had not heard him.[89]

For anyone with an interest in the history of Soviet tourism, monuments and museums, or the cities of Moscow and Petersburg, *Faina* will hold special interest as a result of such scenes. It provides a remarkable depiction of the Soviet tourist industry at an early stage of development.

Literary discussions also fill *Faina*'s pages. Demonstrating considerable erudition, Formakov weaves together references to Soviet and émigré literary scandals and to the work of both major and minor literary figures. The opinions that characters voice on literature and the way they wield literary citations help characterize them and elucidate the cultural spaces that they inhabit. In some places in the novel,

88. On the early Soviet excursion tradition, see Emily D. Johnson, *How St. Petersburg Learned to Study Itself: The Russian Idea of Kraevedenie* (University Park: Pennsylvania State University Press, 2006), 97–123.

89. *Faina,* 120.

Formakov even seems to turn a knowing gaze on his own poetic work: in a key scene, an old friend mocks the verse written by Formakov's autobiographical main character for its childish naiveté and its obvious similarities to the work of Igor Severianin, effectively presaging some of the central criticism of Formakov's poetry voiced by later critics.[90] While perhaps not an undiscovered classic, *Faina* demonstrates considerable talent and suggests that Formakov might have developed into a more influential writer if his 1940 arrest had not interrupted the trajectory of his career.

Similarly, some of the sketches that Formakov published in émigré periodicals during the 1930s are striking enough to merit republication. "Bab'ia gorka: Ne rasskaz" (The Women's Hill: Not a Story), a sketch that Formakov placed in *Chisla* in 1934, describes the lives of Eastern European peasants who lived amid a battlefield for three years during World War I and who even fifteen years later find shells, mines, and rifles so often on their land that they have developed a profitable side business trading in scrap metal and guns. Fully acclimated to their situation, the peasants casually disarm ordnance and store explosives in their cellars and barns. They relate mishaps that led to the loss of digits as comic stories and express bemusement at the narrator's scruples concerning farming land fertilized by blood and corpses. "Bab'ia gorka" reads as a moving study of how war coarsens man's nature and breaks down societal values. The last section of the sketch relates a single tragic incident from World War I: the desperate offensive of the First Russian Women's Battalion of Death near the town of Smorgon, which ended in disaster in part, Formakov suggests, because war-weary male troops failed to offer any support.[91]

LEARNING TO "SPEAK BOLSHEVIK" IN A LABOR CAMP

To what extent did Formakov's ideological orientation change as a result of his 1940 arrest and the two terms that he served in Soviet labor camps? Was he reforged in camp from a passionate anticommunist

90. Ibid., 80–83.

91. "Bab'ia gorka," *Chisla*, no. 10 (1934): 261–65. On the Women's Battalion of Death, see Laurie S. Stoff, *They Fought for the Motherland: Russian Women Soldiers in World War I and the Revolution* (Lawrence: University Press of Kansas, 2006), 66–113.

into a model Soviet citizen through participation in the activities of the Cultural-Educational Sector, the primary unit in camp charged with the re-education of inmates deemed capable of rejoining society? Did he, to use Stephen Kotkin's terminology, learn to "speak Bolshevik," mastering the language and values of Soviet power?[92] Much scholarship in Russian cultural studies in recent years has focused on the problem of subjectivity and the construction of the Soviet self. Building on the work of Kotkin, historians such as Jochen Hellbeck and Igal Halfin have argued that Bolshevik efforts in the 1920s and 1930s to remake Soviet society and, by extension, Soviet men and women were strikingly successful. They note that in autobiographical statements and even private diaries, ordinary Soviet citizens often used official rhetoric to speak about their personal life experiences and seem to have absorbed the new state's values to the extent that drawing any real distinction between public and private beliefs becomes meaningless. "Even when individuals criticized the regime," Hellbeck and Halfin argue, "the terms of their argument remained determined by Stalinist language."[93]

Hellbeck and Halfin's findings on Soviet subjectivity grow out of close readings of texts produced by individual Soviet citizens whose lives were gradually shaped by Bolshevik ideology and the social changes of the 1920s and 1930s and are controversial even as they apply to that period. Extending them to individuals abruptly absorbed into the Soviet Union in the 1940s is in many respects problematic: Latvian citizens such as the Formakovs experienced "Sovietization" very differently than workers, writers, and young political activists in the Soviet heartland in the 1930s. On the Soviet Union's volatile postwar western frontier, including the Baltic region and Western Ukraine, as scholars such as Amir Weiner have noted, pre-Soviet modes of thinking

92. Stephen Kotkin, *Magnetic Mountain: Stalinism as a Civilization* (Berkeley: University of California Press, 1995), 198–237. For more information on the role of the Cultural-Educational Sector in camp life, see Applebaum, *Gulag: A History,* 231–41; and Barnes, *Death and Redemption,* 57–68.

93. Igal Halfin and Jochen Hellbeck, "Rethinking the Stalinist Subject: Stephen Kotkin's 'Magnetic Mountain' and the State of Soviet Historical Studies," *Jahrbücher für Geschichte Osteuropas,* Neue Folge, Bd. 44, H. 3 (1996), 459. See also Jochen Hellbeck, *Revolution on My Mind: Writing a Diary under Stalin* (Cambridge: Harvard University Press, 2006); Igal Halfin, *From Darkness to Light: Class Consciousness and Salvation in Revolutionary Russia* (Pittsburgh: University of Pittsburgh Press, 2000); and Kotkin, *Magnetic Mountain.*

and patterns of identity persisted tenaciously alongside the new social forms cultivated by Soviet educational and cultural campaigns, repressive measures, and internal migration.[94]

Formakov's labor camp correspondence and other documentation concerning his life during and after his terms in the Gulag offer a complex view of what Sovietization might mean for citizens from the borderlands in practice. Obviously, on at least a superficial level, Formakov did adapt to the Soviet cultural environment in which he found himself following his arrest. Shortly after arriving in Kansk in 1941 he began, on the advice of another inmate, to ingratiate himself with the camp Cultural-Educational Sector by drafting patriotic verse for wall-newspapers and agitational performances and participating in performance groups. In order to succeed in these endeavors, Formakov had to adopt a pro-Soviet stance and internalize both the nuances of official ideology and the norms of Soviet speech. Formakov's unpublished camp narrative depicts the learning curve that this entailed quite explicitly. In a key scene Formakov's narrator makes the mistake of introducing a fellow inmate on stage as a "rising star" in the camp drama circle, only to be sharply rebuked for connecting a powerful Soviet symbol to a lowly prisoner. "Did he not know," the head of the Cultural-Educational Sector demanded, "what the word 'star' meant for a Soviet person?"[95]

In writing home to his wife about his work with the Cultural-Educational Sector, Formakov seems to alternate between sincere enthusiasm and cynical calculation. In both legal and illegal communications, he proudly sends home patriotic verse that he has composed for camp celebrations and details efforts to prepare official holiday concerts. He also, however, admits that sometimes after performances you "head backstage, release your soul, and you just want to wail," noting that, for this reason, he has to make sure his soul is "always in a corset."[96] Moreover, Formakov repeatedly signals that practical considerations, at least in part, motivate his participation in cultural education work. He notes that volunteering gives him access to paper, better rations, and more tolerable living conditions and helps him

94. Amir Weiner, "The Empires Pay a Visit: Gulag Returnees, East European Rebellions, and Soviet Frontier Politics," *Journal of Modern History* 78, no. 2 (June 2006): 333–76.

95. [Byloe], 20.

96. Letter to Anna Formakova dated March 9, 1946.

avoid transfers and onerous work assignments. Although Formakov endured brief stints on logging details during his first camp term, more often than not he managed to evade the kind of hard physical labor that quickly killed all but the hardiest inmates. Instead he punched eyes in sewing machine needles, served as a watchman and an orderly, set work norms for other inmates, and, for a time, cut bread rations. Such "soft" spots were in perennial short supply in the camps and, in order to retain them, Formakov had to defend himself against potential replacements and tirelessly curry favor, an effort that Formakov explicitly chronicles in his letters.

In summer 1945, Formakov was abruptly transferred from a favorable indoor work assignment to a general labor detail moving logs. Although initially, in letters, he put on a brave front and presented this change to his wife as an opportunity for fresh air and exercise, by October his health was deteriorating and temperatures were dropping, and he began writing about his efforts to lobby influential individuals for a return to his old assignment.[97] What exactly did Formakov have to offer to get himself moved back to indoor work at the end of 1945? The criminal case file compiled after Formakov was rearrested in 1949 on the presumably false suspicion that he wrote an anti-Soviet letter sent anonymously to his place of employment suggests an answer to this question that again hints at the role that accommodation to Soviet power played in his survival. Both interrogation transcripts and petitions for clemency associated with this case show that Formakov signed papers agreeing to work as an informer in Kraslag some time in 1945 and, following his release at the end of 1947, continued making regular reports to the Soviet secret police under the code name "Zemlitsyn" at least until 1949.[98] In some petitions, dated between 1949 and 1951, Formakov valorizes his contributions as an informer as part of an appeal for clemency, but in other contexts he makes statements that suggest that he was underperforming, at least while he was back home in Riga between December 1947 and September 1949, and was desperate to placate his dissatisfied handlers.[99] It is difficult to know how

97. See the letter he wrote to his wife dated October 19, 1945, later in this volume.

98. State Archives of Latvia, f. 1986, op. 1, d. P-1545, ch. 2, ll. 34, 40–42.

99. Ibid., l. 13 and l. 121 ob.

long Formakov actively served as an informer or how useful the information he provided the secret police actually proved given that most documentation regarding the work of secret-police informants in Latvia remains closed to researchers, but circumstantial evidence suggests that at least in Kraslag he must have given his handlers something.[100] Unlike most Gulag-returnees, Formakov was allowed to return to a capital city immediately following his 1947 release, a boon that, his 1949 case file suggests, was issued in return for his promise to join the army of informers that the Soviet authorities relied on in Latvia as part of its efforts to pacify the newly reassimilated region and root out pockets of resistance.[101]

In signing an agreement that he would serve as an informer, Formakov was by no means unique. As noted earlier, up to 8 percent of the camp population in the postwar period made similar compromises: often this was the only way to survive.[102] Even Solzhenitsyn, by his own admission, caved to pressure and signed an agreement to serve as an informant in camp at one point, although he notes that he managed to avoid providing information.[103] "Trusties" like Formakov, who finagled work assignments indoors instead of on general labor details, made easy marks for recruitment pitches: camp security officers could always threaten to take away the inmate's privileged job in the case of noncooperation.[104] Particularly in years like 1945, when the security officers in labor camps needed to replace informants released in a large postwar amnesty, individuals such as Formakov would have faced considerable pressure.[105] In Latvia as well as in the world of the camps, many individuals agreed, often under duress, to serve as secret-police informants. Soviet records suggest that the number of secret-police informers on the books in the Soviet Union grew by over 200 percent be-

100. High turnover plagued informer networks in the late 1940s in the western borderlands: anti-Soviet partisans killed informants if they caught them, and the secret police dismissed those they found useless. Alexander Statiev, *The Soviet Counterinsurgency in the Western Borderlands* (Cambridge: Cambridge University Press, 2010), 235.

101. State Archives of Latvia, f. 1986, op. 1, d. P-1545, ch. 2, l. 40.

102. Zemskov, "GULAG (istoriko-sotsiologicheskii aspekt)," *Sotsiologicheskie issledovaniia*, no. 7 (1991): 3–17, as cited in Barnes, *Death and Redemption*, 182.

103. *Gulag Archipelago*, 2: 359–67.

104. Ibid., 357.

105. Alexopoulos, "Amnesty 1945," 289.

tween 1943 and 1951, with much of the increase in newly reconquered areas such as Latvia.[106]

Formakov's service as an informant, his work for the camp Cultural-Educational Sector, and his ability to "speak Bolshevik" when the occasion demanded, however, do not tell the whole story. In other respects, Formakov's labor camp letters, records associated with his life in postwar Riga, and even the reminiscences of family and friends suggest that he resisted Sovietization. Formakov's letters document his elaborate efforts to continue to celebrate religious holidays in camp, his daily prayer life, and continued identification with interwar Latvian and Russian émigré culture. In the letters he sent home from the camps, Formakov writes in the language of the bourgeois world at least as often as he "speaks Bolshevik." He continually cites the songs of the great émigré cabaret artist Alexander Vertinsky, reminisces about his comfortable prewar domestic life, and identifies signs of divine providence in both the natural world and the lives of family members. Following his 1947 release, Formakov clung to the remains of his prewar library, which neither he nor his wife ever purged of obviously anti-Soviet materials. This carelessness came back to haunt Formakov after his 1949 arrest when a search turned up portraits of the martyred Tsar Nikolai II and his son Alexei clipped from prewar newspapers, along with anti-Soviet joke anthologies and copies of Formakov's own anti-Soviet novels.[107] During the 1960s, Formakov cultivated an apparently warm friendship with Aleksandr Solzhenitsyn, hosted the author on several of his research trips to Riga, and served as one of the original witnesses who provided Solzhenitsyn with information for *The Gulag Archipelago* before apparently retreating from the connection as official pressure on Solzhenitsyn intensified.[108] Under the influence of Solzhenitsyn's *One*

106. Dzheffri Burds, *Sovetskaia agentura: Ocherki istorii SSSR v poslevoennye gody (1944–1948)* (Moscow: Sovremennaia Istoriia, 2006), 41. See also Statiev, *The Soviet Counterinsurgency in the Western Borderlands*, 233–38.

107. State Archives of Latvia, f. 1986, op. 1, d. P-1545, ch. 2, ll. 8, 41–42.

108. Solzhenitsyn, *Gulag Archipelago*, 2: 135. See also the list of witnesses included in recent Russian editions of this work: *Arkhipelag GULAG, 1918–1956: Opyt khudozhestvennogo issledovaniia* (Ekaterinburg: U-Faktoriia, 2007), 1: 18. Solzhenitsyn's first wife, Natalia Reshetovskaia, suggests that Solzhenitsyn met Formakov in a transit prison in Kuibyshev. After the publication of *One Day in the Life of Ivan Denisovich*, Formakov wrote to Solzhenitsyn, renewing the acquaintance. *V kruge vtorom: Otkroveniia pervoi zheny Solzhenitsyna* (Moscow:

Day in the Life of Ivan Denisovich, Formakov started to write his own camp narrative, which, though cautious in comparison to many other survivor accounts, represented a brave act in the context of the period. There is no evidence that any of Formakov's post–Stalin-era acquaintances believed he was an informer. According to Formakov's family, he remained religiously observant until his death in 1983.

So who was Formakov after 1945: someone who had reluctantly served as a secret-police informant but who in other respects remained true to prewar cultural norms and, by the Thaw era, wanted to testify to the abuses of the Gulag, or a mole leading a double life who briefly infiltrated dissident circles in the 1960s? Or is the truth, like so much of Eastern European history, a little greyer? Was it all too possible in a postwar detention site, or for that matter post-Stalin Riga, to be both fundamentally complicit in state mechanisms of control and yet, in other contexts, something other than wholly Sovietized? To what extent did Soviet citizens in the Stalin period engage in code-switching, alternating between "speaking Bolshevik" and less official modes of communication depending on the context, their interlocutor, perceptions of risk, or just their mood?[109] Were Soviet communicative practices in the Stalin period really as "hegemonic" as has sometimes been alleged, or, if we look closely enough, can we perceive on the margins of society (populations hailing from the western borderlands in the 1940s) and in private life something that almost anticipates the discursive diversity of the late Soviet period?[110] How much did sincerity really matter? Did the Soviet state always demand true belief, or was it sometimes perhaps enough, as Stephen Kotkin suggests, to just "participate as if one believed"?[111] Both Steven Barnes and Miriam Dobson note instances in which individuals on the fringes of Soviet society in the immediate

Algoritm, 2006), 117. On the cooling of Formakov's relationship with Solzhenitsyn, see Fedorov, "O russkom soznanii Latgalii."

109. On code-switching in the Stalin period, see Michael S. Gorham, *Speaking in Soviet Tongues: Language Culture and the Politics of Voice in Revolutionary Russia* (DeKalb: University of Northern Illinois Press, 2003), 131, 227.

110. On late Soviet discursive practices, see Alexei Yurchak, *Everything Was Forever, Until It Was No More: The Last Soviet Generation* (Princeton: Princeton University Press, 2006).

111. Kotkin, *Magnetic Mountain,* 220.

aftermath of Stalin's death (nationalists from the western borderlands taking part in labor camp rebellions, labor camp returnees) "spoke" or tried to "speak Bolshevik" in interactions with the Soviet authorities, perhaps out of practical considerations, while simultaneously displaying adherence to alien values.[112] Perhaps Formakov's communications represent an earlier example of a similar phenomenon?

Formakov's labor camp correspondence, his 1949 criminal file, and the conflicting facts that we know about his later life raise all these questions. Formakov may not have been a stalwart hero who managed even in the worst of circumstances to remain true to principles, but he was a loving husband and father, and he desperately wanted to live and get home to his family. The story of how he managed to achieve this, through luck and calculation, as revealed in his labor camp correspondence, underscores some of the complexity of life in both Stalin's Gulag and the Soviet Union as a whole: survival often involved "cruel choices"; the Soviet system functioned, to the extent that it did, precisely because it succeeded in coopting ordinary, "decent" people, who yielded to persuasive rhetoric, social pressure, threats, and incentives.[113] And yet, from many points of view, the Soviet regime proved incapable of fully realizing its vast aspirations to reshape society and to control every aspect of the daily life of its citizens; vestiges of the past remained evident in Soviet culture alongside evidence of change.

LATER LITERARY WORK AND FAMILY LIFE

Formakov's literary production in the post-Stalin years was limited and, by and large, relatively cautious. He generally tried to work in fields that had offered more opportunities to disgraced writers, such as radio, children's literature, and translation, and employed the tone of reflexive patriotism that typified the verse he composed for Kraslag's Cultural-Educational Sector during the 1940s or relied on the stylistic and thematic norms of mature Socialist Realism. In radio skits, short

112. Steven A. Barnes, "'In a Manner Befitting Soviet Citizens': An Uprising in the Post-Stalin Gulag," *Slavic Review* 64, no. 4 (Winter 2005): 823–50; Miriam Dobson, *Khrushchev's Cold Summer: Gulag Returnees, Crime, and the Fate of Reform after Stalin* (Ithaca, NY: Cornell University Press, 2009), 11–12.

113. Solzhenitsyn, *Gulag Archipelago*, 2: 265.

stories, and essays, Formakov satirized life in bourgeois Latvia; exposed negative characters for their ignorance, laziness, and greed; and promoted the Soviet cult of high culture, including specifically classical music. Even the fictionalized memoir of his camp years that Formakov drafted in this period valorizes labor and features carefully developed patriotic themes. In it, the inmates themselves, demonstrating all the enthusiasm of Stakhanovites, lobby to cut their lunch break in half so that they can aid the war effort by increasing production, and lengthy passages describe successful efforts to introduce labor-saving innovations.[114] Scenes depicting mentor/mentee relationships appear periodically throughout the text, as do direct references to Soviet classics such as Nikolai Ostrovsky's *Kak zakalialas' stal'* (How the Steel Was Tempered).[115] Over the course of the narrative, in part thanks to the models of heroic behavior provided in such Socialist Realist novels, Formakov's narrator gains a clearer understanding of the advantages of the Soviet system and frees himself from his bourgeois misconceptions.[116] Viewed in terms of its structure and themes, Formakov's account of his camp experiences, in other words, in many respects resembles a production novel, the most orthodox and safest form of self-expression available to a Soviet author.[117] Perhaps by cloaking his daring subject matter in this traditional form, Formakov hoped to increase the chances that his manuscript might, like Solzhenitsyn's *One Day in the Life of Ivan Denisovich,* win the approval of official censors and reach Soviet readers legally.[118] No record, however, exists that For-

114. [Byloe], 30, 54–57. Stakhanovites were model Soviet workers who, following the example set by the coal miner Alexei Grigorievich Stakhanov in 1935, worked to break production records and, by means of enthusiasm, advance the construction of socialism.

115. Ibid., 34, 106.

116. Ibid., 94–95, 116–21.

117. Production novels were the most common type of Socialist Realist novel. They describe the efforts of a group of workers to complete a construction project, fulfill the plan, or revive production at a dormant site and, like other Socialist Realist works, often feature a "positive hero" who achieves greater political consciousness over the course of the novel, frequently thanks to the guidance of an older, more enlightened communist mentor. Katerina Clark, *The Soviet Novel: History as Ritual,* 3rd ed. (Bloomington: Indiana University Press, 2000), 255–63.

118. *One Day in the Life of Ivan Denisovich* itself represented a careful work, written and edited with an eye to the demands of official censors. Solzhenitsyn com-

makov ever tried to submit his text for publication: it seems likely that he began writing it in the brief period following the release of *One Day in the Life of Ivan Denisovich,* when publishing on the Gulag seemed feasible, and then abandoned the project as the backlash against de-Stalinization intensified. A 1969 essay describing Formakov's friendship with the poet Igor Severianin, which in part reworked material that he had written in the 1920s, represented his biggest postrelease publishing success. It offers an insightful and in places biting portrait of an aging literary celebrity in exile, and beautifully captures the realities of Russian cultural life in the Baltics during the interwar period.[119] Otherwise Formakov supported himself after 1955 primarily by translating the work of Latvian writers into Russian: most of his postrelease original manuscripts languished in desk drawers.

Family represented Formakov's greatest priority in the last decades of his life. In her memoirs, Solzhenitsyn's first wife, Natalia Reshetovskaia, cites a letter that Formakov sent Solzhenitsyn some time after the publication of *One Day in the Life of Ivan Denisovich,* which highlights his attitude: "I can tell you who all writers owe a pressing debt to—it is to their wives, to wives like yours and mine and thousands of others. A monument should be erected to them—built of words, marble, and music."[120] Although very few of the letters that Anna Ivanovna, whom Formakov characteristically addressed using the pet name Niusha or Niushenka, wrote to her husband during his two terms in labor camps have survived, she nonetheless looms large in the correspondence that follows. As Formakov acknowledges time and time again, she played a key role in sustaining him during his sentences by sending both emotional support and packages. She also essentially singlehandedly raised the family's two children, supporting them and financing her efforts on behalf of Formakov on a modest teacher's salary.

Little information exists on the biography of this tough-willed, resourceful woman. She was, as Formakov notes in one of his letters, a former student of Formakov's and had grown up in straitened material circumstances in an Old Believer home in Daugavpils. As a result,

---

promised in order to get the work published legally: Alexander Solzhenitsyn, *The Oak and the Calf: A Memoir* (New York: Harper Colophon Books, 1980), 1–49.

119. "Vstrechi s Igorem Severianinym," *Zvezda,* no. 3 (1969).

120. Reshetovskaia, *V kruge vtorom,* 7.

perhaps, the relationship seems to have retained a certain paternal cast at least until the time of Formakov's first arrest: Formakov took pride in having helped "raise" his much younger wife and in ensuring that she developed proper literary style.[121] They married in 1932 and had two children: Dmitri (1935–1951) and Evgenia (1940–2013). Left on her own after Formakov's arrest in 1940, Anna faced repeated crises. After a bomb destroyed the Formakovs' home in Daugavpils, she first found shelter with a friend and then relocated to Riga, where she rented a private house with her parents. The rent was exorbitant, and making ends meet was a challenge, but somehow she managed. When Formakov returned from his first sentence in 1947, she met him enthusiastically. He spent nineteen months at home with his family in Riga, getting acquainted with the daughter he had never met and working as an economist for a forestry trust before being rearrested. According to family accounts, a jealous coworker had placed compromising material in his briefcase.[122] Formakov's status as a camp releasee made him inherently suspect: given the large-scale roundup taking place in Latvia in 1949, it is likely that he would have been rearrested and taken from his family in any case.

Formakov received a new ten-year term for political crimes and was sent to Taishet and then to the Irkutsk region before finally ending up in Omsk. Threatened with the loss of her job as a teacher, the family's sole means of support, Anna Ivanovna reluctantly agreed to a divorce. She nonetheless faced such persistent pressure from the school in which she worked that she returned to school part-time to requalify as a speech therapist, which allowed her to change her place of employment. In August 1955, two years after Stalin's death, Formakov won release from the labor camps and returned to Riga. He and Anna Ivanovna officially remarried in 1957, in the presence of Evgenia, their only surviving child. Although Formakov faced several major health crises in the decades that followed, the family, by all accounts, lived happily and managed, despite everything, to come together again as a strong unit. In the memoirs that she wrote at the beginning of the 1990s, Evgenia Formakova noted about her father, "For me, he was not just a father, but also a great friend. When I wanted to talk about my misfortunes

121. See, for instance, his letter dated February 6, 1945.
122. Meksh, "A. I. Formakov (1900–1983)," 356.

and even what I was going through personally, I always went to him."[123] Formakov died in 1983, Anna Ivanovna two years later.

A NOTE ON THE EDITING APPROACH EMPLOYED

This edition contains only part of the labor camp correspondence from the Hoover Institution Archive's Arsenii Ivanovich Formakov Papers. I have abridged some letters with an eye to eliminating passages that seem of purely personal interest and also obvious repetition: because letters frequently arrived out of order or went astray, both prisoners and their relations often repeat essential information in multiple communications. Although, particularly in early letters, I have retained some repetitive elements with an eye to giving the flavor of the correspondence as a whole, in later sections of the book I have cut somewhat more to enhance readability. The places where I have abridged letters are marked with bracketed ellipses.

Where possible, explanatory notes flesh out references to individuals, places, and works of art. Some allusions in the letters, however, remain difficult to trace. The cultural world that the Formakovs inhabited is now a distant memory, obscured not just by the passage of time but also by repeated invasions and changes in political boundaries, values, and social norms. The Soviet Socialist Revolution of October 1917 and the later Soviet takeover of the Baltic region are often treated as fundamental rifts that destroyed historical continuity and disrupted normal processes of cultural memory in the societies they affected. On a small scale in family documents such as the material from the Arsenii Ivanovich Formakov Papers at the Hoover Institution Archive, we see something similar: either because the pace of change was so frenetic that few landmarks remained to anchor memories or because parents chose, out of caution, not to talk about aspects of family history that seemed at odds with the new order even with their children, much remains obscure. Even the Formakovs' daughter Evgenia could not answer many questions regarding the documents in her family archive.[124] In this respect again, perhaps the holes and silences that disrupt our ability to fully understand individual documents are telling: they reflect

123. Ibid., 351.
124. Fedorov, "O russkom soznanii Latgalii," 95.

the communicative limitations that shaped the lives of Soviet families and that continue to some extent today to complicate efforts by Latvia's inhabitants to fully understand their past.

A small selection of letters from Aleksandr Solzhenitsyn to Formakov is included in this edition. They are published with the permission of Natalia Solzhenitsyn.

LETTERS

1941–1944

A Letter Home

To my daughter Evgenia

You are a year old today . . . You are already babbling[1]
And running about like a wind-up rabbit.
You are my bright-spirited daughter, who lives so far away
And whom I've never seen.

Having trusted false portents,
For two months, I thought: it's a son again.
I sent greetings to you through the stars as if through the mail,
And called you to come play with me, of course, only in dreams.

Later, my child, you became real to me,
In an agonizing and incredible moment,
When I was brought to life by the sharpest joy,
And then immediately descended into spasms of tears . . .

I did not tremble at your birth,
I did not stay awake nights hovering over you,
I merely touched the pink blanket
In which you now sleep with my hand.

1. Formakov's daughter Evgenia was born on December 31, 1940. This annotated poem is on plain, water-spotted paper with no obvious censorship marks.

All the cares, anxieties, and sorrows
Of your infancy's unrepeatable days,
To my misfortune, passed me by,
And were no delight to me.

I know your mother, pressing her hand to your hurts,
Will sing you my songs,
And endlessly repeat stories
About your father, who will suddenly appear out of nowhere.

I won't make the sign of the cross over you when you go to bed at
    night,
And won't be kissing you on the forehead in the morning . . .
But I have asked, and good-hearted San Ivanych will see
That your dreams are filled with everything bright.

And in the day, your mother will watch over you . . . my darling,
    my dear!
A great heart; bitter sorrow . . . Today,
My daughter, wishing you well, I bow
To the earth, while my soul longs for home, so far away.

It is so wonderful that I am on duty tonight,
That, in our homeland, you are not yet asleep,
And we can see each other more clearly than if face-to-face,
And we can speak to each other in this quiet.

May the New Year again be not without hope,
Trust in your heart, but do not rail against reason.
Caring, faithful, tender, I am with you forever,
My only, my marvelous darlings . . .

The night of December 30, 1941. Kansk.

P.S. When I arrived, I found myself assigned to heavy labor, wood-
cutting work. Even before I got out of the quarantine section, I managed
to make my way to the club, where I established myself as a versifier and
started working on the wall publications of our settlement [*poselok*].[2]

---

2. When writing home, Formakov often uses language that obscures his status
as a prisoner: in illegal communications, this was important because, if caught, he
would have faced significant consequences. How careful he is varies, which may
reflect how secure he felt a particular communication channel was, how recently

I immediately distinguished myself. After a while I began to whine about how tired I was getting, to say that I wasn't capable of writing when I got home from work, and the administration of the club got me a place as a night watchman at the garage for the whole winter, from 7:00 p.m. to 7:00 a.m. I had to clean various outbuildings and facilities, patrol the courtyard, have four pails of boiling water ready by morning, and light five stoves. But then I had the dispatcher's room at my disposal: it was light and warm, there was a clock, a stove, and a wooden couch. That is where I composed these two poems. I have managed to save the original manuscript pages that I wrote them on, which I now send you.[3] Senia.

♦ ♦ ♦

I Wish You Health, Knowing There Will Be No Answer

For Niusha

Everything is as it should be: the frosty night,
The bright oval of the moon,
A scattering of stars on the dark blue velvet,
And the clock in the middle of the wall.

Firewood hisses in a hearty chorus
Behind the little cast-iron door with its quadriga.[4]
I am alone with my faithful book as always,
But I scarcely take in the words.

This night, which for me is New Year's,
For you has not yet begun.
I will not mark the twelfth hour today
With a wish for your health that will go unanswered.

I will wait; let the earth turn a little,
Let the moon start shining above you

---

a crackdown on illegal mail had taken place, and differences in his attitude and mental acuity as a result of changes in circumstances.

3. This postscript appears to refer to both the preceding and following poems. These sheets were presumably mailed as enclosures in one of the letters Formakov sent home after he located his wife in 1944.

4. Formakov supplies an explanatory note in the margins of the manuscript page: "A quadriga is an ancient chariot, harnessed with four horses."

And the children bid you goodnight.
At midnight, I know, you will be alone.

And not knowing my midnight,
Knowing only our dawn,
Taking my last portrait in your hands,
You'll fill the appointed hour with conversation.

You'll remember everything as I do, you'll feel regret,
You'll cry and send your blessings,
Your gaze, dimmed by sorrow, will clear,
Stillness will soothe your heart.

We will no doubt hear each other
And will feel in the air that blows
Through measureless time and space
The passage of a familiar kiss.

So, midnight, be on your way!
You've a long way to go, but I will wait,
So that, toward morning, I can wish my darling
New happiness in this New Year.

                                        1/1 1942
                                     12:47 a.m.

P.S. I sat up until 5:00 a.m. and then sent my New Year's wishes to you and the children. At that time the difference in time zones between us was five hours: you are an hour ahead of Moscow, right? Since then, I haven't had another New Year's like that ... In April, I lost my position, but I managed to find something even better: I got appointed as orderly in the club. There I was the closest assistant to the head of the club: I helped other people, and I didn't live so badly myself. But envious people appeared. Denunciations followed, and in the autumn I was tossed out and sent to perform hard labor. The winter was hard: I was working out in the open the whole time, loading logs onto sleds. I took apart piles of gigantic logs that were as high as three- or four-story buildings. Once a pile suddenly collapsed, and I barely managed to move aside. I ran, but I fell, and the falling logs covered me. Your prayers saved me then. People came running over and freed me, and I was only a little bruised. They thought I would be ground up like hamburger ...

♦ ♦ ♦

Kansk. July 6, 1944.[5]
My dear, priceless Niushenka!
My darlings, Dima and Zhenichka!

I send my best wishes to you in connection with your liberation, be-cause I feel sure that by the time this postcard reaches Dvinsk, it will al-ready be in our hands. I am alive and well because I had to live at least until we could correspond. I am working in a needle-manufacturing workshop. I fulfill norms by 200–300 percent. I live in a dormitory with very good neighbors.[6] There is a radio. I lead a dramatic group at the local club, where they show movies—even talkies. In a word, everything is fantastically good despite your doubts and grave con-cerns, Niushenka. But three years without any word from you—it's been horrible! I am eager for pictures, letters in limitless quantities. If you can, please send a package of groceries (fats, sugar, soap, whatever you have) and money. Send parcels of old newspapers, magazines, and books to read for entertainment. I don't need clothing or shoes. The only thing I don't have is socks—they all wore out or were lost. I am wearing footcloths. I would like to write many tender words, to convey all the intensity of the love that grips me, but I will do that later, once I have really found you and know your address. I send kisses to all of you together and then to each of you separately. I bless you and wish you every happiness. My address is on the reverse. It is for both letters and packages and everything else. Yours, Senia

5. Written on the kind of official postcard used to confirm delivery of a piece of registered mail. Formakov's letter covers one side of the form; the other side contains his wife's last known address in Latvia and Formakov's official camp ad-dress in pencil, and then, in a different hand, the note: "The house burned down; addressee unknown to the City Information Bureau." The address side of the card is overwritten at a diagonal in black ink with a rough copy of part of the later letter with the header "Two New Year's Tangos." Both sides of the postcard are postmarked. Most likely this postcard was returned to Formakov as undeliverable and then used as scrap paper before being mailed out again in an envelope.

6. Formakov's vocabulary again obscures his status as a prisoner. Presumably he hoped to shield his wife from repercussions: this was a postcard and the mes-sage might have been read by anyone. The fact that Formakov provides his official address, the post office box number signifying the camp in which he was held, suggests he mailed this postcard officially although it bears no obvious camp cen-sorship stamp.

♦ ♦ ♦

The city of Kansk
July 28, 1944[7]
Hello, my sunshine, Niushenka!
Hello, my darling Dimochka and my daughter Zhenichka!

This morning I at last heard the joyous news on the radio that Dvinsk had been taken, news that I had dreamt of all these three long years. It was still only 1:00 a.m. where you are, but it was 6:00 a.m. here— that is how far to the east I am from you now. The workday is now over: I completed a double norm. As always, I had supper, watched a talkie in our club, and now, when it's relatively quiet in the dormitory (some have gone to the third screening, others are asleep, some are darning . . . there are forty of us in the section), I am writing a letter, and everyone is asking: who are you writing to? Are you writing home? And they all smile affectionately.

I am so happy, and I am writing on the paper that was given to me in 1941, and my heart keeps leaping: some day an answer will come! Will it come? If it does, what sort of answer will it be? Many of my comrades are already getting letters from their families who have survived the fascist catastrophe . . . But their relatives knew their addresses, and you, my long-suffering Niushenka, do not!!! Write to me as soon as you can without delay as much as you can. I am eager for photographs of you and of the children, and of all of you together. If you can, telegraph your address. After that, you can send me (in a wooden crate covered in canvas) a grocery package (fats, proteins, sweets, tinned food— anything at all), enclosing an inventory of the contents. I am eager for

7. This is the earliest example in the collection of a kind of letter known as a *treugol'nik* (little triangle): a sheet of paper folded into a self-contained triangle, the inside of which holds the text of the communication, and the outside of which serves as the envelope (see illustration). Soldiers in wartime and prisoners often mailed such communications, but ordinary Soviet citizens also did so in some periods: envelopes were sometimes hard to obtain. The sheet bears a military censorship stamp and Formakov's return address but no camp censorship stamp. A note in indelible pencil on the address side, presumably made by a postman, again notes that the addressee's house has burned down. The date December 28, 1944, was added to the address side in blue pen at some point. This seems to be a mistake: a family member cataloguing the collection added composition dates to some letters and misread Formakov's Roman numeral. Punch holes show that at one time this letter, like many others in the collection, was in a binder.

"Little triangle" letter (*treugol'nik*) from Arsenii Formakov to Anna Ivanovna (Niusha) Formakova, July 28, 1944. Arsenii Ivanovich Formakov Papers, Hoover Institution Archive, Box 1, folder 2.

you to send, in a small parcel, old newspapers (anything Soviet), which I will use as gifts for my friends who smoke, and books for entertainment.[8] In terms of clothing, I only need a pair of shirts, both undershirts and shirts to wear on top, thick and thin socks, and handkerchiefs. Out of all the handkerchiefs from home, I only managed to hold onto one, but it is scented with your perfume, my darling wife!

What can I say about myself? There is so much I should say! We left Dvinsk on June 24, 1941, arrived in Krasnoiarsk in sixteen days, and then a month later left on a barge down the wondrously beautiful and majestic Enisei for the city of Eniseisk. In October, after passing through Krasnoiarsk, we arrived here in Kansk, where I have performed various kinds of work. Right now I help manufacture needles for sewing machines. I spend my leisure time at the club (I lead a dramatic group and recite poetry at concerts). This last sphere of activity gives me certain privileges, which are not insignificant in my current circumstances. Of course, I have lost weight and have aged. I was close to death twice last year (I had bloody diarrhea for five weeks and then, after a week of feeling better, got diphtheria). Our wonderful medical men alone saved me—that and your prayers and those of the children.

There has not been a single day in the last three years when I failed to think of you, reverently praying that all was well. Even though I don't know if this letter will reach you, I can feel my heart constrict, and I can't seem to find the right tender words. Instead I feel tears welling, but I don't cry. Men don't cry (that's for Dima!). What happened at our two visits after my arrest doesn't count: those were exceptional circumstances.

I wrote a great deal of poetry for all of you and for each of you individually. I sent letters out in all directions in search of you until I became convinced that you were not evacuated [before the Germans took Dvinsk]. In my search for information, I located Liza Frolova. She is having a hard time with Kotik (Taniusha is getting on very well in Komsomolsk), but her regular letters once a month brought me a lot of joy. In general, during these four years, many good people have crossed

---

8. The Russian mail system distinguishes between small parcels of goods wrapped in butcher-paper and twine (*banderoli*) and larger packages mailed in boxes or crates (*posylki*). Small parcels typically contain reading material, although they are sometimes used for mailing other items.

my path, who have really helped me survive and stay alive at least until I could send you letters. Oh, how I love you!!!

My address is: Krasnoiarskii krai, city of Kansk, P.O. box 235/8, and then my name. There are no limits on how many letters you can send. You can also send money. If the post office won't accept a grocery parcel, say that it is for a *prisoner*: they are obliged to accept it then (there is a special circular from the People's Commissariat of Communications— No. 1637, dated February 29, 1944).[9] All the requests (except the request for letters, which are essential) have been made without any knowledge of your affairs, Niusha, and it goes without saying that I don't want you to make any sacrifices that will affect you or the children and will not accept it if you do. I have managed to survive and, now that I have established communications with you, I will continue to live . . . After all, the 30th is the fourth anniversary of the blackest day in our lives.[10] If they had told us then what we would have to bear, I would have committed suicide . . . and I would have been a fool.

There are no other Russians from Dvinsk here with me and only two or three Latvians. From Rezhitsa, Serezha Zubov, Minai Morozov, Misha Krutov, and Ukhtin [are here].[11] I am all alone as I always am: I do not form close friendships easily, and all my cultural work is like a narcotic. I first learned a lot about [what had happened to] you from Dania Frolov, with whom (and with the younger Sidorov, your neighbor) I lived in Eniseisk. They both stayed there and probably will be there forever.[12] During a transfer, I also met a Jewish tradesman who was your student and praised you, and I was so pleased! . . .

---

9. The word "prisoner" appears in Latvian. During and immediately after World War II, rules intended to spare overtaxed transportation networks banned Soviet citizens in many areas from mailing packages. By spring 1942, however, exceptions began to be made for packages mailed to inmates: the war had exacerbated pre-existing supply problems in the Gulag, producing soaring mortality rates among prisoners that the central authorities considered problematic. Even long after this new policy appeared, however, in areas deemed sensitive (for example, newly liberated regions and centers of government operations such as Moscow and Kuibyshev), an absolute ban on packages was enforced, with no exception for prisoners. "Tsirkuliar No. 52 ot 13 fevralia 1942" and "Tsirkuliar No. 99 ot 9 marta 1942," GARF, f. 9401, op. 1a, d. 127, ll. 25, 69.

10. Formakov means the day of his arrest.

11. The city of Rezhitsa is now known as Rezekne.

12. Perhaps an allusion to their deaths.

Of course, give my very best wishes to Anna Ananievna and Ivan Tarasievich: I hope they don't hold a grudge that I have brought you so much unhappiness.[13] After all, there were some happy times! I will write to you at no. 94 Kovenskaia street and also through our parish [obshchina].[14] I will also write to you in Riga, although I have forgotten that address. Perhaps my letters will reach you. Niusha, of course you probably don't believe I am alive. You were so concerned about my heart even in Dvinsk, but you see that it continues to work despite the diagnosis: myocardial ischemia.[15]

From the things that you so lavishly supplied me with from home (my dear, I still lovingly save the inventory list that came with the last package that you brought me [at the investigative prison in Dvinsk] on June 15, 1941), I still have the fur coat and the hat, one mitten, a jacket and a pair of pants, the boots, sandals, towel, the sack, the dark-blue short-sleeved shirt (I am in it now!), and the toothbrush (oh, if you can, could you send me a piece of soap and my little pillow?). Here I got work clothes and footwear—felt boots for winter—thin and thick gloves, a hat, a blanket, a pillow, a pillowcase, a mattress, which I fill with wood shavings, a quilted jacket—in a word, everything a person really needs.

I sleep on a lower bunk. My neighbors are cultured. On our table, we have a ceramic mug with violet and white Siberian cornflowers and your favorites, Niushenka, carnations (they grow in beds by our houses). My page is coming to an end, and I still haven't said anything at all. Love me and don't be ashamed. Children, listen to your mother. You have a wonderful mother—there isn't another like her in the whole world. In all the places I have been—not one. Do your lessons well: both your mother and your father did well in school. Be neat and clean;

13. Anna Ananievna and Ivan Tarasievich were Anna Ivanovna's parents.

14. Formakov presumably means the Gaikovskaia parish in Daugavpils, where he acted as a lay church leader (nastavnik) and filled other leadership positions in the 1930s. N. V. Pazukhina, "I. N. Zavoloko: Vekhi zhizennogo puti," Pamiati Zavoloko Ivana Nikiforovicha: Sbornik statei i materialov, posviashchennykh 100-letiiu I. N. Zavoloko (Riga: Rizhskaia Grebenshchikovskaia Staroobriadcheskaia Obshchina, 1999), 59; "Gaikovskaia staroobriadcheskaia obshchina vybrala novyi sovet soglasno instruktsii k zakonu o staroobriadcheskikh obshchinakh," Nash daugavpilskii golos, June 25, 1935.

15. Reduced blood flow to the heart, usually because of blocked arteries, that causes a lack of oxygen.

don't be fussy. When I get back, you can be naughty and fuss as much as you like. I kiss you all and embrace you warmly. I thank [God] that he has allowed me to live to this joyful day [when I can write to you].[16] And when I receive an answer from you, I will spend the whole day shouting "hooray!" with joy. Your Senia. Your papa. I send my respects and greetings to all who remember me and who have been kind to you!

♦ ♦ ♦

The city of Kansk
August 10, 1944[17]
My sweet, unforgettable, one and only Niushenka!
My dear children, Dimochka and Zhenichka!

I write to Dvinsk again and again and congratulate you on the city's liberation from the yoke of the despicable invaders and have not lost hope of at last receiving some word from you and of learning that you are all healthy and safe.[18] But perhaps you are in Riga, and then the uncertainty may continue for God only knows how long.

We have the day off today. The sun is out, but it does not burn too hot during this short Siberian summer. By October it is already winter here. It lasts until April or May with terrible Siberian cold snaps and temperatures to minus 40 or 45. In point of fact, however, these aren't so terrible, and, given the dryness of the climate here, are comparable to temperatures of minus 20 to 25 in Dvinsk. Last winter I worked

16. Formakov leaves a blank with a single period-like dot where the word "God" should stand. Perhaps he wanted to avoid explicit religious references in this early letter, but he does not follow this protocol in later communications. Formakov's openness about his religious convictions may reflect the relaxation of restrictions on religious life that took place in the Soviet Union during the war years. I have found no documentation suggesting that Latvian Old Believers employed a special notation system for the word "God" similar to that used here.

17. Written on plain paper with no obvious censorship marks or stamps.

18. Formakov often uses phrases from Soviet war propaganda in letters mailed both officially and illegally. Although inmates had an incentive to employ such language in letters that they knew would be censored, in Formakov's case the sentiments were probably sincere. Solzhenitsyn notes that Formakov remembered how passionately most inmates in his camp wanted to contribute to the war effort. Aleksandr I. Solzhenitsyn, *The Gulag Archipelago, 1918–1956: An Experiment in Literary Investigation*, 3 vols., trans. Harry Willetts and Thomas P. Whitney (New York: Harper and Row, 1974–1978), 2: 135.

loading and hauling logs to the lumber works. I spent the whole work-day (from 7:00 to 6:00) in the open air with the exception of the lunch break (from 12:00 to 1:00), when I would go to the watchman's booth and would even sleep there in the warmth. I was dressed warmly: felt boots, a quilted cotton jacket, and the same kind of cloth overcoat, warm mittens, and a hat with ear flaps, the long "ski"-scarf knitted by your very own skillful hands, Niushenka, and also the green sweater-vest. On particularly cold days, I would wear my fur coat over the quilted cotton jacket instead of the cloth overcoat. My underwear is the only thing that has gotten really tattered from washing. Also, my stockings have gotten stolen or worn out, of course. [. . .]

In other words, in respect to all this, everything is just fine. I visit the bath house every week. The day after we go to the bath house, we turn in our underthings for laundering. When I need to, I get a shave at the barber's. None of that costs me anything. Last autumn I started wear-ing my hair grown out as I used to, and I got a bronze comb.[19] I read a great deal, I write for the wall-newspaper, and I have a little book that identifies me as an exemplary worker, along with a certificate thanking me for my contributions to amateur cultural activities. As a member of this last collective (and not the least of its members), I can go to our sound-movie house for free whenever I like. I took a break from writ-ing this letter to go see the American comedy *Sun Valley Serenade* with Sonja Henie, the famous skater, in the lead role.[20] I sat through two showings back-to-back. It was bittersweet to remember how we had seen her in other pictures together, my dear Niushenka.

I sleep, I read, I go to the movies, and, most important, I try to think as little as possible, because I can think only of you, and not knowing anything is just unbearable! [. . .] Write to me (and have Dima write to me) at the following address: Krasnoiarskii krai, the city of Kansk, P.O. box 235/8. You should figure that on average it will take a month for a letter to get here. Write to me regularly, let's say twice a month (no less!). You can send the letters C.O.D. Write to me about everything. I will also write regularly, but probably less frequently. You can send telegrams to this address and packages and money. I know little about

19. In Formakov's autobiographical camp narrative, the narrator explains that, as a privilege, members of the camp cultural brigade could wear their hair grown out, as opposed to shaved close to the scalp: [Byloe], 38.

20. The Soviet Union purchased this film in 1944: "Spisok amerikanskikh fil'mov v sovetskom i rossiiskom prokate, 1929–1998," *Kinograf,* no. 16 (2005): 176.

your material circumstances, but I need letters and old newspapers and whatever books you can send for reading. Don't ruin our sets of collected works (if they have survived) [by sending individual volumes]. Please be sure to send at least one copy of *Vstrecha* [The Meeting].[21] In a grocery package (packed in a wooden crate and then wrapped in canvas), enclose an inventory listing everything you are sending: if possible fats, protein, soap, a toothbrush (I lost mine yesterday; it held up for four years), tooth powder or paste. In a clothing package, send: socks, both thin and thick, a set of long underwear for winter, and that is it!!! Don't bankrupt yourself buying things; don't leave yourself without. I wanted to add "or the children," but I know you wouldn't do that. This accursed war is at last coming to an end. On July 30, I completed half my sentence. I don't have any hope of a visit soon, but if I could just get a letter . . . And please send photographs of yourself and the children, whichever you can and as many as you can.

Give my best wishes to sweet Anna Ananievna, dear Ivan Tarasievich, and the marvelous Aunt Pola, the Nemtsovs, and to everyone who remembers me. The only person from Dvinsk here is Jānis Kūliņš, whose parents lived in our building on the corner of Zelenaia street and Kreslavskaia.[22] Stop by to see them. Also, not far from us there is a farming operation. Alik Katalymov has tuberculosis but has gotten stronger there.[23] I exchanged letters with Lida Frolova, hoping to learn your whereabouts. Her address is: Krasnoiarskii krai, Novo Ingashskii district, post office Kucherovka, Zabadovskii Chemical and Forestry Complex, Garevka zone. Things are pretty bad for her. I send hugs and kisses and my blessings to you with all my heart, Papa Senia.

♦ ♦ ♦

The city of Kansk, September 20, 1944[24]
My dear, long-suffering Niushenka!
My sweet children, Dimochka and Zhenichka!

Soon two months will have passed since our valiant Red Army liberated our native city of Dvinsk from the accursed invaders, and by that time, I had anticipated, my dear ones, that I would receive the

21. The book of poems that Formakov published in 1934.
22. Formakov provides the Russian spelling of this Latvian name.
23. Alik is a nickname. As becomes clear later, the prisoner's full name is Oleg Katalymov.
24. A *treugol'nik* marked with camp and military censorship stamps.

first letter from you, which would either bring me indescribable joy by containing the news that you are all alive and well or bring with it something horrible, about which I am afraid even to think.

As you see, I am alive and well (my myocardial ischemia does not count!), and through all these terrible years have lived only in hope of, if not a visit with you, at least the possibility of correspondence. Everyone calls me "the old man" or "father"—even those who are two or three years younger than me. I weigh seventy-five kilos, shave twice a week, and wear my hair grown out. I haven't lost a single tooth, and I have very little grey in my hair. My eyesight is fine. I spend my free time reading or writing poetry. I have not become mentally decrepit. In fall 1941, in Krasnoiarsk prison, I set out to learn how to play chess and, in the space of two weeks, mastered it so well that I started beating my teacher.

From August 28 to September 16, I traveled sixty-five kilometers by car to State Farm No. [ ] as part of a group of seven, the agit-brigade of our camp (the Kansk autonomous campsite of the NKVD's Kraslag).[25] There we gave concerts for the inmates, labor armyists, free laborers, and also those who were there to help with the harvest.[26] The fresh air, sunshine, physical activity, and good food greatly fortified and refreshed me. I work from 7:00 to 6:00 here (with a break from 12:00 to 1:00) in the wire shop, where I use a special machine to punch eyes in sewing

25. An agit-brigade put on propagandistic skits and concerts. Formakov leaves the state farm number blank: censorship rules barred inmates from revealing information that might betray their camp's theoretically secret location. In referencing inmates, he first uses the abbreviation z/k and then, in parentheses, gives the full term, zakliuchennye, in case his wife has not understood. On secrecy regulations in the Gulag, see Mark Harrison, "Secrecy, Fear, and Transaction Costs: The Business of Soviet Forced Labour in the Early Cold War," Europe-Asia Studies 65, no. 6 (August 2013): 1112–35.

26. During World War II, Soviet citizens deemed potentially disloyal, including many ethnic Germans, were conscripted into NKVD-run forced-labor projects. Known as the "Labor Army," they endured conditions that differed little from those experienced by regular Gulag inmates. Irina Mukhina, "'The Forgotten History': Ethnic German Women in Soviet Exile, 1941–1955," Europe-Asia Studies 57, no. 5 (July 2005): 740–43; G. A. Goncharov, "'Trudovaia armiia' perioda Velikoi Otechestvennoi voiny: rossiiskaia istoriografiia," Ekonomicheskaia istoriia. Obozrenie, ed. L. I. Borodkin, vol. 7 (Moscow: Tsentr Ekonomicheskoi Istorii pri Istoricheskom Fakul'tete MGU im. M. V. Lomonosova, 2001), 154–62; http://www.hist.msu.ru/Labs/Ecohist/OB7/goncharov.htm.

machine needles. The norm is 900 per day, but I systematically fulfill double that, which gets me a ration of 700 grams of bread, 750 grams of soup, and 200 grams of hot cereal in the morning; 200 grams of hot cereal at lunch; and 750 grams of soup and 150 grams of hot cereal in the evening. Moreover, I get about 100 rubles as a cash bonus each month. I get up at 6:00 and go to bed after 10:00 (sometimes earlier: it depends on how things go).

In our barrack, the plank bunks are set up in the train-car system [with separate bunk beds that each hold two inmates on top and two on the bottom]. I sleep on the bottom, by the window. Right now I am there writing at the night table, which is why the letters are not so even, but I don't want to go to the common table. My neighbors are sleeping. Today we have the day off. We have one every ten days. [. . .]

[A censorship mark blacks out about five words] in Moscow to eight years in a labor camp.[27] I have already served four. I have earned a special document identifying me as an exemplary worker and also the gratitude of the camp commandant for my cultural work. It is possible that I may be recommended for a reduction in my sentence. [. . .]

You can write and send me things as often as you like and whatever you like (or, more accurately, whatever you, my darling Niushenka, are able to). I can only send you so many letters from here. For this reason, don't start keeping accounts, but write to me systematically at least once a week. This will be a great joy. In a small parcel, send me old Soviet newspapers: for my friends who smoke. Here you can get a whole dinner for a newspaper. I know that you won't be satisfied with this, and you will want to help me more, but in terms of this there is one stipulation: first take care of all the children's needs. If it will not in any way be to their loss or to your detriment, then and only then you can wire me several hundred rubles to the same address or (this would be beyond a luxury and in no way essential for me—after all, I

27. Camp censors rarely left marks on letters: generally they either accepted or rejected them wholesale. In a letter like this that passed through both camp and military censorship, there is no way to determine with certainty which censor made a mark. Judging by the context, Formakov probably referenced the body that sentenced him, the Special Board (Osoboe Soveshchanie) of the People's Commissariat of Internal Affairs, the date of his sentence, and perhaps the alphabet code under which he was sentenced, but such information would not seem likely to concern a censor.

have survived these four years without anything!) send me a grocery package. A special circular allows this for inmates in labor camps. The things I need are soap, a change of warm underwear, a toothbrush, two outer shirts and a tie, thin and thick stockings, and handkerchiefs.[28] If the sweater you knitted at the end of 1940 still exists, send this precious item. I still have your (ski) scarf.

I am ashamed to be writing all this about myself, but I know this is the most interesting thing for you, and it would be a waste of time to ask questions about you. I know *nothing*. When the correspondence gets going, then we will really be able to start talking. And I will send all my poems, and I will torture you with all my questions and demands for more information. Also, more than anything else, I need your pictures. I will send you mine in return: an artist comrade of mine will draw it.

At the state farm, I saw Alik Katalymov. If someone wants to write to him, they could send the letter to my address. [. . .] Greetings to Ivan Taras[ievich], Anna Anan[ievna], to the Nemtsovs, Mania, Petya, to everyone who remembers me. May Chr[ist] keep you. Yours, Senia

My dear son Dimusha: This accursed war has separated us.[29] I am now so far from you that it takes the sun four hours to get from Kansk to Dvinsk. At 6:00 in the morning, I listen to the radio broadcast from Moscow, and there it is only 2:00 a.m. You probably already can read and write. Read this. Love your mother and mind her. Don't be mean to your sister. Write to me and draw something. Do you sing songs? I send you, your mother, and Zhenichka big kisses and hugs. Your loving father.[30]

---

28. The necktie is not a frivolous request: Formakov needs it because he participates in shows staged by the camp Cultural-Educational Sector. Owning the right wardrobe will make him more valuable and will help him retain the privileges that participation in cultural work brings.

29. Written at the bottom of the communication in large block-printed letters.

30. Formakov includes a small drawing of a girl's face surrounded by flowers with the heading "A picture for Zhenia."

◆ ◆ ◆

Kansk, October 1, 1944[31]
Dear Aunt Mania:

Yesterday evening, on what was indeed the day of saints Vera, Nadezhda, and Liubov, I finally received your first postcard and both laughed and wept with joy when I learned that my precious Niushenka was alive and well and had succeeded in nurturing Dima and Zhenia despite the exceptionally difficult circumstances.[32] That my son is very literate and my daughter is a high-spirited little girl is the most precious news for me. May Ivan Tarasievich's memory live on forever! It's too bad that our house burned down, but that is a minor thing. It is sad that Niusha got stuck for so long in Riga. It is already autumn, and she probably did not pack for winter.

Two days ago snow fell here, but today is again a nice sunny day. Bright sunshine always illuminates my soul now. After all, for four years I knew absolutely nothing about my family! If you had sent Niusha's Riga address, I would send a letter there as well. By the time it made its way there, Riga would again be ours. But all the same, she will hear from you that I am alive and that my thoughts are only of them. I have already sent three letters to her on Varshavskaia or Kovenskaia street in Dvinsk (July 28, August 10, and September 20), and I also sent a postcard dated July 6 to the Nemtsovs and the priest in Gajoks.[33] I did not remember your address. I also had forgotten the name and patronymic of your husband: my memory has started to fail me in regards to some things.[34] But, in general, I don't have cause to complain about my health.

Experience shows that it takes about a month for a letter to reach me from where you are. Mine should reach you in two weeks. Try to get all three of the letters that I sent Niusha and pass them on to her.

31. A *treugol'nik* addressed to Mariia Ananievna Vysotskaia in Daugavpils with a military censorship mark, but no camp censorship stamp and no return address. Presumably mailed illicitly.

32. The women's names Vera, Nadezhda, and Liubov mean faith, hope, and love, respectively.

33. The name of the street where the family had lived changed in this period. Gajoks is a region within Dvinsk/Daugavpils.

34. A symptom of poor nutrition.

The war will end soon. Hitler is done for. Perhaps peace will bring us joyful events.[35] Tell Niusha to be sure to send me photographs of herself and the children as soon as she can. She can send them registered mail. [. . .]

I will write to you every ten days, on the 1st, the 10th, and the 20th [of each month]. But if one of these letters doesn't reach you, don't worry: the road is long, and letters can go astray. Just let Niusha write in this case that there was no letter from such-and-such a date.

Why is Grandmother living in Riga? How is Niusha supporting herself? How are your other sisters? Where are Niushenka's brother and sister? Where are Serezha and Iura Nemtsov?

I have everything I need, and I ask you to convince Niusha not to try to help me if it is to her detriment. In fact, if necessary, I can send home about one hundred rubles a month. Give the relatives of Liza Frolova (the one with the son named Kotik) her address: Krasnoiarskii krai, Novo Ingashskii district, post office Kucherovka, Zabadovskii XLX, uchastok Garevka—although I have not had word from her in more than three months. Her sister Lena is not far from her, and so are the widow of Jansbergs (Smolianova), Lielais-Zykova, Hrebtova, Čapļa, Krūmiņa, and Augustāne—they are all widows.[36]

I send my warmest greetings and thanks to you and your husband for all the help and concern you have shown Niusha and the children. Thanks and warmest greetings to all there who remember me. Arsenii.

♦ ♦ ♦

Kansk, November 9, 1944
Niushenka, my sunshine!

I wait so impatiently for your lively lines. The postcard that Aunt Mania sent on August 30, which was so short on facts, made me really

35. Formakov hints at the possibility of a broad amnesty, which prisoners hoped would follow victory over Germany. An amnesty did take place in 1945, but it primarily affected common as opposed to political offenders; see Golfo Alexopolous, "Amnesty 1945: The Revolving Door of Stalin's Gulag," *Slavic Review* 64, no. 2 (Summer 2005): 274–306.

36. The last four words explain the fate of the male breadwinners of these families: none survived Soviet imprisonment. I have replaced Formakov's Russian spelling of these names with the Latvian orthography listed in the State Archives of Latvia database: http://www.itl.rtu.lv/LVA/dep1941/agram1.php?param=6.

happy, but since then she has fallen silent. Olia Chernova's letter also brought me a lot of joy.[37] I learned something important and new about you and Dimochka and Zhenichka from it, and the sweet characterization of them that she, as an outsider, penned really touched me. Aunt Mania wrote that the house in which we lived on Varshavskaia street burned down and when, but were you living there at the time? Such a great subject for my thoughts! Olia wrote to me that this took place on June 26, 1941, and that [since then] you have lived in Slobodka and in many other [places]—I am so grateful to her.[38] She sent the letter registered mail. She behaved like a real human being, just as one should.[39]

On June 24 in the morning, when they were evacuating us from Dvinsk, we stopped alongside the viaduct, and I saw all the windows of our apartment. In the rooms closest to the end [of the façade], the shutters were closed. There were no paper strips on the panes as there were in other apartments.[40] It was clear no one lived there. We were moved to the passenger train station. I hoped I would see Slobodka and the house where you were living, my dears, but, alas, they did not take us any further than the station, and then they sent us back in the other direction past Kreslavka, Bigosovo, Smolensk, Kaluga, Kulikovo Field, and Lev Tolstoy station, to Samara, Ufa, through the enchanting Urals, and then here.[41]

When we were going through Dvinsk on the train, we were passed by Lugovskoi and Milovskii, who were on foot, but they did not notice me. The only person to whom I managed to say goodbye through the

37. Olia Chernova was the acquaintance who spotted the letter that Formakov sent general delivery to the Daugavpils post office and took the time to reply.

38. *Slobodka* means "settlement" in Russian. In Daugavpils it referred to an area where many Old Believers lived.

39. To say that someone "behaved like a human being" is high praise in Russian. It implies acting against self-interest to help another. Olia earned this distinction by claiming a general delivery letter from an "enemy of the people" and writing back even though this might have led the Soviet secret police to question her loyalty. Sending the letter registered mail cost extra and created even more of a paper trail linking the sender and recipient.

40. A common wartime defensive measure meant to limit damage from explosions.

41. Kreslavka (now Kraslava) is in Latvia. Kulikovo Field, in the Tula region, was the site of a fourteenth-century Russian military victory over the Mongols. Lev Tolstoy station is the site where the author spent the last week of his life in 1910 under scandalous circumstances.

window and who recognized me was Lisov, who was on his locomotive. Did he tell you about how I said goodbye at that time?

Dimochka's days are approaching, his birthday, with which so many unforgettable memories are connected, and his saint's day . . . During the week of October 20, I mailed a special greeting for these occasions in verse, my portrait, and a story in verse about the fox and the hare to him at Aunt Mania's address. If it got lost, let me know, and then count this as the special greeting: with all my heart I hope that you find your reward in the children for all the distress that I have brought upon you. [. . .]

I remember that on November 19, 1941, I held a real celebration (we had gotten here a month earlier and were living in quarantine, where it was dark and cramped).[42] I managed to buy a handheld pie [*pirozhok*] from someone on special hospital rations, got a cube of sugar from someone else who still had some that he had brought from Latvia, skipped lunch and supper, and managed to get a small onion.[43] As a result, my guests found, on a clean white handkerchief (scented with your perfume), a handheld pie with six matches stuck into it, with the heads up (I lit them later), [and then for each individual] a piece of bread with a piece of salmon and small slices of onion, and a fourth of the cube of sugar. There were three guests: a Russian resident of Dvinsk [who had worked for] the city water system and then most recently in Talperin's house (later he was sent north to work on a train line); a high school student, a Latgalets from Aglona who took Russian-language lessons from me all the way here (now he is here working on a farm); and my "roommate" from Dvinsk, Pakers-from-around-Nīcgale . . . It was all so bitter that later on I did not invite "guests" on such occasions, but I always celebrated that day as best I could, and only once did I have to get by without a handheld pie . . .

Now I have rendered butter (I bought a kilo for 300 rubles at our grocery stall a few days ago with my bonus from the last few months), a small pot, and some potatoes, and the fact that I will be on duty in the cafeteria on November 19 means that I will get a double portion!

42. Here Formakov describes a celebration in honor of his son's sixth birthday.
43. Handheld pies with a filling of meat, fruit, or vegetables are a common snack in Russia. At best, such pies are three inches long. Here this small serving, like the lone sugar cube, is shared.

. . . But the biggest holiday of all will be when I get a letter from you. Lord, when will it be?

I am healthy and look better than I did last year, when I was trying to cope with three abscesses in a row on my fingers.[44] Finally they all healed! Don't send me anything—no food and no money—until you are settled yourself and know what is possible, but do start putting together a parcel of clothing and household goods. [. . .][45]

[In the margins:] Shouldn't you think about staying in Riga? It would be better than living amid the ruins of Dvinsk.

◆ ◆ ◆

Kansk, December 1, 1944[46]
My dear Niushenka and my beloved children!

If not today, then tomorrow I expect to receive the first letter from you, which I have been awaiting for so long. How I long, Niushenka, to see your sweet handwriting and "hear" your voice, your intonation, your account of everything that has happened to you during these four long years in which we have been totally separated. Most of all, I long to hear about our children, our big and greatly respected Dmitri Arsenievich and the lively, vivacious Zhenichka. Did Dima get the birthday greeting that I sent, which contained my portrait and the story "The Fox and the Hare"? November 19 was a happy day for me.[47] At work I kept humming songs to myself much of the day. I was on duty at the cafeteria, so I got to eat my fill. Then I spent a long time stretched out reading and fell into a wonderful sound sleep. Then a big freeze suddenly set in, much colder than anything last year. For five days the temperature hovered between minus forty-five and minus forty-seven, so we did not have to work outside. [. . .]

I also tried to make a kind of holiday for myself on Dima's name day.[48] In the evening I treated myself to some potato pancakes with butter. Well!, wasn't that something! And in the name-day cake (250 grams

44. A sign of poor nutrition.
45. The letter, which is badly torn, breaks off.
46. A *treugol'nik* with camp and military censorship stamps.
47. Dima's birthday was November 19.
48. The Formakovs celebrated both birthdays and name days (saints' days): the feast day of the saint in whose honor an individual was named.

of bread), I stuck nine matches in place of candles, which I lit to great effect. They burned beautifully and, I think, portend only the best for the future. The very next day I learned that a letter had arrived for me with a photo of my "father" and of some ruined houses. As soon as certain formalities are completed, I will at last get it.[49] Hooray! [. . .]

On the 21st, I conducted a show on the camp radio network in honor of the hundredth anniversary of the death of Krylov. I delivered a short paper, which was a great success, judging by the number of responses we received. After that, people read fables that I had helped them prepare, with added sound effects (the barking of dogs, the whistling of the nightingale, the sound of a quartet) . . .

When sending me books and journals, don't focus too much on quality. Choose things according to the "good enough" principle: packages frequently go astray.

My dear son!

Always do what your mother says and keep doing well in your studies, as you have to this point. Your father really loves you. Write to me and draw me a plan of the room where you live with all the furniture. The very warmest hugs and kisses to you all, Papa Senia.[50]

♦ ♦ ♦

Kansk, December 8, 1944[51]
My dear son, Dimochka:

Thank you so much for your beautiful letters. You write and draw very well. I sent a happy name day letter to you in Dvinsk because I still did not know your Riga address. It contains my portrait and a story in verse. Here in the taiga [dense forest], I cannot get any toys or books for you, but you are already a big boy and understand this.

---

49. Formakov alludes to the camp censorship process.

50. At the bottom of the first side of this letter, Formakov added his full name in large clear letters, last name first. Below this two words are blacked out. In this early attempt to use the official postal service, Formakov probably misunderstood the regulations and added identifying information deemed sensitive.

51. The original date in black ink reads: XI/8/1944. A hand-correction in red pencil alters the Roman numeral for the month to XII. Whoever made this correction acted reasonably: Formakov did not receive letters from his wife and children until December and could not have sent this reply in November.

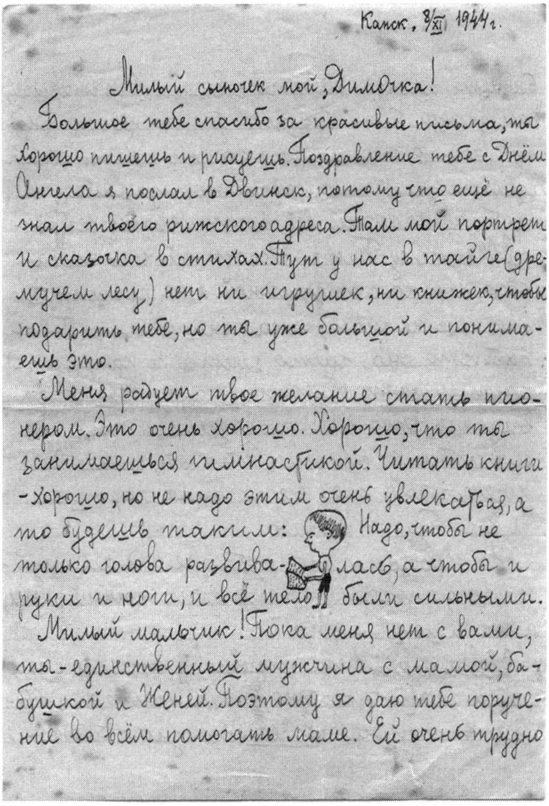

[Handwritten letter in Russian]

Letter from Arsenii Formakov to his son Dmitri dated [December] 8, 1944.
Arsenii Ivanovich Formakov Papers, Hoover Institution Archive, Box 1, folder 1.

I am pleased that you want to become a pioneer.[52] That is very good. It is also good that you practice gymnastics. Reading is good, but you don't want to get carried away with it, or you will end up like this:

You do not want only your head to develop—you need your legs and arms and your whole body to be strong as well.

My dear boy, until I get back home, you are the only man [there] with your mother, grandmother, and Zhenia. For this reason, I am giving you

52. The Young Pioneers was a Communist youth organization for children ages ten to fifteen.

the assignment of helping your mother however you can. It is sometimes very hard for her to do battle with you. As the oldest child, you need to be a role model for your sister. I know that sometimes you will be naughty, but as soon as your mother corrects you, you must obey her. Don't talk back to her, and help her rear your sister Zhenichka. You tell her [Zhenia] that I won't send the little box with an air hole [that she asked for] because I don't know what kind of a little girl she is just yet. I have heard that she often gets angry, throws tantrums, and is even mean to her mother. When you see that she is getting out of line, kiss her on the forehead, and say, "That is from Papa. He wants you to always be good." Then everything will be all right. [. . .]

Chess is a very adult and serious game. It would be better if you didn't start playing it just yet. Checkers and dominoes are a different story.

I am very pleased with your grades. Write and tell me which subjects you like best in school and why.

Of course, I would be very glad to see you. But the war isn't over, and I must work here. We produce cross ties for the construction of new railway lines to replace those destroyed during the war, and we also have factories that make special beams needed for the construction of airplanes, and saw boards for crates used to pack shells and other things. Also, the railroads transport troops, artillery, and military equipment. They don't have time to haul fathers and children so very far. You traveled from Dvinsk to Riga, right? Okay, from Riga to the city I live near is twenty-five times as far. Just try traveling from Riga to Dvinsk twenty-five times! That's how far it is! Of course, when the war ends, that will be a different story.[53]

Keep saying your prayers as you have always said them. May God keep you safe, my precious son. Give Mama, Zhenichka, Grandmother, and Aunt Mania a kiss from me. Yours, Papa.

---

53. Here Formakov draws two maps illustrating the distances involved.

♦ ♦ ♦

"Thou alone, my dove, my dearest"[54]

Kansk, December 10, 1944
My darling wife, Niushenka:

Our People's Commissariat of Communications is an amazingly quick-witted organization: it measures out letters to me no worse than you dispense photographs. Really, on the 2nd [of December], I was told that funds had been wired to my account, and I was allowed to read the lines you had written [on the form]—the first [written communication from you] in four years! Two days later, I received your first and third letters, which contained pictures of the children, our darling children. This was my first glimpse of Zhenichka: before that, when I crossed myself at night [during my prayers], I could not imagine her. But here I see that she is all that I could hope for! Then a day later: newspapers, envelopes, and paper. And finally, the second letter, which contained the tragic summary of all your ordeals. Oh what a martyrdom you have suffered! And then your two postcards and the two letters from our son. That's how richly I have been supplied. Now I can write directly to Riga; in the past, I always sent my letters to Dvinsk.

The only thing that has gotten lost is the volume of Stanislavsky. It's too bad, but it still isn't hopeless: perhaps it will still arrive. [. . .]

Reading about everything that you went through was painful for me, and I felt such shame that I was not there and could not be by your side, that I, in essence, spent those terrible years in tranquility and safety.[55] And then at the same time I felt pride for my Niushenka, my one and only, who is such a wonderful wife and mother.

54. A citation from "No Sleep, No Rest for My Tormented Soul" from Alexander Borodin's opera *Prince Igor*. In this aria, Prince Igor, a captive of the Polovtsians after ignoring an omen and suffering military defeat, rues his fate and addresses his thoughts to his far-away wife, who alone, he believes, will not blame him: "Thy tender heart will tell thee/All my bitterness and sorrow;/I shall win thy sweet forgiveness." Obviously this text would have personal significance for Formakov. A. P. Borodin, *Prince Igor: An Opera in Four Acts with a Prologue* (New York: Fred Pullman, 1915), 29; http://books.google.com/books?id=ehsQAAAAYAAJ&printsec=frontcover&source=gbs_ge_summary_r&cad=0#v=onepage&q&f=false.

55. Such sentiments were common in letters mailed from the camps during and immediately after World War II. Although the privations prisoners suffered

Yes, of course, Zhenia is a hard child to raise. But thank God that this is all we are dealing with! After all, what [a challenge confronts] young life in such a beyond-abnormal situation!

By the way, sitting up late and not getting enough sleep is not good, but when you go to bed at 1:00 a.m., say "good morning" to me: it will work out almost perfectly.

In answer to your purely practical questions, our most experienced specialists in correspondence here say that it makes no difference whether you send letters by regular post or registered mail, so don't waste money on registered letters. We have to sign for small parcels [*banderoli*] of all kinds here anyway, so it isn't necessary to send these registered mail either. It takes about three weeks for your letters to reach us, and in the other direction it varies, but it usually does not take longer. I read *Izvestiia* regularly.[56] There is a great deal of interest here in Riga publications (if possible in Latvian). Everyone who is from Latvia reads the newspapers that you send, but I ask you to send all kinds of newspapers—not just papers suitable for reading, because, in our settlement, newsprint is the best paper for rolling cigarettes. For a newspaper the size of *Pravda* or *Izvestiia,* smokers will pay seven to eight rubles or trade a coupon for a two-course dinner, so I have been making wise use of the newspapers you have sent after reading them (the Latvian papers are still being read).[57] Some I have given away and some . . . well, you understand the situation. Don't send me any more money right now. Don't worry about sending big packages [*posylki*]. It's unlikely they will be accepted [by the postal system] from a region that has been recently liberated, and moreover from a capital city.[58] In any case, none of the Latvians here who managed to get into contact with their families far earlier than I did have received newspapers, let alone packages: they gesture in amazement at my dear wife's tenacity! [. . .]

The page you wrote about grandfather really touched and moved me. You did a great job describing all this. I will write a poem about

worsened as a result of wartime shortages, they often described themselves as comparatively "safe" because they were far from the front.

56. *Izvestiia* (The News) was the official newspaper of the Soviet government.

57. *Pravda* (The Truth) was the national newspaper published by the Central Committee of the Soviet Communist Party.

58. Riga was the capital of the Latvian Soviet Socialist Republic.

the train whistles. I loved him a lot too, and, while here, have suffered pangs of guilt before him and Anna Ananievna on more than one occasion for dragging their beloved Niushenka into such an abyss of sorrow.

I took a break from writing: I went to the bath house. Here, as in Dvinsk, my bath day is now Sunday. I often put it off until Monday but not always, because we all turn in our laundry the day after we have our bath. In the evening I am going to the club to see an American film. I will have an envelope with the photos [you sent] in my pocket, and I will show all my acquaintances here who have been good to me the pictures of my children with great pride. But when they ask me, "What about your wife?" I will just answer very sadly: "I don't have one [of her]." Everyone here is very taken with Zhenia. People argue about whom she takes after. Some say she has my nose. Everyone is unanimous that Dima gets the top half of his face from me (at least in the big picture [it seems that way]; in the small photo he looks different).

It was hard to look at the pictures of the ruins of your little nest. I imagined it as a wooden structure, but it was made of stone and two stories tall! The piano, which was overturned onto the bookshelves, and our wedding bed covered in debris—you yourself know how these images stabbed painfully at my heart. But the pain from these images, like so much else that is painful in the past, is dulled now by the joy of getting into contact with you.

Ninety percent of our conversations here revolve around food. "To be full" is the most important injunction here, and to stuff oneself "to the gills" is the ideal.

[In the margins:] Does Zhenia have blond hair?

[In the margins, mostly upside-down:] I just got a letter from Savelich dated October 30.[59] It was a good one with information about everything, including the fact that they had Lilia take my letters to you. I will send them a holiday greeting in reply and will thank them very, very much for everything they have done for you, my precious. 12/XII.

59. Presumably Savelich, who is identified only with an abbreviated version of the patronymic formed from his father's name (Savelii), is a relative. This form of address suggests intimacy. A first name and, often, the full form of this patronymic (Savelievich) would be used for someone at a further remove.

♦ ♦ ♦

Two New Year's Tangos[60]

For my one and only

This New Year's Eve my heart is with you, my darling.
The stars sing gently, not lamenting anything.
Racing from the moon on high, beams turn silver
And cut a path to you, far, far away, across the Urals.

My friend, you know that in my heart and soul I am with you.
You believe, as I do, that the hour we've been longing for will come,
And I will hold you, not in daydreams, but in reality, in my arms,
And on them something will shimmer, perhaps teardrops from your
   eyes.

Oh, if there are tears then, they will only be of joy!
Oh, if there are words then, they will be like a child's murmurs of
   delight!
Believe me, my sunshine, believe me: soon all the rough weather will
   pass,
And there will be many joyous days again in our life.

On New Year's Eve I've laid bare my soul in daydreams,
And, invisible, sat next to you. Pour me
A little wine, so I can say a toast for you, my darling,
So I can drink with you to the swift arrival of happier times.

New Year's Eve. Siberia's distant reaches gleam like silver.
The stars are scattered on the sky's velvet in an unfamiliar way.
Leaning over me, you softly whisper: "There is no need for sadness!"
And your gaze sparkles with an ardent and familiar love.

Yes, my darling Niusha, all this flies by as swiftly as an arrow, and
   passes,
Just as smoke disappears, giving way to what is new.
These difficult days doubtless are already almost past:
Hope and faith fill my breast.

New Year's Eve, just like that first night, the night of our wedding,
Endless love, our pledge, the summation, the farthest limit . . .

---

60. Formakov again mails out poetry composed earlier in his sentence. This
letter is incomplete and undated but, judging by its contents, was written before
December 18, 1944.

Happiness has passed so quickly; oh, what an unfortunate life!
Did I really know? Could I have supposed? Did I want this?

Please understand, dearest, and forgive me for everything!
Be like that tiny star that peeps in the window, not lamenting.
Racing from the moon on high, beams turn silver
And, like a path, stretch into the distance, to the river Dvina, to you.

Happy New Year, my beloved! Let us clink our glasses in friendship.
We'll exchange kisses in our dreams, and we won't grieve.
If only I could be with you and the children again . . . I need nothing
    else . . .
Happy New Year, my darling! May your life be easy.

January 2, 1942

I will send Zhenia a picture of some kind for her name day. I will manage to get a drawing done . . . I kiss your hands tenderly. Senia

[In the margins in pencil:] Auntie's letter made it even without a stamp. And for "Formakov" not even . . . Well, enough said . . . I send my kisses, Arsenii

[In the other corner:] Savelich writes these terrible things about you. Take care of yourself for the children, for me. I don't need anything except letters. The letters are everything: they are my life, they are the air I breathe.

II.

So now for the first time in three years I feel morally sated. At the same time, despite everything you may be imagining, I am also not starving physically. Our basic ration is sufficient, given my work assignment, and we also get all sorts of extras. Moreover, I have now gotten back to normal after the two illnesses I suffered last year, which forced me to trade my summer coat and boots for food. [At that time] I had no way to satiate my spiritual hunger, except perhaps by expressing my emotions in verse. Now I am sated by your letters, what Dima writes, "fatherless" Zhenia, etc.

I am not doing very well with holiday letters, however. It took so long for communication with Riga to be reestablished that I missed

Dima's birthday. I have managed to wish you happiness on yours, but my greeting will only just make it on time, and now I have to wish Zhenia a happy birthday, and then we have New Year's, Zhenia's name day, Christmas . . . Oh!

So, I send my compliments to you in connection with the birthday of our daughter, who was first conceived of by me and then made flesh by you. I am not afraid of meeting her: your concerns are groundless. I believe that blood tells: there is great power in it. If only God will allow . . . !

Please tell her happy birthday for me and kiss her warmly on my behalf. Tell her I love her so much . . . Oh! so very, very much. But I cannot send her anything. You understand how it is . . .

I went to the movies at 4:00, had dinner, and now am continuing my conversation with you. The picture was *The Hurricane,* an American film.[61] It was a little like the film *Taboo,* which we saw together at one point, except that in that one the setting was Hawaii and the storyline was better. In this case, I was distracted at first, but, then, what do you know: Terangi escapes from hard labor and returns to his wife from whom he has been separated for eight years and who had a child after his arrest. How do you like that plot?

Thank my colleagues for remembering me and their good wishes. I remember them all. I even remember Ershova's first name and patronymic: Virineia Emelianovna (is that right?), but I can't recall Zutov at all. Is he old with a grey beard? Tell Ershova (if this seems appropriate) that I am so sorry about her sister's terrible death.[62]

On Dima's name day, it was warmer here: [minus] 15 to 20 degrees Celsius. Today the temperature suddenly returned to minus 34, but it's again getting warmer. It is good that I work in an enclosed space that is only two or three minutes away and that I am dressed better than required. [. . .]

---

61. A 1937 film directed by John Ford and Stuart Heisler that was purchased by the Soviet Union in 1944: "Spisok amerikanskikh fil'mov," 176; "Spisok kinofil'mov, zakuplennykh za granitsei v 1941–1948 gg," Rossiskii Gosudarstvennyi Arkhiv Literatury i Iskusstva (hereafter RGALI), f. 2456, op. 4, d. 152, l. 78. Thanks to Sergei Kapterev for this information.

62. Antonina Emelianovna Ershova was shot by the Germans along with several other family members for feeding prisoners of war. B. V. Pliukhanov, *RSKhD v Latvii i Estonii: Materialy k istorii Russkogo studencheskogo khristianskogo dvizheniia* ([Paris]: YMCA Press, 1993), 289.

I am not doing anything at the club; I am not reading anything. I spend all my free time with you and the children: with your letters, in which I always find something new, new nuances and details.

May Christ protect you and the children! I embrace you warmly and kiss all three of you and Grandmother as well. Give my greetings to everyone who remembers me. Yours, Arsenii.

[In the margins:] What is going on with the dacha in Stropy?[63] If you need Mania's wedding photo, I can send it back. If you have the chance, send me a pocket calendar.

♦ ♦ ♦

Happy Name Day![64]

For Zhenia's name day,
I waylaid two reindeer:
"Fly to her without delay,
Bring her this bouquet!"

The reindeer set out,
Ran and got tuckered out.
Then a big bear replaced them,
An excellent racer.

But the road just dragged on,
And the bear's feet started to ache.
He passed the bouquet to a fox:
"Urgent, run away quick!"

The fox, sneaky and sly,
Gave it to rabbits running by.
And they, a hundred strong,
Grabbed the bouquet and charged on.

A white-sided magpie
Flew it far away,
And then an orange-tailed squirrel
Took its turn with the bouquet.

63. An area with many summer houses near Daugavpils.
64. A pressed flower and line drawings decorate this poem (see illustration). Formakov mimics the meter and structure of Kornei Chukovskii's 1926 children's poem "Telefon" (The Telephone).

An illustrated name day poem for Zhenia. December 18, 1944. Arsenii Ivanovich Formakov Papers, Hoover Institution Archive, Box 1, folder 1.

They all carried and brought the flowers
For my Zhenichka with best wishes.

The road was not easy;
It was a long journey;
And Papa's bouquet

Suffered along the way.
It withered and thinned,
But still it flew on.

After the squirrel ceded the course,
Next up was a horse.

And then at last (alas! that's how it goes!),
The bouquet passed to a crow.

The crow!—an ill-fated bird—
Cost the bouquet its whole form.
He was ready to zoom
But lost all the blooms.

Only one sad little pansy fell
Onto the ground you know so well.

A mailman, out making deliveries,
Picked up the lost bloom,
Which he stuck in my letter
And delivered to you.

To my dearest daughter Zhenichka. I wish you a happy name day! Papa. December 18, 1944.

♦ ♦ ♦

Kansk, December 29, 1944

Wait for me, and I will return
In spite of all the perils.
Those who would not wait for me,
Let them wonder later at my luck.[65]

My dearest!

Our correspondence broke off for a whole month, but then today there were two letters, one from you (dated December 5) and one from Dima (December 27) with a wonderful picture of a tank shooting at an airplane! Only again there is bitterness and torment and I am buffeted by the fates in minor ways: it seems that your fourth registered letter, which was sent between November 8 (the last I received) and December 5, has gone astray. Also, Dima's third letter never reached me, if you

65. From Konstantin Simonov's 1941 poem "Zhdi menia, i ia vernus'" (Wait for Me and I Will Return).

were talking about independent letters . . . In addition, there was your reproach that my tone seemed somehow cold in the letter I wrote on November 9, which, though fair, pained me. Well, that was one of the letters that I sent out into empty space before I began receiving replies from you. I have saved the most awful thing for last. Don't ever write that Zhenia is alien to me. She is as much in my heart as Dima. I have already sent a special greeting to her. I always mark her name day and birthday, and on the 6th I will have a name day cake in her honor, although it will only be a hunk of black bread with four matches blazing on it. And I am writing to you about how bitter all this is, and that will embitter you once again, and there is just no end to this vicious cycle, and how can we discuss anything when six pieces of correspondence sent later separate each letter from its answer? Therefore, my dearest, the correct thing to do is to carry on our correspondence primarily in the narrative mode, which you manage so marvelously, but which, I sense, I do not always employ to such great effect. The reason for this is clear: my absolute spiritual isolation. You at least have some opportunities . . . For goodness sake, this is not envy (what you wrote about that was strikingly true: people have always envied us, and, even now, some continue to envy you and, even more incredibly, some here envy me!).

The epigraph is from Simonov (the third to the last stanza in the poem I sent you in your birthday greeting).[66] I often sing it to myself in my mind to the tune of the ballroom waltz from *The Gypsy Princess,* our favorite operetta![67]

I write to you whenever I have the chance, and I ask you to do the same. People say that postcards reach us more quickly: they are easier for the censors to process because they don't need to be opened and then sealed again . . . But real letters are such bliss, so it would be best if you alternated. It'll be as though you're firing one heavy, long-range missile and then a bullet from a machine gun . . .

On your name day, I was in the most wonderful mood for some reason. In general, my mood has been like that since receiving your first letter, and nothing throws me off balance or makes me lose my general

66. In most print editions of Simonov's poem, these lines appear at the beginning of the final twelve-line stanza.

67. By the Hungarian composer Emmerich Kálmán.

good humor. Several days ago I moved to a new barrack. In my last barrack, with the brigade, things were really uncomfortable for the last month: it was cold, filthy, dark, and there was constant swearing. The place where I am now houses our settlement's "bureaucrats": book-keepers, norm-setters, and so forth, people among whom I have many good acquaintances.[68] They have been inviting me to come live with them for a while, but I was deterred by the fact that the only vacant places were on the upper bunks. [. . .] But now I have moved, and I am very glad. I have my own little footlocker instead of just a half. It's light, warm, and clean; the people are polite; there are plenty of books, newspapers, and a good radio!

It also really used to bother me: everyone here ate a lot and really well, and I used to go hungry. Now that is no longer the case: that is all behind me. I get 700 grams of bread, and in the morning I also get 700 grams of thick soup and 200 grams of hot cereal, stewed vegetables or pancakes, or a handheld pie. In the afternoon I get 250 grams of hot cereal or something else. In the evening I get the same kind of rations as in the morning. It is quite enough to keep oneself going, but I almost always get a double portion at least, and that makes everything really fine. And then, in addition, I get butter with the money you send and what I earn, and potatoes. Sometimes I can't eat everything.[69]

You still can't send packages here from the Latvian Soviet Social-ist Republic, just as you can't from many other regions. If you can't manage to come for a visit in the spring, perhaps you can go to Pskov or Ostrov and send me a package from there, because I don't need anything all that immediately. I really ask you not to send any money

68. Norm-setters were responsible for determining how much labor prisoners were expected to perform in specific work assignments. If prisoners did not meet the designated norms, they received reduced rations.

69. The improvement in Formakov's living conditions and access to food partly reflects the parcels and funds he has received from home. Presumably he can take advantage of the opportunity to live with the most privileged inmates in the camp, as opposed to in a common barrack, because he can offer bribes. By the end of the war, living conditions in the Gulag had also improved considerably, and mortality rates were down from the highs recorded in 1942 and 1943. Steven A. Barnes, *Death and Redemption: The Gulag and the Shaping of Soviet Society* (Princeton, NJ: Princeton University Press, 2011), 158; Alan Barenberg, *Gulag Town, Company Town: Forced Labor and Its Legacy in Vorkuta,* The Yale–Hoover Series on Stalin, Stalinism, and the Cold War (New Haven: Yale University Press, 2014), 92.

right now. Send newspapers. I don't really need books either: they are too expensive, and they will just get lost. Everyone who gets packages complains about this.

A specialist has taken over the leadership of our dramatic circle. He is a real professional: in the past he was the head of a literary department [in a theater]. For the New Year's concert, I am going to read my own poem: "Happy New Year, friends, happy New Year! I wish you peace and joyful reunions! . . ." (I didn't think that last phrase would be allowed.) In advance of the first of January, I've pledged to increase my work tempo like a Stakhanovite: I am exceeding norms by 250 to 290 percent every day.

Everyone here, including especially me, is eagerly waiting for you to send a photograph. Please send at least a small one! If you did, and it was lost in the fourth letter (which went missing), that is just awful. Regarding the Stanislavsky that was lost, you should absolutely submit a complaint to the post office along with the receipt showing that it was mailed.[70]

These are all practical details! In the next few days, after New Year's, I will write you a proper letter. May he to whom we all owe our salvation amid the common lot of death and illness protect you all. Hugs and kisses, Papa. [. . .]

70. Both the postal system and labor camps could be compelled to pay senders compensation for lost packages. Who paid depended on whether the camp postal clerk had signed for the package at the local postal station. Rossiskii Gosudarstvennyi Arkhiv Ekonomiki (hereafter RGAE), f. 3527, op. 4, d. 628, ll. 12–14; GARF, f. 9407, op. 1, d. 1634, l. 55; GARF, f. 9401, op. 1a, d. 316, l. 141; GARF, f. 8360, op. 1, d. 1, ll. 9–10; GARF, f. 8131, op. 37, d. 363, l. 14.

1945

January 1, 1945

> With its dust, the long road beckons,
> Spring too calls and intoxicates,
> But so little life remains before me,
> Grey hair already lightens my temples.

(Vertinsky)[1]

Happy New Year's, my dear Niushenka!

After we came back from dinner at the cafeteria, everyone went to bed. I am sitting quietly at the table all alone. I am clean-shaven and am in a white sweater, striped trousers, and my black jacket. From the jacket's pocket juts the corner of a snow-white handkerchief, perfumed by you, my sweetheart, for March 15, 1941. I am writing to you without hurrying and am not anxious at all about the need to provide a "report on my condition on the 1st of January of this new year."

Ever since I got into contact with you, I have been in a remarkably serene, tranquil, cheerful mood. I am more good-humored than I have

---

1. Formakov cites the first verse of the song "Palestinskoe tango" (Palestinian Tango) by the great cabaret performer, poet, and composer Alexander Vertinsky inaccurately. I have translated it as it appears in Formakov's letter. The contents of this letter indicate that it traveled illegally.

ever been. I carry inside myself my own (mine and yours) reclaimed world [мiр]—not peace [мир], but, of course, it leads to peace and tranquility as well.[2] I pay absolutely no heed to all the surrounding trivialities and rubbish. Physically I now feel my condition is completely satisfactory: recently we had our latest quarterly medical inspection, and they found absolutely nothing wrong with my health (except for my heart, but whose heart is in good shape nowadays?).[3]

On my sleeping spot, I have a mattress, which is stuffed with hay, a sheet, a wool blanket, and my old quilted jacket (a short overcoat) for softness. [I also have] a straw-stuffed pillow, my green knit jacket, quilted trousers, and a soldier's blouse, in the pocket of which I have about sixty rubles in cash and fifteen assorted vouchers for breakfasts and suppers that have been left over from days on which I was on duty. The thing is that food is issued to us through a little window from the kitchen by voucher as a general rule, but for the best workers (a new list is drawn up each day on the basis of the work results from the previous day) there is a cafeteria. Its entrance is manned by several of those active in cultural work (this is a bonus that we receive for our work in clubs and circles in the evening). I am on duty more frequently than anyone else, eight times a month: in the morning from 6:00 to 7:30, in the evening from 6:00 to 8:00, and, on days off like today, also at lunch from 12:00 to 1:00. I man the door and check off visitors against the list. Our orchestra plays there. At my request, my dearest, it treated me to melodies from our [favorite] *The Gypsy Princess* ("Do You Remember the Happiness That Passed Us By?").[4] At one time, the food [in this cafeteria] was better [than regular camp rations]. At the end of each

2. In 1918 the Russian orthography system was simplified, and words that had contained different vowels—"мiр," which meant "the world" or "the universe," and "мир," which meant "peace"—came to be spelled the same way: "мир." Here Formakov references this old distinction. As a member of a diaspora community that used the old alphabet long after the reform was implemented in Soviet Russia, he would have retained a fresh memory of the old spelling difference.

3. On medical screenings and the classification of prisoners by their labor capacity, see Dan Healey, "Lives in the Balance: Weak and Disabled Prisoners and the Biopolitics of the Gulag," *Kritika* 16, no. 3 (Summer 2015): 538–40; and Golfo Alexopoulos, "Destructive-Labor Camps: Rethinking Solzhenitsyn's Play on Words," *Kritika* 16, no. 3 (Summer 2015): 505–12.

4. Formakov references the duet between Sylva and Edwin from the second act of Emmerich Kálmán's operetta.

shift, the person on duty at the door and the musicians receive two or three portions of both the soup and the main course without having to turn over any vouchers. You can keep the vouchers for another day. This is our enduring hard currency here. So, for instance, I was on duty yesterday (in the place of one of my comrades who declined the job) and today. As a result, I saved five vouchers, and in my footlocker I have two rations of bread that I haven't even started, a handheld carrot pie from breakfast, and two liters of wonderful New Year's soup. In the other pocket of my soldier's blouse, I have the booklet that identifies me as an exemplary worker, which I received in 1942 (it is given out to model workers and comes with certain privileges—you can go to the hair dresser's and the kitchen whenever you like, and you get the best housing and clothing . . .). In it, I keep my supply of postage stamps and the key to my chest.

Yesterday at the start of the New Year's concert, the head [of the Cultural-Educational Sector] conducted the ceremonial part of the evening. She summarized our annual achievements and, in conclusion, listed those receiving awards. For the third time, I received commendation and a note was made in my personal file regarding my cultural work, and then, for the first time, I was nominated for privileges dispensed by the state, specifically a reduction in my sentence.[5] It will take about three months to get an answer (the decision is made in Moscow). Only half of those nominated receive a reduction. Sometimes six months is subtracted; sometimes even one or two years. But the first step is the hardest. If they do not reduce my sentence now, I will just get nominated again and again. Anyway, there is a chance: it's like buying a lottery ticket . . .

My felt boots are under the bunk. The coat I got from grandfather and knit mittens hang on a hook. A hat with ear flaps and the scarf you knitted are on top of it. In hotels, I used to use it [the scarf] as a pillow—I would just fold it over several times.[6] But the most important thing is that it was made by your adroit and skilled hands. I also have a set of two-ply arm warmers that I wear for work . . .

5. Formakov is finally eligible for a reduction in his sentence because he has served half of his eight-year sentence.

6. Formakov often uses the word "hotel" as code for prison in his correspondence. It is likely that in this passage that is what he means.

This morning, by the way, our guys [the people from my workshop] were also led out [of camp] to help with loading. This is hard work on the railway line. In order to ensure that the train cars aren't detained any longer than necessary, all available workers are mobilized. The foreman, however, did not send me because we are "on good terms": "Say that you are busy in the club!" (In fact, those who went at eight returned in time for lunch.)[7]

I return to the contents of my little nightstand [*tumbochka*] (a kind of bedside table).[8] On the top shelf of it, I have a glass jar with rendered fat (isn't that something!), which should last me until Christmas, even taking into account the feast I have planned for Zhenichka's name day, two ceramic mugs (one of which contains salt; the other today contains spruce sprigs), a green enamel mug, a new aluminum spoon, and an old wooden spoon that is in good condition, as well as the bread that I already mentioned. On a small hand-made shelf [that I added to the nightstand], I have a scrub sponge and a piece of soap in the lid [of a jar]. In the lowest section [of the nightstand] I have a bottle of ink, a pen, a box containing the stubs of colored pencils, needles, thread, buttons, drafts of my poetry, and, in a special stiff folder, letters from you, my dears, paper, envelopes, manuscripts, and books for reading. Also: in the inner pocket of my soldier's blouse (I sewed it [the pocket] myself), I keep an envelope in a hard cover made from the outside of a notebook that contains your photographs. This is the most precious part of my inventory!

I mentioned my key. I have a little black wooden chest on deposit in the check room that I bought last year for 800 grams of bread. That is where I keep my dress suit when I do not need it, a change of underclothes (I have two towels with me! I forgot to mention this), old manuscripts, letters (that treasure from the past: the first postcard that I received in the summer of 1941 from the Central Information Bureau

7. Formakov hints at the palm-greasing that was a constant feature of camp life.

8. Formakov uses a colloquial term that was common in Soviet Russia but perhaps unfamiliar to Latvia's Old Believer community. The word *tumba*, which is etymologically related to the English word tomb, was introduced into Russian relatively recently from German (*tumbe*), and initially referred to a grave or road marker. Over time, the diminutive, *tumbochka*, came to mean a squat nightstand. A. G. Preobrazhensky, *Etymological Dictionary of the Russian Language* (New York: Columbia University Press, 1964).

on the Affairs of the Evacuated in Buguruslan—it was the answer to my inquiry as to whether you had been evacuated.[9] "We know nothing. [The inquiry] has been registered. If we learn anything, word will be sent immediately."), a big old wooden suitcase, containing various junk, and the canvas travel bag that you sent . . .

This is all trifles and trivialities, but I know, first of all, how interested I am in even the most trivial aspects of your life and, second, I want you to have a clear sense of how I am living here, to see that I am not living so badly . . . The only thing that really threatens me is an accident of some kind, which is no more likely to occur here than anyplace else, or else being moved to a site where the living conditions are worse and the work is harder, but this last eventuality is the lot of those who don't pull their weight at work or who face disciplinary sanctions.

About two weeks ago Alik Katalymov was moved to another settlement where they cut timber, one of the hardest forms of work for those unaccustomed to physical labor. He was somehow never really able to settle into work, was very run-down physically, and was always filthy. He came down with tuberculosis here. They treated him for a while and sent him to an area farm. There he drove a tractor, and he started to look a lot better. He returned here for the winter, but he wasn't found suited for work in the garage, and then he was shipped off. A few days later, I got a letter for him from Valentina Rosiskina-Katalymova in Prel.[10] The doctor has been slowly dying for six months, is practically blind, and knows nothing of the fate of any of his children. He has pneumonia and asthma. I forwarded the letter to Alik.[11]

For now I am valued at the club, irreproachable in my personal habits, and am an exemplary worker. There has been talk of appointing me foreman. For New Year's I received a hundred-ruble bonus in my workshop for the achievements of the previous year. Moreover, I was allowed to redeem a third of the bonus for goods. In other words, I could use thirty-three rubles to buy groceries (vegetables) at state prices (fifty kopecks for a kilo of potatoes instead of five rubles)! Again, that's

9. Buguruslan is in Russia's Orenburg oblast.

10. Formakov uses the old German name for the Latvian city of Preili.

11. Alik Katalymov displays all the traits of a *dokhodiaga* (goner), a camp inmate so weakened by hunger and hard labor that he can no longer pay attention to elementary hygiene.

not bad! And I have about 150 rubles on my personal account. And soon I will get my pay for December! In other words, I am in clover! Really, by God, Niushenka, without the slightest irony, I can say that I always feel a little guilty for leading such a quiet, "old-fashioned life" while you, with your visor raised, singlehandedly do battle with life all alone. I just stand off to the side in awe.

Yesterday at the club there was a big New Year's concert. On the proscenium there were two pine trees (they couldn't get firs) decorated with cotton from the sewing shop and tin foil from the engine shop, lit up with electric lights. I opened the concert joyfully and energetically by declaiming my poem with Dunaevsky's song "Youth" ("Can one be a zealous Komsomol member/And spend all spring sighing at the moon?") playing in the background.[12] This was received not just with applause but also with shouts of "Very good!" because it fit so well with the general mood:

> Happy New Year, my friends, happy New Year,
> Best wishes for 1945, which will bring to an end
> Both the war that ruined our nations,
> And the man who started it all.

> We'll make it to Berlin and Vienna;
> We'll return ancient Prague to the Czechs
> And light up the fascists' torture chamber
> With the victory flame of our scarlet flags.

> Happy New Year, my friends, happy New Year.
> To a year of peace and joyful reunions.
> May our protective sword always
> Defend freedom.

> We will rebuild damaged buildings,
> And plant gardens of gold
> So that the people of the star we call earth
> Are the happiest of beings in the universe.

> The thunder of stormy battle will die down,
> The sun will sparkle again in the garden . . .
> Happy New Year, my friends, happy New Year!
> May you find new happiness in the New Year!

12. Formakov has the composer wrong. The song "Molodost'" (Youth) featured lyrics by Iurii Dantsiger and Iurii Dolin, and the music of Matvei Blanter.

The concert lasted until midnight. Then all those who had participated in it had supper in the cafeteria: we each got a large potato pancake and a spoonful of stewed cabbage. Because it was so late, there was no dancing at the club, but now a dance is being held, as Volodia Shen just came and told me. He just recently joined our brigade. He is sixteen. His mother is Russian, and his father is Chinese and a teacher. He lived in Harbin until August of this year. He ran away from his parents and then came here on a mission for the Japanese. He was caught and got a fifteen-year sentence. In terms of his character, he reminds me of Nikolai Iv[anovich] Kharlap.[13] Perhaps he isn't being entirely truthful, but he caught my interest because he knows a lot of verse by heart, including many things by Vertinsky. Take the epigraph I used today: "Who are you writing? Your family?" "Yes, and I have taken the epigraph from [the verse] that you dictated." "If I were your wife, I would answer: 'This is all such nonsense . . . just a fig leaf coquettishly drawn.'"[14]

A very witty comment! And, of course, to some extent, it is true since Vertinsky's funereal mood is not at all in accord with my own disposition right now: I am not looking towards the grave but rather out of it.

I went to the dance. They are showing the cinematic fairy tale *Vasilisa prekrasnaia* [Vasilisa the Beautiful] in the evening.[15] If only I could take Dimusha with me. Oh! . . . . But let's not think about that! I now have a "*hinterland*," and I am standing more firmly than ever before.[16] [. . .]

A comrade who left here not long ago told me that after his arrest in 1937, he did not write to his family at all for four years in the hope that they would think he was dead and would "rebuild their lives to suit themselves." Then, when he finally did write because he wanted to learn the fate of his son, his wife gave him such a dressing-down that his head still shakes as he recalls it. I couldn't understand him. How

13. Nikolai Ivanovich Kharlap was a Latvian educator. See Tat'iana Odynia, "Fedor Fedorov: Nam nado osoznat' edinstvo mira . . . ," *Inye berega* 22, no. 2 (2011); http://www.inieberega.ru/node/323.

14. An abbreviated citation from the Vertinsky song "Femme rafinée."

15. A 1939 film by Alexander Rou.

16. In the original, the word "hinterland" appears in German. Formakov seems to misuse the term: he presumably means something closer to "homeland"—real connections and relationships outside the camp.

can you love someone and do that? But when I, through no choice of my own, had no contact with you for three and a half years, I allowed that there was a one-hundredth of a percentage chance that I might receive a letter from you informing me that your life had changed. On a theoretical level, I allowed that it was possible. But in my heart I always knew that you were the kind of woman who would only love once, my dear, that you would never bestow on anyone the kind of love that you conferred on me. My dearest! My one and only love!

People have come [to get me]. They say that the auditorium is full, and they are going to start the film. I don't care. I will just go at 8:00. But I will hang onto this letter until the third. Perhaps tomorrow evening, on the second, I will receive a letter from you. Then I will make a note here, so that you know that I got it.

We get all worked up and worry that letters are getting lost, but it is just marvelous to have such constant news from you, to know about the children, their growth and development . . . This is so priceless!

Also, a few words about our settlement (the site where we live): it is about three [square] blocks enclosed by a solid fence (guards are on the watch towers).[17] Inside there are wooden one-story buildings scattered around and then another building set apart as the zone of confinement for the women (with a locked gate and a special guard). You see them at work and in the club. You can talk with them and go for walks, but you can't go into their places of seclusion, and they must be home when the call to quarters sounds (10:00 p.m.). This makes it difficult to carry on a romance. There are pairs of lovers that act like married couples. For instance, the wife of Dr. Grishak . . .

The windows of our barrack are nothing special; the doors are always open. We go to visit each other freely and in the evening you can go to any of the bathrooms. In other words, inside our settlement, we are almost free. Most of us leave under guard in the morning for work in the warehouse or factories (half a kilometer away) and come home as it is getting dark. But I always work here on site [*v zone*]. All our correspondence undergoes a special censorship process in the settlement. The packages are opened in the presence of the recipient at our post office. Citizens of both genders often come here to the warehouse from

17. The phrase "guards are on the watch towers" appears in Latvian.

the city, both staff and also those who used to be like us.[18] Some of us send letters and sometimes even telegrams through these individuals. Things can go astray: the person forgets or doesn't put the letter in the mailbox!

It is getting dark. In the barrack, things are getting livelier. The Armenians are playing backgammon. Next to them, some others are playing checkers. The bookkeepers are busy with the end-of-the-year accounts and even work on them in the barrack. One person is reading; another is drafting an official complaint. I have put the soup from this morning on the stove. It is particularly tasty today with powdered egg in it. I will drink it down just before 6:00 as I head off to the dining room . . . The radio is not on yet . . . It comes on at 5:00 p.m. and is on in the morning from 6:00 to 9:00.

Looking back, I recall with what stubborn determination I, painfully slowly, over the course of three and a half years, won for myself this place in the settlement. Now almost everyone knows me by sight, and I am in the good graces of the authorities here and even the central administration in Kansk knows me well. This means that when, on some indescribably marvelous day in the future, Niushenka, you come here, perhaps they will allow us to have a visit . . . "Dreams, dreams! Where is your sweetness?"[19]

January 4
At the very last minute

Well, I said that it would take a while for the mail to get moving again after two days off. Today, it is true, only small parcels arrived, but two of them were for me. The magnificent New Year's present that you sent from the whole family (how wonderful that sounds!), the Pavlov book with the color engravings, reminded me of the views of Mos-

18. Formakov means former prisoners. This passage, like many others in Formakov's correspondence, highlights the porousness of the Gulag. In most camps, some prisoners mixed regularly with free laborers and even residents of the surrounding area, which facilitated the smuggling of mail and personal packages and the exchange of goods and information. See Wilson T. Bell, "Was the Gulag an Archipelago? De-convoyed Prisoners and Porous Borders in the Camps of Western Siberia," *Russian Review* 72 (January 2013): 116–41.

19. The opening lines of Alexander Pushkin's poem "Probuzhdenie" (Awakening).

cow that hung in frames in our apartment at one point. It has really captivated everyone with its abundant illustrations: we have so few visual stimuli here. I have already looked through the whole book after stealthily kissing the inscription that you, my guardian angel, made. Then I quickly looked through the newspapers. Oh! It is so interesting! Even the movie listings are interesting. They showed us *Zoia* here too yesterday.[20] It is a very harrowing film . . .

All December was unusually warm here, and now it is only minus ten. So much for Siberian frosts! . . . In a few days I [expect?] letters.[21] [. . .] I send the warmest hugs to you and kisses for the eyes of my dear ones, the foreheads of my clever darlings, and the hands of my busy bees. Yours, Senia. Hugs and kisses for the children and Grandmother!!! Write to me. Write to me! Write to me! [. . .][22]

The last page for this time   January 7, 1945

I did not mail the letter when I thought I would because my mail carrier got sick and will be back at work only tomorrow.[23] Well, at least there is a bright side . . . As the workday was ending on the evening of the sixth, Zhenia's [name] day and Christmas Eve, I received your registered letter, a parcel dated the 17th, and two postcards dated the 10th and 11th of December. Everything was postmarked Riga, December 17, 1944.[24] Your New Year's greeting touched me deeply and gave me great joy. You understand: what an evening it was! For the first time I had a real open line of postal communication with home, and I received both your greeting card and a series of photos of the children. I was dazzled by the sight of it all, and my heart started to race: [I was so affected by] the way it was all put together, the humor in the inscriptions, my dear little children, and your captivating, as always, inventiveness. I bow before you [in gratitude]. And so, my holidays turned

20. A 1944 Soviet film about Zoia Kosmodemianskaia, a Moscow teenager who joined a partisan unit that crossed enemy lines to fight against the German invaders. She was caught and executed by the Nazis in November 1941.

21. A punch hole makes a word difficult to decipher.

22. At the bottom of the page, Formakov includes a note to his son, describing a word game for children.

23. "The letter carrier" is the person who smuggles letters out of camp for Formakov.

24. Eastern Orthodox Christians celebrate Christmas Eve and St. Evgenia's Day on January 6.

into a real holiday, and then it was the day when we could buy things at the camp kiosk, and I was on the list, and I had more money than I expected in my personal account. I brought "home" a kilo of butter for 250 rubles (I hadn't finished the last of the old stuff yet either), and I am making pea porridge (I brought peas back from the farm in October and I saved them for the holiday, and I still have enough for one more meal!).

I keep looking at the faces of my dear ones: again I look at the full-length picture of Dima in his dark blue shirt, then at [a photo of] the same familiar boy laughing at the pool, a good little boy with a good little girl, and then, in another picture, I see another boy who is all grown up and, although familiar in some way, does not completely correspond to the previous images. Perhaps it is the way he is biting his lower lip? I don't know. But I love him in his entirety and wholly, even down to his bitten-to-the-quick fingernails. Zheniurka is a very nice little lady in the shot where she is crying, and where she is reclining, and where she is just being good, and of course in the supremely successful photo of her at one and a half with cheeks like ripe apples . . . My own darling daughter is becoming part of my soul, yet you say she is alien [to me]! What foolishness!!

Dima's educational level is astonishing. How is it that he, by the age of 14–15, wants to graduate from a ten-year school, surpassing his father and even his mother?![25]

Of course, such a series of photos will create a sensation in my workshop and dormitory. I need to show them off, both because they are my pride and joy and because I spent four years looking at other people's pictures, sighing hopelessly and enviously. In regard to the letters, of course you are right, and how could you even think this? I won't show them to anyone. They are secret and sacred for us. These are your revelations to my loving heart, and I won't let the stupid eyes of anyone else fall on them. Not on your life! And I won't show your photo if you don't want me to. But I still don't have one. I hope to get one on

25. In the Soviet Union in this period, seven-year schools provided a base level of education. Ten-year general-education schools prepared students to go on to higher-educational institutions and more skilled professions. Between 1940 and 1956, Soviet parents had to pay tuition if they wanted their children to attend grades 8-10 either at a general-education school or at a trade school that prepared students for a specific vocation.

Monday. The money should come then too. There wasn't any paper or envelopes in with the newspapers. When I receive everything, I will send a telegram. It turns out that it only takes three days for them [telegrams] to reach the addressee, although I was told that because of the war it was taking weeks. If I had known, I would have wished you a happy holiday [by telegraph] . . . This is what happened with the stamps: I noticed that Dima's photo wasn't attached very well, so I decided to look behind it to see if there was some kind of inscription, and I saw that there were stamps there! Thank you, my beauty! But there was no reason for this: we have stamps in our post office, and in an extreme situation, I can mail a letter without a stamp . . .[26]

By the way, don't write USSR as part of the address. That is understood and writing it adds nothing. You also don't need to write RSFSR [Russian Soviet Federative Socialist Republic] . . . I officially learned that packages were impossible on your saint's day. They announced it over the radio: they are accepted only in district post offices everywhere except in Moscow, Leningrad, Stalingrad, the Murmansk region, Latvia, Lithuania, and Estonia, the Moldavian and Ukrainian Soviet Socialist Republics, and the western regions of the country. You don't need any special documentation when you send one. Just use the regular address. You just need to write before the last name "ieslodzitajam." (Darn it, I forgot the ending! However, I read *Cīņa* amazingly easily even though I haven't read in Latvian for four years.)[27] So sit tight and don't bother until the circular is rescinded, and I will hear about that first. And please don't send me any more money until Easter. If I need any, I will ask. Along with the newspapers, send a small calendar and one or two magazines into the spines of which you have sewn a few pens.[28] My friends have past experience with this . . . !

26. Gulag inmates could both send and receive letters mailed collect-on-delivery: even outside the camp system Soviet citizens sometimes struggled to obtain stamps; whole categories of the Soviet population (collective farm workers; special settlers) had little access to cash. Because Gulag officials often could not collect postage due, detention sites incurred debts to the postal system, and camp bosses periodically tried to ban such correspondence. In the 1940s, the Ministry of Communication tried to regulate this situation with an eye to stemming its own losses. GARF, f. 9489, op. 2, d. 5, l. 399; GARF, f. 9489, op. 2, d. 19, l. 94; GARF, f. 9414, op. 1, d. 327, ll. 41–46.

27. "Ieslodzitajam" means "prisoner" in Latvian. *Cīņa* (The Struggle) was a Latvian-language newspaper published in Riga.

28. Pens were not banned in camp, but like stamps, envelopes, and paper, they were easily filched from parcels.

On the 5th, I visited the island where our medical unit [*sangoro-dok*] is located. This is where they send the very weak to improve their health. In the largest barrack there, we restaged much of the New Year's concert that we presented here, which really cheered up the sick. They are pretty bored. I acted as the master of ceremonies and opened the concert with my "Happy New Year!" [. . .]

Today and yesterday I have had a spruce bouquet and pictures of our children on my table. And you, my beloved, are in my heart.

The lines you send me sometimes sound desperate, and your position is unbelievably difficult. I can't offer you any help—not even advice. I am as helpless in this respect as Zheniushenka. I can just stroke your head ever so gently, stroke your tired hands "like the ones of those just lowered from the cross," tell you about all sorts of insignificant things, and remind you of happy times in the past.[29] And there were happy moments! I can also very, very cautiously dream of a future that, although difficult and arduous, will be bright because we will all be together.

Today, after dinner I lay down on my bed and read Pavlov until the bell rang. I read it all evening too, because fortunately there have been no film showings, rehearsals, baths to get to, shifts on duty, and so forth. Right now I am finishing this letter. Then I will go to bed. It is too bad that I can't manage to see you in my dreams! . . .

I sent Aunt Mania and F. S[aveli]ch a holiday letter and warm thanks for all the help they have given you. If you have been in Dvinsk, you yourself know this, of course . . .

I want to remind you that I still haven't received any information about the children and how they have been growing and developing.

In the expectation of the arrival of some sort of commission tomorrow, our settlement has been decked out with spruce and pine trees as if it were a skating rink.[30] This has made things seem cozier.

With all my heart I wish you success in getting settled into a house of your own and sleeping better and finding some peace.

29. Formakov cites Alexander Vertinsky's "Seroglazochka" (Grey-Eyed Girl).

30. In memoirs, many Gulag survivors describe efforts by Gulag officials to spruce up camps in advance of inspections or the arrival of an official delegation. The clean-up that took place at the Solovetsky labor camp before Gorky's visit in 1929 is particularly notorious: Iu. I. Chirkov, *A Bylo vse tak . . .* (Moscow: Izdatel'stvo Politicheskoi Literatury, 1991), 102–5; Dmitry S. Likhachev, *Reflections on the Russian Soul: A Memoir* (Budapest: CEU Press, 1997), 110–13.

In terms of real friends, I have none here. I am pretty well acquainted with five or six of the men engaged in cultural work and two or three of the women from the drama group, all of whom have husbands here and children elsewhere.

And so, best wishes! Tender kisses and hugs so intense that your back pops. Greetings to the children and Grandmother, Mania, and Zorenka. Senia

♦ ♦ ♦

The night of January 20, 1945
Dear Niushenka:

Yesterday the Christmas season ended, and I removed the bouquet of spruce sprigs from my table. Now it is about 4:00 a.m. Since 3:00 a.m. it has been my turn on duty in our tent (that is what we call houses made out of panels and boards as opposed to barracks made of logs). One of my comrades was on duty from evening until 3:00. You need to keep the fire going in the stove and maintain order. We used to have to guard against thieves, but lately there haven't been any reports of big thefts. Everyone is asleep. One of the two light bulbs is burning. Between 10:00 p.m. and 12:00 a.m. they broadcast Stalin's order and the celebration that took place in Moscow in honor of our latest brilliant victories: since Warsaw fell, Krakow has been captured, and there has been a great breakthrough in Eastern Prussia. If only this terrible war would end soon! . . .

The head of our library is leaving for another settlement, and the day before yesterday they let me off work in the afternoon, and now I give out books from 8:00 to 9:00 p.m. twice a week (on Wednesday and Friday). We have about 700 [volumes]. They are really dog-eared, but, nonetheless, what joy they bring to us! Only the best workers get to check out books. Tomorrow was supposed to be a day off, but in our workshop we have fallen behind the plan, so they say we have to work . . .

I have the portrait of you with the very nice inscription on the back in front of me. I waited and waited for it and, like a criminal, feared looking my victim in the face. But when I got it, I smiled with joy. My darling, you are just perfect. My dear, mine in everything, you're the same—although of course you have changed too—you are my own familiar darling in all ways. Only your smile betrays your suffering a little. That letter [the one with the photo] is the last one I received. On the 6th, I got your postcards, the series of [photos] of the children, and the newspapers from which the stationery and envelopes had been stolen. Next time write your address on any envelopes you send, but don't write a return address.[31] That way no one will steal them. Also send me some postcards preaddressed in this same way. We don't have any of those here and won't in the future either. I have plenty of stamps, thanks.

On January 10 the New Year's story with the portrait finally arrived. Oh, how overjoyed I was! I immediately let you know about everything that I had received and wrote at the same time that the money too had arrived. You had written that you sent it.[32] According to the rules in place now, funds are transferred to our settlement once a month, at the very beginning of the month. Because the money [you sent] did not make it here by the beginning of January, it won't get here until early February, but I told you that I had received it so that you wouldn't worry . . . Then I didn't get anything for ten days. If I don't get something today, something will come tomorrow. I am eager for mail. [. . .]

January 25

Time flies at the end of the day, and by 6:00 I jump every time someone knocks on the door to our workshop, until finally our brigadier enters and, passing by, says: "There's nothing for you." [. . .] Today is my first free evening [in a while]. During the hard frosts of late January, temperatures dropped to minus 35, but now the weather is again more temperate, minus 15–20, which is typical for this "mild" winter.

On Monday, we had a concert in memory of Lenin. I opened the program by reciting some poems about him. All those who participated in the program received two kilos of potatoes yesterday . . . Alik Katalymov said to me once: "Arsenii Ivanovich, to whom are you reciting poetry now? Do you remember the concert hall in Dvinsk?"[33] He really

31. Formakov hopes to use some of the envelopes for illicit letters. If his camp address is on them, this will not be possible—it would be too obvious that the letter was from a prisoner.

32. Formakov provides inventories of what he has sent and received, so his wife will understand what has gone astray.

33. Formakov regularly read verse, often to musical accompaniment, at concerts in Dvinsk.

oohed and aahed over Dima's photo, remembering, in surprising detail and with real warmth, how the three of us came by row boat to visit them [the Katalymov family] at their cottage on Stropsk[ii] Lake.

Here we subsist primarily on our memories. Just now Serezha Zubov of Rezhitsa, who just got out of the hospital following a bout of jaundice, came by. Everything his family had both in the city and in the country burned up. His father is staying with strangers. His Latvian wife left for Libava . . .[34] He looked at my pictures, and he also began to remember [the past]. He told me that in the fall a woman traveled with her eight-year-old son from Arkhangelsk to the village settlement where he lives (twenty-five kilometers from here) in order to visit her husband. She had not done any preparatory work, and they did not get permission for a visit. Her husband waved to her from the roof. They looked at each other, and that was it. There is no point in seeing each other that way.[35]

I often reread your letters . . . Each time I find new nuances. Lately I have been thinking that it is good that you don't always come off in them as perfectly composed, businesslike, and serene. It is good that you do not hide from me your tears, bitter thoughts, and anguish. Who better to complain to than to me? [. . .]

I will write Dima a special letter of his own soon. I will also resend the poems that went missing from the holiday letter, but I haven't managed to get a second copy of the portrait yet. The artist is busy and keeps begging off. Oh, but it must be soon!

Many people here have taken such a fancy to the pictures you sent of our darling children that from time to time they ask to see them again. A comrade of mine named Anatolii Teize, who is active in cultural work and who is a poet and plays the accordion for our ensemble, even composed a lullaby for an imaginary child "like yours" (as he put it). I attach the text and the score, although, of course, our children are big already and no longer need lullabies.

I warmly kiss Zhenia's eyes, Dima's forehead, your lips, and Grandmother's hand. May Chr[ist] bless and preserve you all. Your papa

34. Libava is the pre-1917 name for the Latvian city of Liepaja.
35. Formakov is cautioning his wife against trying something similar. Usually camp officials turned away visitors who had not secured permission in advance.

♦ ♦ ♦

Kansk, February 6, 1945

"Don't cry, don't cry, my long-sufferer,
Don't be sad, my darling wife."[36]

My darling Niushenka!

You did not receive my first letter in which I described the unforget-
tably wonderful moments when I received the first lines from you and
when the faces of our children looked out at me [from their pictures].
I also wrote about what you were to me in the past and who you are
to me now. This all happened on December 2, when the head of our
records department [raschetnyi otdel] came up to me at work and said:
"Let's see you dance, Ars[enii] Iv[anovich]!" In his hands he had the
form from the wire transfer you had sent with your address in Riga (finally!) and the tender words you had written. In the evening I went to
pick up the mail. The post office is just opposite our workshop. I pick
up the packet of letters, head back [across the street], and then start
loudly reading off the addresses: and there's one for me, and there's a
second, and there's a third from Dima. And I open one at random and
I find a photo of the children together in my hands, and I am pierced
to the depths of my soul, and I cry tears of joy and sweet sorrow . . .
I described that for you, and I also told you how I had to show everyone in the workshop the photo and how taken they were with it and
how wonderful everything was . . . And then I wrote that you are my
life and light and that you entered my life like a scarlet sunrise and gave
me so much unforgettable happiness that I could subsist on memories
of it alone for a little more than four years. I repented of my sins (from
the notorious Chaliapin [incident] to crowding you with my proxim-
ity and thus inhibiting your development and self-sufficiency) . . .[37] I

36. Formakov modifies lines from Vertinsky's "Pesenka o moei zhene" (A Song
about My Wife): the original reads "Don't cry, don't cry, my beauty/Don't cry, my
darling wife."

37. On March 29, 1930, Dvinskii golos, the newspaper Formakov wrote for,
informed its readers that Feodor Chaliapin would be passing through town in
several days. An excited crowd showed up at the train station to greet the singer on
April 1, but he never arrived. When the paper published a short note congratulat-
ing itself on its April Fool's joke, it angered many people. Z. I. Iakub, Daugavpils v
proshlom: Publikatsii kraeveda (Daugavpils: AKA, 1998), 258–59.

wrote a great many things. Can I really be expected to recall all the words? But my feelings remain and will remain the same until the day I die. You really expressed this well in your letter when you spoke of mutual feelings of guilt and the "competition" to assuage [each other's] suffering. [. . .]

Yesterday, after an agonizing month-long interruption [in the mail], I received a letter and Zhenichka's drawing of the women and a small parcel with newspapers, envelopes, paper, postcards, and a marvelous little notebook. And then today several wooden crates that packages had arrived in were brought to our workshop from the post office, and in one of them I found scraps from a torn-up postcard that you had sent on January 16. Two-thirds of it reached me, so I read all that and could guess at the rest. I was very angry: that meant that someone had stolen one of the parcels you sent and had destroyed the postcard that informed me that you sent two. The thief! And I am not the only one who has had this happen. This is where things are going astray! . . .[38]

You plan to send money since you can't mail packages. Please don't raise this issue again. When I wrote to Dvinsk the first few times and asked for all those things, I assumed that you still had a settled way of life and a home, that even if your cup wasn't completely full, you at least still had a cup.[39] Now everything is very different. I am better off than you are. It is awful, but that is how things are. Dimusha's lines about his slippers and waiting for Father Frost and about how Father Frost left him two notebooks burned me like the lash.[40] You will manage to send me money by my name day, I don't doubt, and I will accept it humbly, but after that, not a single kopeck more! If you send it, I will return it. Honestly! I have plenty of envelopes, stamps, and paper for February and March. (By the way, when is Easter?)

38. Formakov guesses that someone in the camp post office is stealing, which was a common problem.

39. Formakov references the Russian saying "My house is a full cup" (Moi dom—polnaia chasha), which means that one finds perfect contentment in one's home and, depending on the context, suggests either material good fortune or domestic harmony and love.

40. In many European countries children leave slippers or shoes out on Christmas Eve, and Father Christmas places small presents in them. In Russian culture, Father Frost is the closest analogue to Santa Claus or Father Christmas.

In the evening, three letters in dark blue envelopes were brought over from the post office, yours from the 1st and 15th of January and two from Dimusha [. . .], and all my anger at the post office dissipated.[41] Your letters contain many bitter truths and a very pointed analysis of our situation, but I am not worried that we will feel estranged when we meet. [. . .] Yes, there will be some external problems and even large ones, but in terms of our private life there will not be any serious difficulties, I know. Our love is too great! This is how the wives of the Decembrists loved, this is how Turgenev loved: once and forever, until the grave.[42]

If I said to you, "Forget me and get on with your life!" that would just show that I did not understand your heroic temperament, which is so reminiscent of the martyrs of the earliest period of Christianity. (By the way, in all this time the censor has only blacked out one line in your letters: a quotation from what you yourself described as a sentimental German poem.) We Old Believers are flinty people in spirit, and perhaps this is what Aunt Mania's son-in-law cannot understand: the breadth of spirit and great range of our internal life. He is a primitive person: yes, yes, no, no. But for us, yes does not always mean yes and no does not always mean no. [. . .]

The question "What [did this all happen] for?" really ceases to be important when you remember what is happening all around: how separation and death roam among mankind and how the tears of human unhappiness have long since filled the seas. And fire rains down from the heavens . . . And curses uttered against God and the Mother of God pierce the air hourly. [. . .]

Officially our mail is picked up from the settlement once every one or two months and sometimes even once every three months, so I often have to ask someone to take letters out for me, and you yourself understand how unreliable this is and how often things get lost. We should be glad that some things get through.[43] [. . .]

41. One of the four letters was presumably an enclosure.

42. The Decembrists were army officers who led an abortive revolt against the tsarist state in St. Petersburg in 1825. Some received capital sentences, others hard labor and exile in Siberia. A number of the officers' wives voluntarily joined their husbands in exile, earning admiration. The writer Ivan Turgenev remained devoted to the opera singer Pauline Viardot, although she was married to another man.

43. In other words, he sends a lot of mail illicitly.

Our troops arc approaching Berlin. If not today then tomorrow the Germans will abandon Hitler, and the terrible war in Europe will end. Some of my fellow countrymen are preparing to leave [for home]. They have spent five years here. [. . .]

Another comment about the prose of life: when I wrote to you about the package, we did not have a grocery stand in the settlement, but now we do. For cash and also money from our personal accounts, we can buy butter, honey, tobacco, and milk there, and of course it costs less than it would for you to buy these things and ship them. I have money, and I have been seriously thinking about whether I could send you a hundred rubles a month. This would give me such moral satisfaction that you cannot even imagine!

No, of course this isn't true: you can imagine it, because you yourself live only for such "moral satisfaction."

Yes, my dear, our life has turned out quite badly, but at least we have memories, but the young people . . . Well, of course, they have the future! Our great motherland will rear them, our own native Russian people will raise them up to the crest of its waves, and a little part of us will live on within them and will continue the struggle. We will cross over into new generations. May their lives be brighter than ours![44]

February 10. My letter was delayed. It is the evening of our day off. I have reread all your letters. They are better than mine, smarter and deeper. Why? It is hard to say. In general, perhaps because these years for me have been a lethargic dream, but for you they were life in the largest sense, as difficult as a course of study at the university.

I recopied Dimusha's story and will send a special letter for him to-morrow. On the 1st of March, I will almost certainly be sent for two weeks to our local "house of rest" since it is my turn as one of the best workers in our brigade. I will get better rations and a chance to do nothing. So that is where I will be on your celebrations. It's wonder-ful! [. . .] Warm kisses to you and the children. Greetings to Mania and Grandmother. Yours, Senia.

---

44. Formakov again employs Soviet rhetoric.

♦ ♦ ♦

February 12, 1945
Dearest Niushenka:

I couldn't bear it and decided to add a page just for you.[45] I hope Dimusha isn't offended. I sent you a really long letter yesterday. I've been sick with the flu for the last several days. On the 1st of February we had the premiere of a contemporary play staged by our drama circle: *Poedinok (Kapitan Bakhmet'ev)* [The Duel (Captain Bakhmetiev)], and I had a small part.[46] It is terribly cold in our club, and everyone got sick. We performed the play four times. Soon the projector will be repaired, and they will start showing films again. [. . .] And as a reward for our labors, everyone who participated in the play got three kilos of potatoes, so today for supper I am having mashed potatoes.

In our workshop, we have pledged to fulfill the monthly plan by February 23, so there is a lot of work to be done, but the main thing is that my job isn't too much for me [physically], and it is indoors. The cold doesn't affect us.

My mood is always good now despite the very sad news that I received from you. [. . .]

I have enough envelopes for the next two months. I still have paper, and more is coming. In the future, when you send envelopes, write your address on them so that no one covets them. When you send newspapers, number them so that I know how many you included in the roll.

Like you, I have no idea what the future holds. We'll know when it happens. There is no sense in trying to make plans for your personal life now! The main thing is to win the war—then everything will be clearer. In terms of the lack of affection that our children suffer, we want for it even more, isn't that so? I hunger after the touch of your hand. No one close to me has touched me in five years—not even with their side or their knee. In addition to all the other forms of loneliness [that affect me], there is this physical form, although, in truth, there is nothing physical in this longing for primitive affection.

In the mornings and evenings my heart is with you and I yearn for you.

45. Presumably this was sent as an enclosure in a letter addressed to Dima.
46. A spy drama set during World War II by the brothers Tur and Lev Sheinin.

I embrace you, kiss you, lift your spirits, and pray for you. Your husband who is made happy by the past.

[In the margins upside-down:] Experience has taught me now to note down not just the date of each letter I send but also its contents so that, if it gets lost, I can repeat what I have said. I recommend that you do the same . . . I can't get the portrait redone right now. It was for you and the children. As soon as I can win over the artist, I will get one made and will send it to you by registered mail. Well, I'll manage it!

♦ ♦ ♦

February 20, 1945

"From your high tower
You looked out to the distance . . ."[47]

My distant star, my darling!

I somehow missed Candlemas. And then the next day unexpected circumstances arose, and I was almost transferred to a new living site. At the last moment, I was left behind on the grounds that I was an irreplaceable specialist (what do you say to that!) in my workshop. Now all this is in the past and is unlikely to arise again, but just in case, I have made arrangements for a telegram to be sent to you in such an instance, so that you will know not to write to me anymore until I send my new address. Although, of course, any letters you did send would be forwarded on from here.[48]

Transfers, like moves in general (in this instance we would be talking about a move on foot), are hard in and of themselves (more than 150 kilometers in winter), and also because you have to get settled in a new place. Well, glory to G[od] that it worked out. Things will be clearer in the future. Like you, I have gotten out of the habit of planning things very far in advance (I didn't like it much to begin with).

On the 16th I moved into new quarters, and then I moved again (to the place where I am writing this), and now I am dreaming of an-

47. Formakov cites the Prince's aria from the Borodin opera *Prince Igor*.
48. Camps were supposed to forward mail to transferred prisoners, but the system worked imperfectly.

Arsenii Formakov before
his 1940 arrest. Arsenii
Ivanovich Formakov Papers,
Hoover Institution Archive,
Box 4.

other possible move, inasmuch as having sixty men
housed in a single section,
and most of them poorly
brought up, makes for
most trying companions.

I am writing at the com-
mon table after supper.
It's warm, I am full (I am
not saying this to make
you jealous, Mother to us
all, but to reassure you), I
have my materials spread
out around me, and, of
course, I have to show everyone my photo (what a wonderful idea it
was [to send this]. I look with wonder on my old self). Their reactions:
You sure have aged a lot! That must be your younger brother after a
stay in the sanatorium! . . .

Now, about your letters, I received them both in one day: the long
one that you sent on January 21 and also *The Meeting*. This was a
wonderful new present! You formatted the book so tastefully: pink like
the color of hope and scarlet like our passionate love, and the poems,
some of which I had been able to remember only after great torment
and a long struggle (and sometimes not completely) and some of which
I had forgotten entirely, suddenly came to life, like fish in a thawed
stream, so (well, now this is a sentence!) that it turned out better than
if you had sent the original [book]. Of course, I did not ask for it to
gratify my pride (vanity). I needed it.[49]

49. The poems will solidify Formakov's reputation as a poet in camp.

Now "let's talk about the peculiarities of love": you write very well, too cleverly, and a little anemically about my "right" to have affairs.[50] My attitude to this is the same as yours would have been (you probably did not receive that letter) to my statement that you have the right to get divorced and make a new life for yourself (and the children) without any thought of me. My brigadier sent a letter like that home, and now his wife is married to someone else, but they still continue to correspond . . .[51] It is nonsense!

But I do not want to talk about that but instead about us. I am proud that, since the day of our marriage, I have not been unfaithful to you in word, deed, or thought. Here in Siberia, after stays in various places where the food supply was meager and after my first years of hard physical labor, I was so weakened physically (but not morally!!!), that I could not get an erection until the winter of 1944–1945. Now I get one very rarely in my sleep, as adolescents do. So for this reason alone . . . well, I think you understand what I mean.

Second, I think that everything that has happened to me is only retribution for the great sins of my youth. This does not bring upon me a spiritual depression or estrangement from life. No, it is my atonement. Judge for yourself: given this mood, would I really sully myself in some sort of dirty relations for a piece of bread or the sort of copper ring that our machinists trade in here?

Third, this is punished quite severely in our situation, and there are other reasons as well. I am glad that you answered in such detail concerning the icons. The icon you have in Riga belonged to my Rezhitsa grandmother Praskovia Osipovna. It was [given to her as] a blessing on her marriage, and when she died in 1912, my father gave it to me. Until the war (the First World War), it hung in the room where I studied and slept with Misha (the nursery). I remember it very warmly. And then

50. Formakov cites Alexander Pushkin's bawdy *Gavriliada*. For the original passage, see A. S. Pushkin, *Polnoe sobranie sochinenii v desiati tomakh,* 4th ed. (Leningrad: Nauka, 1977), 4: 108.

51. The Formakovs themselves ultimately entered into this kind of fake divorce. Such cases show that Soviet citizens sometimes responded to political pressure in a more nuanced way than has been understood: they yielded publicly to demands that they break off relations with a traitor but then privately continued the relationship. See also the V. V. Georgievskii Fund, Memorial Society Archive, Moscow, f. 1, op. 3, d. 1049.

later it was in our marital bedroom, but I don't have to tell you about that. My [. . .] grandmother was short, gentle, wonderful . . . and very unhappy in marriage: my grandfather loved to enjoy himself.

As much as I hated our Dvinsk houses, I loved our summer house, the place where we spent our honeymoon and the first years of our marriage and where our Dimusha took his first steps. By the way, has the album that covers his first five years also been destroyed?

It really makes me sad that Dima is causing such rows and is distressing you and Grandmother. Tell him for me that it is time that he understood when his naughtiness goes too far, and he needs to stop the first time you admonish him. In sending the tale of the fox (registered mail), I, foreseeing this issue, wrote to him about discipline (using Chkalov as an example).[52] Our son should not grow up to be a hooligan, and I believe that he won't become one! Isn't that right, Dimochka?

Judging by the prices [you listed], food in Riga is one and a half times to twice as expensive as here. So what is the point of sending packages? Now I always have plenty to eat. I buy butter (one kilo a month is plenty as an addition to our basic ration). The extra potatoes that I receive as a bonus never leave my table. For Shrovetide I will again make pancakes out of grated potatoes. Easter is April 29. How do you like that plan?

My moves and some other changes (the closure of the club and the cafeteria) have all taken place because new arrivals are expected, and they will need to be housed somewhere temporarily.[53]

On February 22, we are giving a concert outside our settlement in the red corner of our local village.[54] I will read my poem "Rus[skii] Soldat" [The Russian Soldier] and also a new piece titled "Na Berlin!" [To Berlin!].

I would be interested in hearing about the following topics: 1) how Dima learned to read, 2) his first days at school, 3) what he remembers and says about me, 4) Zhenichka's experiences at kindergarten, 5) her

---

52. Chkalov was a famous Soviet test pilot.

53. A huge influx of new prisoners entered the camp system at the end of World War II as territory once occupied by the Germans was purified of elements the Soviet state deemed potentially disloyal.

54. A "red corner" was a special building, room, or portion of a room that was set aside for agitation and propaganda work.

early childhood in general. Don't let them forget me; have them remember me in their prayers. Perhaps they have saved me even now. [. . .]

I did not tell you about our trip here. On the afternoon of June 22, [1941,] we saw German airplanes outside the window [of our prison cell in Dvinsk] and understood from the sound of strafing that the war had started. We wrote letters home, but they were never mailed, as we later learned. At dawn on June 24, they started organizing us for transport. There were many sudden and unexpected meetings. In our train car there were many people who had been picked up for evacuation that same night. We immediately started to call them "Jāņa bērni" [the children of Jan's Day]: the director of the Conservatory Freils, some people from Kraslava, the brother of Obraztsov's wife, Danka Frolov, the administrator at the government high school, a high school student by the name of Cherniavsky, who is the son of the man who runs the "typing courses," three schoolboys from Aglona, and many, many more.[55] What news we learned! What stories we heard!

In the forest by Stropy, the train stopped, and many people thought we were done for. Then we started moving again. We passed Bigosovo, Polotsk, Vitebsk, and Smolensk . . .[56] Everywhere we saw the results of enemy aircraft raids and bomb shelters. Then we passed through the Kaluga gubernia, the places that Turgenev extolled.[57] We passed Kulikovo Field station. Then, after moving almost straight east on a horizontal line across the country, we moved north. We passed Lev Tolstoy station, where there is a monument to him [the writer]. This is where he died. We traveled right up to the Volga (in Balakhna, I think), and then we moved north again. Finally we reached Samara. After that, we spent a full day stuck on a railway siding as we waited for it to be our turn to cross a bridge, which was occupied by trains moving military supplies. What a broad and glorious panorama it was: the Volga on the right; Samara in the distance.[58] The sun burned down mercilessly.

55. June 24 was the summer solstice holiday Ivan Kupala, known in Latvia as Jan's Day, or Ligo.

56. Bigosovo (Bigosava) is a Belarusian city, as are Polotsk (Polatsk) and Vitebsk. Smolensk is in Russia.

57. A gubernia was a Russian territorial division roughly equivalent to a province.

58. Kuibyshev, the name used for Samara from 1935 to 1991, appears over the word "Samara" in different ink.

And all day we got no water (although we were right by the Volga!) and no bread (although we were by Samara!). That night we crossed the Volga over a two-kilometer bridge. The blindingly bright moon cut a silver path across the waters. The beauty was almost unreal. Despite everything I had gone through, it delighted me. In the morning, the river looked white. Ufa, spurs of the Urals, reddish-orange sand and clay (from the iron content), all under the green of vegetation. It was so aesthetically striking! There is a pillar that has the word "Europe" inscribed on one side and the word "Asia" on the other. It is a marvelous mountain route, which takes you by a river and through a pass (in general, it wasn't so high; I thought we would get higher up). We went by Cheliabinsk, the Irtysh river, and Omsk, which I remember because the water [we got] there was mixed with kerosene. We were horribly thirsty all the time under the red-hot roof. I gave away my bread for an extra mug of water (we had a limited amount). After a journey of sixteen days, we finally arrived in Krasnoiarsk, which is a big, prosperous city, where we stayed for exactly a month.[59]

From the stories [of others] I learned a great deal. Stories about the special trains of evacuees chilled my soul. I still had in my possession (even now I have it) the receipt for the last package you sent me, which was dated April 15 and featured your intricate signature, and I wanted to think that you and the children had escaped the horrors of evacuation. However, once I got settled in here and learned of the existence of the Central Information Bureau on the Affairs of the Evacuated in Buguruslan, I wrote there, and then, after I had lost any hope of receiving an answer, I suddenly heard: "There's a letter for you!" My heart skipped a beat. A warm wave rushed to my head. But the stamp of the bureau caught my eye: "We know nothing. Your inquiry has been registered. If we learn anything, we will inform you . . ." And then I spent almost three years completely without letters. And then, through the Dvinsk native Glik, who ended up here for a while, I wrote to the daughter of Zykov. After that I poured my heart out a second time to Liza, and then I sent a third letter to Aunt Mania, and then finally the unforgettable delight that I experienced when I began corresponding with you.

59. Here Formakov notes that his letter writing was interrupted, and it is now February 23.

You see, my sunshine, always, everywhere, and in all things, I think only about you and the children.

"Because you and I—
Our features blur together"[60]

I got up to go to work when there were still stars in the sky: three in the west were in a straight row like this: ***. At work, I sometimes became completely exhausted as a result of my physical weakness. I returned after dark to eat and then immediately collapsed into sleep. I lived like an animal, but I did not turn into an animal, because, as soon as I returned to consciousness, "you appeared before me, the promise of a dream for exacting, faithful souls."[61] You gave me the greatest happiness in life. I gave you what I could—everything. What happened later was fate. The devil take it! I disdain it as I do the cold, which has dropped to minus 45 for three days in a row. [. . .] I kiss you tenderly and passionately, bless the children, and kiss Grandmother's hand. Senia. 23/II

[Upside-down in the margins:] Today it is minus 46, so we did not work outside. We are working so that we can take the day off on the 23rd.[62]

♦ ♦ ♦

Kansk, March 6, 1945[63]
My darling Niushenka!
After a great delay, today I finally received your letter from January 28, which was about school and Mania, the Sunday voluntary labor day, the cold, and hunger, and which also contained the graveside verses from *Mtsyri* [The Novice].[64] I grieve, shudder, and blame myself that I sent you nothing except some whiny poems and can send nothing apart from this. Of course, I understood that it was hard for you to live and struggle on your own, sick with small children. With every

60. From Formakov's poem "Odnim dykhaniem" (With One Breath) in *Vstrecha* (Daugavpils: Zar'ia, 1934), 34–35.
61. The source of this citation could not be identified.
62. February 23, Red Army Day, was an important Soviet holiday.
63. A registered letter with military and camp censorship stamps and Formakov's official return address.
64. A long poem by Mikhail Lermontov.

letter, the veil [that obscured my vision] lifted, and you (thank you for this) revealed the truth to me little by little. But what was in the last letter is enough to make one wail with horror. You don't even have anything warm to wear! Oh, my poor darling, what can be done? The fellows here see that I have grown despondent after reading your letter (at work) and are asking [what's wrong]. I answer: things are bad at home; hunger and cold. One fellow came up to me just now and said: Ars[enii] Iv[anovich], let's take up a collection! You can put in what you have, and I will put in all my pay up to August, and we'll send it to your family! . . . It is touching and absurd. With great difficulty, I can probably get permission to send you a wire transfer, but what meaning do my hundred rubles have given how unfortunate your life is? Just in case, I want to repeat my threat: don't send me any more money, or I will return it to you with mine added for good measure. Seriously.

Don't get upset about the letters. I am not allowed to write any more frequently. Also, either you yourself tore off part of the second page of your letter at the last moment, or it got cut off in transport, beginning right after the line: "I even for my father feel e . . ." (envy perhaps?) and to "whom can I tell?" (my sorrows?).[65] I am ashamed of my peaceful, well-supplied life here. I can only sympathize with your suffering from a distance. Hearing about the cold January day on which you cried so bitterly, I am horrified, but it is already almost March. Is there really no one in Dvinsk who can sell what possessions you still have? (Uncle wrote, for instance, about the desk.) [Here three lines are blacked out by a censor.] I treated him to some supper. He told me about his native city. And he recognized me, which means that I haven't changed so terribly yet.

I write and chatter on, but I cannot find the words I need. And how exactly would I go about finding them? [. . .] I cannot advise you and see no way out. I am blind and stupid. But my heart, soul, and my entire internal "I," everything that is not just flesh, body, bones, and skin, streams toward you and is with you day and night. If human thoughts, will, and love can fly, like an airplane, and reach a distant target with

65. The phrase Formakov cites from his wife's letter, "whom can I tell" (komu povem?) uses an archaic verb form. The object Formakov inserts suggests that he thinks she may be referencing a poem, often sung in Old Believer communities, "Stikh placha Iosifa Prekrasnogo, egda prodasha bratiia ego vo Egipet" (Verses on the Lament of Joseph the Magnificent, Who Almost Sold His Brothers in Egypt).

lightning speed like an artillery shell, then my thoughts surround you and my prayers too. I kiss you passionately and bitterly. On the 9th, I will turn forty-five. And I will again be alone. Kiss the children and Grandmother [for me]. Senia

♦ ♦ ♦

March 24, 1945
From the house of rest
My dear Niushenka!

It is so wonderful! A clean white room with two windows, five beds covered in white blankets, a radio playing the song "Suliko," and pictures on the walls.[66] Over the head of my bed, I have the new photo of you and the picture of the children under glass in a frame decorated to look like oak. I am writing with the pen that you sent by a roaring fire (after some springlike days, it is again minus 27) and under bright light. This is such joy after everything that has happened, and if I did not feel such terrible pain at the thought of your life, things would almost be good. We must believe in miracles.

So, allow me to report, Mother-commander: I arrived at our house of rest not on the 1st, as I had expected, but rather on March 20.[67] This means that I get to spend two weeks doing nothing while all the while getting enhanced rations and 800 grams of bread. All the bedding is provided here. The lavatory is heated! Those of us who reside in the small room, in addition to all the other advantages we enjoy, are also freed from the obligation to perform two hours of labor [a day]. If I were allowed to live like this for two months, as opposed to two weeks, I would again look like my 1940 photo. We sleep in until 8:00 a.m. Then we have breakfast: a bowl of thick cabbage soup, mashed potatoes, and fried fish. Dinner is at 1:00 p.m. We get the same kind of soup, a meat cutlet with potatoes, and a white-flour handheld pie with carrot filling. Supper is at 7:30 p.m. We get a bowl of "Polish" soup and then

66. A popular Georgian song.

67. Generally in the Soviet Union, a "house of rest" (*dom otdykha*) was understood as a place of rest and relaxation for fundamentally healthy people. Unlike sanatoriums (*sanatorii*), such facilities did not offer specialized medical treatments. Formakov's description suggests that the "house of rest" in camp also primarily provided nutritious food and rest, although some light medical services were available. For information on rehabilitative sites in the Gulag, see Dan Healey, "Lives in the Balance."

some porridge.[68] Everything is completely filling and so tasty it seems home-made. And meat cutlets are a dish I haven't seen in four years!

For the first few days, I was busy with a writing assignment that I had received from the higher-ups: composing all sorts of *chastushki* and so forth for the upcoming sowing campaign (the First Congress of our Agricultural Workers [is coming up]).[69] Yesterday I turned all that in, and now I am a free Cossack for the next ten days. This is one of the paradoxes of our life.

Yesterday I received the first postcard that you sent in March, from which I learned that our post office has been honestly settling its accounts with me and not leaving me with grounds for grievance. [. . .] Dimusha's letter and all the postcards arrived just fine. And today I finally got the birthday letter I had been waiting for, which contained the wonderful picture of you with the marvelous, sad verse inscription, the picture of the children's sweet faces, and then the picture of you in white, in which you are wearing—I just now spotted it—your cameo. Ah! It is all so wonderful. [. . .]

Along with the letter, I received a small parcel: masses of newspapers. Judging by the numbering, I got them all, but this is not what I meant for you to do. It is time-consuming to number each page. Just write the total number of items in the corner where you put the address. And even that isn't essential. In addition to the newspapers, I got five envelopes (one with two pens inside—a real treasure!!!), seven postcards (who colored that one pair so delicately, you?), and a notebook. Thank you, my sunshine. [. . .]

In one of the cards, you asked about Grigorii Savel[iev]ich.[70] I wrote about him in one of the first letters I sent to Dvinsk. Apparently, it did not reach you . . . I met up with him in the bath house when I arrived in Krasnoiarsk (August 1941). He told me how he had seen you in court.

68. Most likely a vegetable soup with sausage and perhaps beans. Traditionally supper is lighter than the midday dinner for Russians. In regular camp conditions, this distinction disappeared: little food was available at work sites outside camp during the day; in camp, inmates received similar servings of porridge and soup at most meals. Formakov's description suggests that the house of rest tried to evoke the food rituals inmates remembered from home.

69. *Chastushki* are four-line humorous poems associated with Russian folk culture.

70. Probably Grigorii Savelievich Eliseev, a prominent Daugavpils Old Believer and former Saeima deputy, who was arrested in 1940 and sentenced to ten years of hard labor: http://www.russkije.lv/ru/lib/read/grigory-yeliseyev.html.

I was very moved by the way that you managed to make all the rounds, never allowing me to leave your sight for an instant. But we [Grigorii Savelievich and I] did not live together and when, a month later, we were moved to Eniseisk, he, along with a small group (about forty), was left behind to be used at another work site. He was completely healthy [at that time]. I haven't been able to learn anything else about him, although I tried to get information, and I have heard about other people.

Here's how things stand with Alik Katalymov. I wrote to Aunt Mania in Dvinsk about him. The doctor found out about this somehow, and his new wife, Raiskina was her maiden name, wrote to Alik here using my address. The letter arrived a few days after he left here. Then a second came. I forwarded both letters to him, but I do not know if they reached him. Then quite recently his aunt, the doctor's sister, who works as a teacher in the Iaroslavl gubernia, wrote to me: describe the character of my nephew, who is working with you. I want to understand "the moral and political countenance of my relations" and why he is not writing to his father, and so forth. Well, I gave her what's what in my answer. She's a fool, and I feel sorry for Alik. Write to him [Alik's father] in Preili at number 5 Lipovaia street and give him Oleg's address: Reshety station, Krasnoiarsk railway, P.O. box 235/5.[71] I can only send so many letters, and I am using them up on all these things, so I can't . . .

Since I got into correspondence with you, my treasures, things have been so good and easy for me that I feel a little guilty and fearful: as if any moment everything may break off and fall to pieces. After all, our life here is like that. At least up to now God has protected me.

Regarding the poems, I have recopied them and sent them to you in a separate little booklet so that you could see that, as always, in every place and every hour, I thought only of you, my one and only, and the children. [. . .] At the end of the booklet, using up the extra space, I wrote out several of the estrada numbers that I wrote for our jazz soloists.[72] Drabinskii is a real original. He is our guitar player and an amateur composer. In his regular life he was an engineer. He lost his whole family in Ukraine. All he has left is a son, who has been taken in

71. Oleg is Alik.
72. Estrada is a kind of variety performance popular in Russia.

by strangers, and he can't discover by whom. He has been living here for a long time and is very quiet, nice, and entirely grey. Tolstov is a wonderfully accomplished bayan player.[73] You'll understand this when I say that he played the entr'acte to *Carmen* and Tchaikovsky's piano concerto by ear: he cannot read music, and others have to notate his compositions. [. . .]

You may recall that I started to write [the poem] "Tchaikovsky" when I was still at home. Then, when I was in the hotel and there were no books and I had no one to talk to, I had no other way to entertain myself, and I made significant changes to the first three parts, which had not satisfied me.[74] The fourth part (the death of Tchaikovsky) had turned out so well at home that I did not want to rewrite it, but I was not able to remember more than two to three lines of it, no matter how hard I tried.

I added a second and third part to "Pushkin," and redid the first and fourth parts, but I think I forgot to copy the last part ("The Funeral") into the booklet. I will send this as soon as I know you have gotten the book.

It seems to me that the results of Grandmother's trip to Dvinsk have really disappointed you. You learned of new losses to add to the innumerable losses you have already suffered. "On poor Makar [all the pinecones fall] . . ."[75] Oh, my darling! We may have to suffer [misfortunes] again and again, but perhaps one day good times will return.

You wrote about the suitcase that contained my things. Perhaps this does not need to be said, but keep in mind that you do not need to save anything for me. Use anything you need for your own benefit and the benefit of the children. I do not need anything, and I will not need anything in the future. And right now every stray piece of fabric matters for you.

I will write to Dima tomorrow and will compose something for Zhenia.

Yesterday my roommates showed me their photos, and I showed them mine. Everyone was particularly taken with the New Year's

73. A bayan is a type of accordion.
74. Formakov uses the word "hotel" as a cryptic reference to the Daugavpils investigative prison.
75. A folk saying that describes how repeated misfortune afflicts the unlucky.

gallery. And one fellow kept asking: "Is your wife also a writer or a journalist? She put everything together so well with the signatures under the photographs—it is just a masterpiece of artistic expression!"

No, I said. She is not a writer or a journalist, although she did study journalism. She is just a very talented person in all respects: at school, at home, in medicine, at the theater . . . And it is true, my darling. You have so much talent and such a light touch along with your unusual assiduity and diligence! Looking back on the past, I remember it all, your ability to make yourself comfortable in any room, your pedagogical talents, and your ability to stage things . . . What we didn't have then! (And he gestured sadly.)

Soon it will be 11:00 p.m. It is 7:00 where you are. I will listen to the latest news, which pleases us with reports of new victories on all fronts, finish this letter, and go to sleep, having put out the light and shut off the radio (two more wonderful aspects of our current "sanatorial" existence). We sleep a great deal both after breakfast and after dinner. Tomorrow is Sunday; it's the third week of Lent if I am not mistaken. I am going to pore over the Riga newspapers and look for familiar names. During a cursory glance at them, I already noticed Kira Verkhovskaia. Here one Riga native told me that she had told him herself that I was her protégé. Perhaps. Isn't it all the same now?[76] May Christ protect you all. I kiss you warmly, my darling (take heart!), and also my wonderful children, our boy and girl.

Yours, always with you in my thoughts, Papa.

76. Verkhovskaia (1907–1980) was a journalist who supported the Soviet occupation in 1940. According to many accounts, she denounced former associates to the NKVD during the occupation and had served as a Soviet agent in Riga in the 1930s. The word used for protégé here, *krestnik,* literally means godchild and has a potentially ominous cast given Verkhovskaia's reputation. *Kum,* a word applied to godparents in Russian, was used in Soviet labor camps as slang for the camp security officer. Perhaps in this passage, Formakov hints at this double meaning and signals that Verkhovskaia played some role in his arrest. Both christening rituals and denunciations involve naming individuals; moreover, in respect to what occupation might Verkhovskaia have claimed Formakov as a mentee, in journalism or perhaps some darker field of activity? There is little sign that Formakov acted as a Soviet secret-police informer prior to 1945. Although he named some names during his interrogations in 1940–1941, by and large he confined himself to giving information the authorities most likely already knew. Russkie Latvii, http://www.russkije.lv/ru/lib/read/kira-verhovskaya.html; Iu. Abyzova and T. Feigman, "Nepravyi sud nad pravovedom P. N. Iakobi," in *Baltiiskii arkhiv,* vol. 4 (Tallinn: Avenarius, 1999), 134, fn. 20; State Archives of Latvia, f. 1986, op. 1, d. P-1545, ch. 1.

♦ ♦ ♦

March 30, 1945
No. 1[77]
Dear Niushenka!

Your postcards are reaching me very quickly. On the 27th, I got the postcard from the 11th, and then on the 28th, a small parcel containing books arrived. Oh, it was just fabulous! Thank you LOTS for both the Stalin and *Stranniki* [Pilgrims], and the little enclosure that you slipped in with the postcards and the packet of tooth powder amused me so much that my laughs filled the whole room.[78] Oh, what you don't come up with, my genius! But the postcard you sent was sad: the children are sick again, and if it is measles, then you are in quarantine, and your heart . . . We're just unlucky, darling! But it will be all right. Some day things will turn our way. I've also gone through such tough times (and will again in the future) that more than once I have thought that I would be better off hanging myself. Your memory stopped me. I overcame everything. You must take heart as well. Everything changes, everything flows.[79] Perhaps we will meet again sooner than we think. Your only February letter went astray. I am not upset—I just wanted to let you know. I am grateful to the post office for the things I do receive. I need it [mail] more than bread or air. I kiss you ardently and also kiss the children. I send my respects to Grandmother. I'll send a new letter in about three days. Yours forever, Senia

♦ ♦ ♦

March 30, 1945
No. 2[80]
My dear!

I had just sent off the last postcard when they brought me your [letter] containing the little calendar and the stamps from the post office. My respects to Lev Serg[eevich] and you for all your efforts. It turns out I celebrated Shrovetide a week early, not to speak of everything else

77. A plain postcard with a military censorship stamp but no return address or camp censorship stamp. Like many camp inmates, Formakov made sporadic attempts to number the letters he sent home. Periodically, however, he loses count.
78. Formakov probably received Viacheslav Shishkov's novel *Stranniki*.
79. Formakov paraphrases an aphorism traditionally attributed to Heraclitus.
80. A plain postcard with no return address and a military censorship stamp.

I got wrong. Your letter softened my heart; it was so good and tender. It is good you were so frank. [. . .]

Don't send money even if you have extra. I promise you that if I need it, I will let you know myself. But do send newspapers from time to time. Here they are read with delight by people from our part of the world, are used for smoking, and in other ways . . . For me they provide a window on your lives . . . Always with you in my thoughts, your Papa Senia.

P.S. Who is that E. or Ye. who has appeared "in your life"? I will break his ribs!!!

♦ ♦ ♦

April 10, 1945
Still from the same place
Happy May 1!

> "You, like a distant star,
> You, like a shining star . . ."

                                                    (my work)

My angel, Niushenka!

Your concern for me is so touching it almost makes me cry; and your kind attention seems endless. Two days ago there was another joyful surprise: a blue parcel containing Latvian journals, four books, and, most important of all, two pussy willow branches, which I immediately stuck in water and then placed in the sun on the windowsill, but whether or not they will grow only God knows: they were pretty dried out and shriveled, although all the "white bunnies" were still firmly attached . . .[81] Two years ago, when I was working far away on the river, I brought home several downy branches of some sort of willow, but we don't have real pussy willows here.

I spent March 20 to April 4 in our house of rest and came back well rested. I wrote you three letters from there, read a lot, and gained 700–800 grams in weight. That is real "material proof" of my spiritual improvement. Now that it is April, the snow has started to melt here,

---

81. In Russian Orthodox paschal ritual, pussy willows substitute for palm fronds.

the sun is burning fiercely, and soon we will be able to change our felt boots for leather ones.

About a week ago someone told me that a person from our part of the world was working in the shoe repair shop. I went over to get acquainted. It turned out to be a woman of about your age from Rezhitsa. She graduated from high school there and had attended my lectures: "You sure have changed!" (that was the first thing she said). They had a farm by the river Malta. That's where her children are now. Her husband was separated from her, as I was separated from you, last August. She [was seized] in October . . . So we talked and sighed together to the extent that we could in the workshop. She knows Zavoloko very well.[82]

Regarding the parcel you sent with *Literatura i isskustvo* [Literature and Art] in two separate packets with an arithmetic notebook, it has landed in a very nice place. I see this as an illustration to the folk tale about Sadko: "we have traveled back and forth across the sea many times, but have not been paying the sea god tribute . . ."[83] Well, we have been paying, but at least our correspondence has not broken off. [. . .]

This is my whole life—the communications that I receive from you and about your life. It takes a long time for these tidings to reach me—at least three weeks—and they are like the rays of a distant star, which take decades to reach earth. We see this star and that one up in the sky, but all that is ten years in the past and what is happening to that star now, we will only see after ten more years. [. . .]

I almost forgot! I scored another success: the post office never delivered the toothbrush you sent—just the tooth powder, but then our consumer goods workshop began manufacturing surrogates, and I bought such a brush for five rubles in the shop that sells our local manufactured goods. It is nothing special, but it is a brush, and it does serve its purpose.

There, you see how everything works out here for me! Now if only your life could begin to go more smoothly, then we could just count off the days that remain.

82. Ivan Zavoloko was a leading member of Latvia's Old Believer community and a pioneer in the study and preservation of its heritage. Like Formakov, he worked as an educator.

83. For the folk epic Formakov cites, see "Sadko," in *Byliny* (Moscow: Khudozhestvennaia Literatura, 1955), 304. The newspaper Formakov received is presumably the Latvian *Literatūra un māksla* (Literature and Art).

My toothbrush from home lasted me four years. I left it on the lid of the wash basin, which was out in the open. I remembered and went back, but someone had already taken it. Your names had been carved into it, as well as the dates of all the gifts I had received from you in Dvinsk and so forth. It wasn't just a brush; it was a keepsake . . . There, you see: you are mourning the chairs, and I pine for my toothbrush . . . Nice, trifling, everyday objects. So much is connected to them, and then they are lost. Remember, I always warned you against getting too attached to things. And, at the same time, I loved these things myself and could not get rid of even trifles. Even now I am saving not just all your letters and all the envelopes that they came in, but also the address slips from your parcels.

After dinner, I sat in the sun for the first time for about two hours reading *Pilgrims*. Then I took a walk, went to visit a friend in the hospital to cheer him up, and then, on the way back, I went by the house of rest where I was not long ago, and I picked up a letter from Dima. [. . .]

Happy, as always after having received mail from you, I returned to the dormitory. A fellow from Riga stopped by. I wrote a letter for him to send home (he doesn't know Russian). Suddenly someone stuck his head in from the entryway (the door was open) and, smiling, called out: "Does F. live here?" Another guy gestured at me, also slyly. I stepped out, and they handed me your letter of March 19 with great ceremony—a marvelous postcard of a young girl with bangs and a braid having a conversation with a sparrow. Immediately there's a crowd [around me]; everyone wants to see. Something so colorful brings joy to everyone. Then Boris is called over. He's a boy of about sixteen. He is 130 centimeters tall. "Boris! Do you like your bride?" "No, she's snubnosed." [. . .]

I am taking a break for supper. Then, when everyone goes to bed at about 10:00, I will continue writing. This is probably the last letter I will send before Easter. For the holiday, I will send a picture postcard "officially" in a few days.

I managed to get settled back down to write a little earlier than I expected: they didn't manage to get a film for us, so they announced that there would be an evening of dancing from 7:00 to 9:00 (one of the paradoxes of our life here). Everyone ran off to get a look. About twenty couples are dancing: it is a dreadful spectacle in every possible sense. Our barrack is pretty empty and comparatively quiet. The electricity is working, which is good because last night the system was damaged, and, making use of the dark and the fact that our door is unlocked almost all night long (as a result of the night shift and people needing to go to the bathroom), someone stole two bags of potatoes, weighing 40–50 kilos altogether. It is a good thing that my spot is far from the door. My bag wasn't taken. They caught the thief in the afternoon, beat him, and brought back one bag unopened, but the second, smaller bag is gone. This is, of course, an insignificant incident, but it gives you an idea of our life here. [. . .]

Our artist is traveling. When he gets back, I will make him draw me. By the way, I am letting my hair grow out again.

Thank you so much once again for writing so frequently and for everything you send. Just don't send any money please. I warmly hug and kiss my wonderful daughter Zhenichka, my dear son Dimusha, sweet Anna Ananievna, and you, my precious friend. Yours, Senia.

♦ ♦ ♦

April 10, 1945
My dear son:

I received the letter in which you promised to correct your behavior. I know that my son cannot be bad, or else how will he look at me when we meet? Your mother writes that in this trimester you will not have any Cs. Good job, son! Both your mother and your father were always good students.

The picture you drew of the airplane bringing Papa a letter turned out very well. The way you drew it, the flowers, the envelope, and the way the parcel was tied to the plane were all very good.

Your choice of rhymes was very artful.

There are many flowers here in the summer. They are extremely bright and many of them smell nice. I will dry both a carnation and some white clover and will send them to you. The ice will break up on the river Kan only in May. The year before last, I saw it: the right bank is very high, steep, and overgrown by the forest, and the current is swift. The pieces of ice swirled in circles, passing by with lightning speed. In the forest here, in addition to the familiar species from back home (spruce, pine, birch, alder, aspen), we also have many larch and Siberian pine trees. On the Siberian pine trees there are very tasty nuts, which are in a thin dark shell that you can easily bite through. In their shapc, they resemble a triangular pyramid with smoothed edges. The needles on these pine trees drop in the winter. The needles on the larch trees turn yellow in fall and then green up again in the spring. There are no edible seeds in the larch cones. The larch's wood is pink in hue and rich in sap, and logs cut from it are as heavy as oak and just as strong. Sap seeps out of cracks in a larch tree (as from our cherry trees), and Siberians chew it just like Americans chew rubber. As a special treat, sometimes they boil it with sugar and milk into what they call "grey." They suck and chew on this for days at a time.

In the winter here you often see what are called sun dogs. I remember reading about this in cosmography, and here I saw it for myself. Because of the refraction of the sun's rays on the snow and in the air, when the sky is clear, a flattened oval forms around the sun, and you can see four false suns on it. It is a mirage (an apparition). [. . .] Most often there are only two sun dogs, located to the right and left of the real sun, like ears. It is a magnificent and somewhat terrifying sight. Kisses to you, my splendid boy. Your papa.

◆ ◆ ◆

April 24, 1945[84]
My dearest Niushenka and my children Dimochka and Zhenichka:

I send you my warmest wishes for the upcoming May holiday. I hope you spend it happily and are in good health. A few days ago, I received your letter to Anatolii, and I do not understand how it is that you have not received anything from here for a month and a half (up to March 30).[85] It is true that I can only write once every three months, but Senia writes every ten days without fail.[86] Of course, his letters go astray more frequently: there is nothing you can do about that. I am not limited in the number of letters I can receive from you, and I get them pretty regularly. Up to this point, I have received everything with the exception of the toothbrush: I got the telegram, and the book, the journal, and the calendar, the newspapers, the tooth powder, the greeting card, the

84. A mass-printed postcard with the text of the Soviet anthem on the front side, a military censorship stamp, and no return address.

85. Anatolii has acted as a courier for the Formakovs.

86. Formakov references a code that he explains later in the correspondence: he tried to sign unofficial letters with the diminutive of his name, "Senia," or "Papa," and to sign official letters "Arsenii." He employed this system inconsistently.

postcard, and the notebook. If I move (which is not in the wind at the moment), my friends will let you know, and the mail will be forwarded. Anatolii is already elsewhere, but people are so good to me that even this postcard made it to me. I kiss you all a billion times. Arsenii.

[In the margins:] Sending a telegram from our backwoods is really a trick.

♦ ♦ ♦

May 1, 1945
From the same place
My dear Niushenka!

The 1st-of-May sun shines down, as is fitting for a holiday. We have been off work for two days. They cleared half the people out of the place where I live yesterday. It's quieter now, and there is more space. At the head of my bed, by the frame that holds the faces of those dear to me, I have two pussy willow branches, which were sent from afar by the dear hands of my own beloved. On my nightstand, I have a sprig of bird cherry that is beginning to leaf out. There's music playing outside. Our victorious flag flies over Berlin. You can already walk around without a hat and with your pea jacket draped over your shoulders. But the main thing is that yesterday I received a parcel from you with the journals *M. and L.* ([a set tied up] with dark blue twine and then two more) and two volumes of *Sputn i agit* [The Agitator's Companion].[87] After all your howls about my silence, I have to understand this as a joyful sign that communication between us has been restored. [. . .] I will continue to write to you once every ten days, but don't forget that all sorts of things can happen in transit from me to the mailbox and in all the disorder of the mail system. I have been counting things up just now, and this is my thirty-sixth letter (since the one I sent to Dvinsk on July 6, 1944). That is not so little! As always, I got the parcel first, so I expect letters after the holidays: perhaps a big one, perhaps a short, lively postcard. It's all the same to me: radiant joy. I am going to try

87. The word Formakov uses for twine, *vluchka,* is not typical for Russian. By *M. and L.* (M. un L.) Formakov may mean the Latvian newspaper *Literatūra un māksla* (Literature and Art). Formakov makes a minor error in rendering the title of *The Agitator's Companion*. It should read *Sputnik agitatora* as opposed to *Sputn[ik] i agit[ator]*.

to get some eggs for the 6th. I will probably have to work. I dream of pulling together a microscopic *paskha* out of cheese curds.[88] There arc several of us "old believers" [*stolovery*] here.[89] They are all envious of my sprigs of pussy willow. [. . .]

Today I went to check on Kostia Smirnov, who is from our parts. He is twenty-two and is the oldest son of the inspector of our Russian high school. Their whole family was evacuated to the Kansk area on April 17, 1941. They think the father is dead. He was working as a tractor driver at a collective farm, but he got two years for spilling fifty-eight kilos of kerosene. He was arrested on January 5 of this year. Kostia said I did not look bad at all. We talked about Dvinsk. I may, it is true, never see it again, but everything there is so much a part of me!

My hemorrhoids aren't bothering me; my mood is confident and calm; I sense your support. I am like a warrior who knows that there are marvelous reserves [behind him]. Every letter you send is like a shipment of vitamins that no professor has ever identified. Anatolii is traveling, so the postcard you sent him, which was marked with his new address, after it was read, wasn't given to me. And that Volodia is running around with your postcard as if it were some sort of rarity: no one writes to him. I don't think he finished high school. He lies a lot, but he is a cultured boy and knows a lot of poetry by heart. I like talking with him (our work stations are next to each other). I often tell him and think to myself bitterly: "Oh, if only it were Dimusha here beside me!"

By the way, about our workshop, forty people work in it (fewer during the night shift; I always work during the day). Two electrical motors that hum, noise, sometimes soot, but plenty of light, and it's not crowded or terribly dirty, and the work isn't physically hard. Many of the workers, the sorters, are women. Our workshop has a small front garden with currant and bird cherry bushes. Later we'll have beds of flowers. A little walkway made of boards runs past our windows to the post office. Even the postman winks as he walks by and beckons in invitation when he has something for a person. When he gave me your postcard from March 30, he said reproachfully: "What is this, F[ormakov]? Your wife is worried!" In short, everyone here knows me, respects me a little, and a wonderful (relatively speaking) feeling

88. *Paskha* is a sweet dish that Russians eat at Easter.
89. Formakov uses a corruption of the term *starovery* that was common in popular speech.

in my spirit prompts me to hum sometimes and to climb the porch steps by twos, which never used to happen. We work from 7:00 a.m. to 6:00 p.m., not counting an hour off for dinner. Since I can make progress toward my output as I choose over the course of the workday, I can take a little time off to run to the barrack to listen to the news, or to the club to take a look at the latest newspapers, or even to go to the barbershop for a shave: after work there is an enormous line.

May 2. In terms of books, [. . .] I would really love some Wallace or anything else adventurous, but that is really from the realm of unrealizable dreams.[90] Don't send the journal *The Agitator's Companion* anymore: the contents are of little interest, and it doesn't work for rolling cigarettes. It would be better to send newspapers, including Russian papers. I still have a lot of stamps.

On the 6th I will spend the whole day remembering only happy things: you dressed up for Easter in your new red dress and black shoes over at our house for a visit; the 1st of May, the Easter Day on which we got engaged; and Dimusha coloring eggs . . . And even my last Dvinsk Easter [in 1941], which I spent without you. I made three Easter eggs of various sizes out of the inside of a piece of bread, dipped them in powdered sugar, and decorated each with a red ribbon and your monogram. I also remember that now . . . My grandfather Kapustin, I remember, brought a linen basket of decorated eggs and Easter cakes to that house [the prison] each year . . .

I congratulate Dimusha on his success in school. I am sure that he is growing up to be a smart and well-behaved boy and soon will be a real help to his mother. I kiss Zhenichka warmly, as I do all of you. I am eager to see her new pictures and her impromptu poems.

Thank you, my dears, for everything. If my spiritual impulses can help you, don't doubt that I am thinking all the time about you, Niushenka, and about all of you. I send you a billion kisses and a trillion warm words of love. Your papa. [. . .]

[In the margins:] By the way, there is no hint of a change of address anymore (see the first page).

I enclose two drawings for Zhenichka to color.

90. The popular English writer Richard Horatio Edgar Wallace (1875–1932) is best known for writing the screenplay to *King Kong*.

♦ ♦ ♦

No. 37[91]
May 9, Victory Day
Hooray, my dear!

I send you my best wishes on this great day of our total victory over the enemy. This morning we had a rally, then a dance, and a concert. Great joy and hope [fill our hearts]. And on Saturday the 6th (you hit your target so accurately), your colorful holiday card and the second letter with postcards arrived. And on the 8th I got Dimusha's letter with the drawing and your note. My heart sometimes is filled with long-forgotten joy and sometimes with total despair (just for a moment), and then, clenching my teeth, I head back into battle again, because you are my inspiration, my example, and model. I go into battle for a better future, for a better place in life . . .

I spent the holiday well. I had a clean towel on my table, your pussy willows and postcard, some eggs and cake made out of bread with a layer of butter and a white inscription . . . done with salt. I had a full glass . . . of cabbage soup.[92] Judging by D[imusha]'s letter of April 14, you got the letter I sent from the house of rest. So a lot of things are getting lost again, including, most important, the book that I sent registered mail on March 4 that contained all the poetry I have written over all these years, and also the fairy tale I wrote for Dima about the fox (for a second time!). I kiss you all countless times. I hope that peace will improve postal communication and our letters will travel better. Hooray! Praise be to victory! Your papa

♦ ♦ ♦

Saturday, May 13, 1945
No. 38
My truly precious Niushenka!

This was a joyous week. A week ago, on Saturday the 6th, such perfect timing, I received your holiday greeting card: the colorful [picture of] the children with the little chick in the hen yard. I had them out on my nightstand for three days, leaning against the mug with my Riga

---

91. A plain postcard with no return address and a military censorship stamp.

92. Traditionally at an Easter table the inscriptions would be done in sugar and wine would be served. Formakov's substitutions highlight his deprivation.

pussy willow sprigs and my Kansk bird cherry sprigs: the vivid colors brightened up the whole room. On the 8th I received Dima's letter, which, although short, I will always hold close to my heart. [. . .] On the 9th in the morning at 6:30, I was listening to the radio and heard about the capitulation of Germany. Hooray! Victory Day—a holiday, sunshine, and merriment. I was even touched: there has never been a victory like this in all of Russian history! Incidentally, it is also good that the Courland peninsula is being cleared out without a battle. On the 11th, I did not work until dinner, and then yesterday I had the whole day off (there was a change of shifts in the workshop). Then finally today I got the long letter from you that I had been awaiting for so long (April 15). It turns out that everything, including the parcel with the Latvian journals, which I received before anything else, was sent on the same day but was delivered in such sensible doses! [. . .] Finally tomorrow I am going to get to see the film *Mart-aprel'* [March-April] for the first time.[93] It's been a long time since we have had a new one [film] here; we've watched the same thing several times over.

In connection with Victory Day and the end of the war, everyone here is rejoicing and filled with the same high hopes that you yourself so well described.[94] So far I have not sensed anything [of this kind], but I have not lost my eternal optimism.

From Dima's letter I got the sense that much of what I have sent has gone astray, but your letter consoled me. Most of all, I am glad that the little book of poems that I worked so hard on reached you. That is wonderful! [. . .]

My life remains largely unchanged: in some ways a little worse, in others a little better, but, in general, entirely satisfactory in an average way. I have, partly on my own initiative, stopped participating at the club, so my main work there is now as librarian. I have free time to read and to take a walk in the fresh air. Today I bought half a kilo of butter for 120 rubles; yesterday I got two kilos of excellent potatoes for four rubles. This is not at all an essential supplement to our everyday diet, although recently that has gotten worse. [. . .]

I have plenty of space to send you kisses for your courage and for mothering our children. You are my beloved, eternally and forevermore,

93. A war film made in 1943 by the director Vasilii Pronin.
94. Formakov again hints at the possibility of a mass amnesty.

and I also give you my respects as my guiding star. Embrace my prank-ster bookworm Dimusha for me: let him be naughty while he's a boy; his mother will get him back into line when it's necessary. In conclu-sion, toss my daughter high in the air so that she squeals with glee and kiss her fat cheeks so soundly that her ears ring. Then kiss the hard-working hands of dearest Grandmother. I do not know if I will ever be able to give her even a drop of thanks. Yours forever, Senia. Husband, father, son-in-law.

♦ ♦ ♦

Kansk, May 20, 1945[95]
My darling Niushenka!

I send my best wishes to you, dear, on our thirteenth anniversary, which I will now, for a fifth bitter jubilee time, spend without you, always in the same sad separation to which I can see no end or limit. Of all the family dates outlined in red in my (your) little calendar, this is the happiest for me. You gave me your hand and blessing, and we set off hand in hand, heart to heart, step by step, along a single path. And even now we move to one tempo, in the same rhythm, despite the fact that we are far from one another. Every second I feel your breath alongside me and your concern shines through my loneliness and en-circles me. I think that the poem "Desiat' Let" [Ten Years], which I sent to you in the little book, fully expressed what June 12, 1932, meant to me.

Today it is 30 degrees Celsius in the shade. The sky is cloudless. The bird cherry has been flowering for two days. So, our short Siberian summer is here already, and we'll hardly have time to notice before it is gone.

Both nature and our living conditions are satisfactory. The hardest thing is the people. It is a miracle that I have not taken up smoking and do not swear offhandedly as everyone else does here, including even the women and children. Coarse, harsh Russian profanity, that defiles mothers, God, the Mother of God, mouths, and who knows what all else hangs in the air from dawn until dusk. The following complaint

95. The first page of the letter contains a poem that Formakov wrote in honor of his anniversary, which is omitted here, and a drawing of a spray of flowers with a banner beneath reading: "1932–1945; June 12."

voiced (angrily) by a female worker is no made-up story: "Comrade foreman, what is this? This wh[ore] called me a *prostitute!*"[96] People treat each other like animals. "Better you should drop dead today and I tomorrow." The main law of existence here is: "Drown ten men if it means that you yourself can climb even a tenth of a centimeter higher [above the water line]!" It would seem that things couldn't get worse, but alongside all this, amid this swamp, this zoo, all the time, throughout these five years I have also found extraordinarily kind people, sensitive and caring, who, like a beacon, bring light to the darkness of bad weather and help you steer your fragile boat through rough waters. In return, I try to help those I can when and with what I can. I never forget the smallest good act. Sometimes a year later I go [to the person] and say: "At one time you did this and that for me. Now here you go [in return]!" [. . .]

Rain clouds passed overhead again. There was talk of closing our workshop and dispersing everyone . . . but then [it all came to nothing] and we stayed in our jobs. The camp shop has been unusually lively. Yesterday I bought five onions and three heads of garlic for ten rubles (vitamins, right?), and they were giving out canned fish at three rubles a can, allowing a can for every two men. We're living it up here!

There is a great deal of talk here, but I don't have much faith in it.[97]

My spirit remains strong, and my body seems in full working order. I am reading Flaubert's letters. Yesterday I watched an American movie, *Give Us the Night* with Jan Kiepura.[98] The rascal sings well! I am preparing to play the producer in the comedy *Svadebnoe puteshestvie* [A Honeymoon Voyage].[99]

I include a song that I heard on the radio for Zhenia.

I really hope that the summer to come brings you at least a little rest. Don't get too overwhelmed with volunteer work: keep at least your head above the water.

---

96. In the original Russian, Formakov politely elides most of the offensive synonym for "prostitute" in the first half of the sentence he cites.

97. Another reference to hopes that the end of the war would bring changes.

98. A 1936 musical by the director Alexander Hall, which was purchased by the Soviet Union in 1941 and distributed under the title *Pesn' o liubvi* (Love Song). Formakov uses the Russian title in his letter. "Spisok amerikanskikh fil'mov v sovetskom i rossiiskom prokate, 1929–1998," *Kinograf*, no. 16 (2005): 176.

99. A 1942 play by Vladimir Abramovich Dykhovichnyi.

I send you and the children kisses and hugs that are warm and sorrowful as always. I kiss Grandmother's hand. My greetings to everyone. Yours, Senia.

♦ ♦ ♦

Kansk, June 1, 1945
No. 41
My darling Niushenka!

I haven't received anything from you in three weeks. I know that all the celebrations and holidays in May took a good deal of your time, and it is exam time for both you and Dima, and letters might have gotten lost, but I am getting more worried and sad because I have been spoiled by your frequent letters. Today it is again a warm sunny day. We aren't working. The orchestra is playing. The young people spent the afternoon dancing at the new dance area around the new fountain. In the evening we watched the film *Nebo Moskvy* [The Skies of Moscow].[100] It's a good picture.

But you are the only thing in my heart. [. . .] I feel hopeless. But the main thing that I dreamed about came true: my children will have something to remember me by—a few lines of love and ideas, several dozen poems that they will reread once they grow up—and you will have one more proof of the great and eternal love that burns in my heart, after having been lit by you, my sunshine. [. . .]

The war, unlike any other in the history of our people, has ended victoriously. How much effort and strength will be needed to smooth over the nightmarish destruction! May our children as quickly as possible acquire the consciousness of peaceful life. That is what I pray for. But of course for you on your own all this is extremely difficult. And for a long time I still won't be any kind of help. I believe that our great motherland will give our children every opportunity to grow and develop. The great Russian people, about whom Stalin spoke so well at the reception of the commanders in the Kremlin Palace on May 24 and to whom they have the good fortune to belong, will open before them (our children) both the limitless expanses of space and extraordinary possibilities.[101] [. . .]

100. A 1944 Soviet film by the directors Iulii Raizman and Aleksandr Ptushko.
101. Formakov references a famous toast delivered by Stalin in which he praised the Russian people as the "most outstanding nation in all the nations that com-

June 3. Someone just passed on greetings to me from Misha K. Do you remember his wife, Frosia Makusova? He is not far from here and came through not too long ago. Perhaps I will see him again. It would be interesting to ask him about everything. After all, he only left Dvinsk three months ago! . . .

The cafeteria where I used to be on duty sometimes has closed. There have been some intrigues against me going on in the club, so I thought it was better to step aside. There has been no answer yet on the petition to reduce my sentence. My living conditions are not yet completely satisfactory. In the past I would have been I can't say how anxious as a result of all of this, but now I am wonderfully calm, with a truly philosophical greatness of spirit because my heart is filled only by you and the children, so there is no room for anything else. "There is no room, citizens!" (like on a tram). "Be so good as to stay on the square." [. . .]

June 4. Today also I got no mail. For fulfilling the May plan I got a bonus card and some [dried] peas. In general, in terms of food, my situation is entirely satisfactory.

May Christ protect you all. What wouldn't I give for one kiss from your lips! (A real one.) Nonetheless, a million kisses to you, Dimochka, Zhenichka, Grandmother, and everyone else.

Your Senia, who is infinitely lonely but at the same time inseparable from his family. [. . .]

♦ ♦ ♦

Kansk, June 10, 1945[102]
My dear Niushenka!

Finally, after a long month of patient, mournful expectation I received your bitter letter of May 22 (it made it in two weeks—a record!) and Dima's postcard of May 25 with the laconic phrase "Mama is quite sick; her whole face is swollen up." [. . .] I am ashamed of my fortunate everyday living conditions, for the fact that I have bread to

---

prise the Soviet Union": "Vystuplenie I. V. Stalina na prieme v Kremle v chest' komanduiushchikh voiskami Krasnoi armii, 24 maia 1945 goda," in *O Velikoi Otechestvennoi voine Sovetskogo Soiuza* (Moscow: Gosudarstvennoe izdatel'stvo politicheskoi literatury, 1947), 197.

102. On plain unlined paper with a camp censorship stamp.

cat and for every possible form of estrangement from the disquiet of family life, that I cannot even really sympathize with you, because I learn of all the problems raining down on your head only much later, although, through this long period with no news, I knew in my heart that something was wrong with you.

A cold fall rain is falling. I sit at the window. It is Sunday evening. I ate two portions of cabbage soup and porridge. That is 1,700 grams—enough volume so that my stomach (excuse me) is swollen. For the third day in a row, I went to the station, our warehouse, after work to load potatoes in a train car. They haven't taken us to town in quite some time. I looked around as always at the children we met with painful curiosity: that one is probably about Dimochka's height; and that one is Zhenia's size! [. . .]

Here I am still terribly lonely, if you do not count my comrades from my daily work under the din of motors, dripping oil, and metal shavings. Needles, needles, and more needles! For the first few months (last winter) I came back from the workshop and pulled dozens of untempered soft needles from my quilted trousers, my felt boots, my sleeves, and hems [. . .]

Soon I will have spent five years in confinement. I have changed a great deal in this time, and I am thankful to the camp for much that I have learned here. I so want to finish my term as quickly as possible, return to the family of Soviet citizens, and live and feel things as one with our great nation, our wondrous, immense country. Here there are many enthusiasts of the Altai region, for instance, [who talk] about what amazing beauty and riches [there are there] and how no Switzerland can hold a candle to it. By the way, a film of Jack London's *White Fang* is being shot there now. Recommend that writer to Dimusha.

June 12. Today it is our anniversary. I have been filled with emotions, which I do not need to describe to you, since morning. As always, you have brought me joy with a surprise: after dinner I received two parcels at the same time. One contained four books, including a novel in Latvian, and two remarkably good issues of *Molodezhnaia estrada* [Youth Variety Shows]. The other contained a huge pile of newspapers, two journals, three postcards, and again a charming drawing of cornflowers and ears of grain. Who drew this? After having supper, I lay down on my bunk, turning the pages of the newspapers with enjoyment, and then on the radio there was a Latvian concert, which opened with the stately sounds of "Dievs, svētī Latviju" [God Bless Latvia].[103] Perhaps this is a good sign, and I will again see the places that are native to me and all of you, my dear ones?

I reread your letter. I am so happy that your 1st-of-May show was such a success! And it is too bad that I could not be there in a hat of invisibility! You again have written that you have become completely different both externally and internally, but I just cannot accept this. I do not believe it. [. . .]

We are living in an atmosphere of all sorts of expectations and hopes, which are voiced in every letter from home. I am glad that you do not write about this. If it is meant to be, we will learn of it, but it isn't befitting to act like children waiting for candies to drop in parachutes from above. One ought to work honestly and bravely wait. That's how things should be! [. . .]

Not long ago, I received greetings from Volodia Lugovskoi and Misha Kallistratov, who do not live far from here. The first is already an energy engineer, but he was once my elementary student!!! Yes, the years do fly by!

I kiss you warmly thirteen times. These, of course, are not roses, but it is from my whole heart. [. . .] Give my greetings to everyone who remembers me. Yours forever, Arsenii

◆ ◆ ◆

June 11, 1945[104]
My dear Dimochka:

With a great deal of difficulty, I found a copy of the book *Rodina* [The Motherland] for you in our backwater. Be a loyal son to our great motherland and serve it faithfully. This will be the greatest joy for your mother and me. Today I received the postcard you sent on May 25. It only took two weeks to arrive, as opposed to three, as used to be the case. I congratulate you, my son, on your entry into the second grade. Take care of your mother and love Zhenichka and Grandmother. I am

103. The Latvian national anthem from 1920 to 1940. Formakov gives the title in Cyrillic letters in his letter.

104. On a plain postcard with camp and military censorship stamps and Formakov's official return address.

mailing the book today in a parcel.[105] Write to me as often as you can. Kisses to everyone. Papa

♦ ♦ ♦

July 7, 1945
No. 45
Dear Niushenka:

For several days now there have been problems with the supply of electricity. As a result, work in our shop has fallen into disarray, and during the day I either sleep or fritter my time away. I work from 7:00 p.m., and since we do not have to sit out the full shift, I go, get my work done by 11:00 or 12:00, and then I come back. I am reading the Latvian-language novel that you sent. All our Latvian men and women read through it before me, gulping it down with pleasure. And then yesterday, as I am wont to do from time to time, I enjoyed what is for me the best literature in the world, the letters of Anna Ivanovna Formakova! [. . .]

I cannot guess the future. People still haven't left here whose contract ended long ago (two to three years ago) but was automatically extended until the end of the war. And those who are leaving our settlement still are not ending up back at home.[106] In short, this is a sore topic and very uncertain, and it is better not to touch upon it at all until the issue is upon us. People say a great deal about the future, and all of it is good.

Today I would like to add some explanatory notes to the poems I sent you in the separate little book. Unfortunately, out of tactical considerations, I did not organize the material in it chronologically as it is in my notebook, and I did not indicate the order. So I will "notate"

105. Prisoners sometimes managed to mail small gifts: such offerings allowed them to participate directly in family celebrations and, in a small way, reclaim familiar roles.

106. "Contract" is a euphemism for sentence. Formakov is warning his wife that even after his sentence ends he may not immediately return home. During the war, political prisoners whose terms of confinement ended were routinely held over in camp because they were viewed as too dangerous to release. Moreover, labor camp releasees could be kept in internal exile far from home indefinitely: Steven A. Barnes, *Death and Redemption: The Gulag and the Shaping of Soviet Society* (Princeton, NJ: Princeton University Press, 2011), 136.

them as they stand in my notebook, and then you will understand how they should go.[107]

"Gibel' Pushkina" [The Death of Pushkin] is a cycle that I began while I was still with you ("At the Duel" and "The Funeral"). [. . .] "Klass[icheskie] iamby" [Class(ical) Iambs] was composed in my head in the hotel in Enis[eisk].[108] It describes what took place in 1940, but now it is always perceived as about the barbaric invasion by the Germans of our great and free country.[109]

"Ballada o 28 geroiakh" [The Ballad of Twenty-Eight Heroes] is about Panfilov's Guards and their political officer Dmitriev at the approach to Moscow in November–December 1941. I declaimed it to musical accompaniment to great success on many occasions. Later on I learned that a great deal had been written about their heroic deed, for instance by Tikhonov.

"Kogda-to" [At One Time] was written on my name day: March 15, 1942. "O nevozmozhnom" [About the Impossible], like many of the other poems, was set to music by our violin player/guitarist and amateur composer Georgii Fedor[ovich] Drobinskii, a Ukrainian and an engineer. [. . .] "Za barakami" [Behind the Barracks] is an accurate depiction of our landscape here. At that time I still could not leave the village. I really like "10 let" [Ten Years]. I wrote it under great inspiration: for days on end my thoughts were full only of you.

"Na volnakh" [On the Waves] was written to accompany music that had already been composed by our former bayan player, as was "Krylatyi drug" [Winged Friend]. All these pieces were sung at our concerts. Then my work in the club came to an end and I had to do heavy physical labor, rolling logs out of the river—"Severnaia tikhaia reka" [A Quiet Northern River] and "Nichto ne izmenilos' v mire" [Nothing Has Changed in the World]—I was out in nature for the first time in ten years. "Naputstvie moriaka" [The Sailor's Parting Words] was perhaps the best thing I wrote during these years aside from "Tri platka" [Three

107. Formakov describes the contents of the 1945 notebook of poems entitled "O rodine i sem'e" (About the Motherland and Family), which is now in the Hoover Institution Archive.

108. "Hotel" means prison here again.

109. The poem in question describes the Barbarians overrunning Rome. By "what took place in 1940," Formakov means the Soviet invasion of Latvia.

Handkerchiefs] (L'Amour, l'amour). It secretly advanced the unsubstantiated rumor that young people were being called up to serve in Latvian units. This period (work!) was not so rich in verse and ended with my forty-third birthday. During the holiday season that followed, I added to my story about Father Frost. "Ia s toboi" [I Am with You] was written for a woman who declaims verse here, as were some other things. This was when I was in the sick bay during my episode of pellagra-induced bloody diarrhea (poetry and diarrhea—now that's a combination!) after I had gotten better. Right there in the margin you see my weight on July 15: sixty-three kilos in my clothes. From August 8 to September 7, I had diphtheria. I was in complete isolation. I reread the books I had out [of the library] three times each. I made up crosswords and played chess with myself. I wrote. I finished the story about Father Frost. One of the people involved in cultural work, breaking through the barricade, brought me a bouquet of carnations. I wrote a poem about your favorite [flowers]. At that same time and in that same place, I wrote "Blagoslovila, slovno na propiatie" [She Blessed Me, as if Sending Me to Crucifixion], which did not make it into the book but was mailed to you earlier (January 20 of this year) in a letter. "Russkii soldat" [The Russian Soldier] was the first poem that I composed while at work in my new job in our needle-making workshop, where I have been working since December 1944. At some point, I am going to rework the ending so that this poem can be declaimed even now following victory.

"Na dne" [The Lower Depths] is a poem for Liza Vasilevskaia, whom I managed to get into contact with by mail, and the first letters I received in four years were really like a knock from outside for a prisoner locked in a sunken submarine. I did not know if I would live to reestablish contact by mail with you, so I sent her several poems in the hope that perhaps they would reach you some day (after two such illnesses, I did not feel so sound [in health]). There they, all women from Dvinsk, got together and read them and wept . . . "Poliarnik" [The Polar Explorer] is a poem that I wrote foreseeing the possibility of making contact with you. "Na uborke" [At the Harvest] was written at a state farm during threshing. We traveled there to put on concerts and stayed about a month, working in the fields, and ate very well. There I regained my physical strength after the illnesses of the previous year and replenished all that I had lost. During threshing I hauled sheaves on yoked oxen. Here people even ride cows in collars. Further on there are poems that were inspired by our correspondence, which is flourishing like a snowdrop in spring.

By the way, I keep forgetting: try to put a blank sheet (one!) of paper for an answer in each letter. I still have envelopes and many postcards, but things are worse with decent paper. This is my next-to-last sheet. Well, I will manage to get some when I need it. There is no sense in guessing the future. Only a few people get paper that way.

Today I received Dima's letter of May 7, which had been delayed somehow. Two months is a record! I am being moved to a new location. May God bless you all. I will inform you of my address.[110]

With my best wishes.

Yours forever, Senia; the children's papa.

July 8. Thank God, I did not leave! They left me behind at the very last moment. This is again your prayers [at work]! The process of moving to a new location, often on foot, is very difficult and, most important, I would lose contact with you, my darling, for a long time! And a new place in the taiga, which is just being developed, far from the railroad with biting midges and with only rare official letters—brrr! This is already a second unsuccessful attempt: I have been saved by friendly connections as head of the library. But still, the journey there (or to someplace different) is inevitable, inasmuch as production here is winding down.

Yesterday at 11:00 in the evening I came back with my things (a wooden suitcase and the sack you gave me, which has been incredibly useful), hung up my photos again, and did not sleep a wink all night. I finally fell asleep at dawn, and then I was woken up at 11:00 to listen to the act of amnesty read over the radio. It does not affect Arsenii at all. He had no great illusions about that. But about half of the people who live with him had every reason to be happy. There will be a separate letter about this.

It is so wonderful that D[imochka] sent his height. He's up to my chest. Wonderful! In our sector there is an eighteen-year-old by the name of Boris Zakovyrkin who ran away from a factory. He is six centimeters taller than Dimochka. I look at him, and I am amazed: Lord! That is how my son looks now! I am waiting to hear Zhenia's height.

---

110. Formakov's handwriting becomes shaky in this paragraph, reflecting his anxiety about the move.

I embrace you all together and each of you individually. I kiss you again and again. Your Senia-Papa.

July 12. Today I received three more letters from the children, which were mailed on June 18. Hooray! I will answer them separately. Yours, Ars[enii]

♦ ♦ ♦

July 16, 1945
No. 46
My precious, darling Niushenka:

On Saturday I finally received your long letter dated June 20, and I have been getting no end of enjoyment from it for three days now. Then today I got two postcards, your no. 1 and one from Dimochka dated the 26th, which informed me that he had received *Our Motherland* and the postcards. I am so glad that the book reached you. And I had so little hope that it would have fit on the tip of my pinky!

Zhenik calls you old. Well, from her point of view, you are a decrepit old woman. I remember very well that I perceived my own father as a decrepit old man when he was about the age that I am now. Everything is relative. [. . .]

I was addressed as "old man" for the first time on an Eniseisk barge in autumn 1941. Now strangers never call me anything but "old man" or "father." I am glad that in June you lived pretty well. For the last two or three months here, the food was bad: we had watered-down sauerkraut as our soup and then sauerkraut without the water for our main course. Then they cut our bread ration by a hundred grams. Then they eliminated the main course at breakfast and supper. But now the menu has suddenly really improved. Just today I got half a kilo of butter for seventy-five rubles (I have been saving my money, because I sensed that I might be transferred).

Don't on any account send me money. I will need it immediately if I am transferred to another place (right now I can get by), and I ask that, if that happens, you immediately send me a hundred as soon as you get my new address without even waiting for me to ask for it. Or if I, heaven forbid, get sick. But right now, this is not at all necessary. I (knock on wood!) feel just fine.

Kostia Smirnov's mother came to see him. She stayed here for three days, but only got to visit with him unofficially for a half an hour because he is in line for the amnesty. She got an official summons from the Council of People's Commissars [Sovnarkom] of the Latvian Soviet Socialist Republic (thanks to the efforts of her Lithuanian sister). If he leaves here soon and ends up in Riga, he swore that he would look you up and tell you all the details of our life here.

Yesterday, after multiple approaches, as a result of a complicated diplomatic game, I managed to secure a sitting with our only local portrait maker, and he drew a fairly good likeness of me in the space of half an hour. The gaze from behind furrowed brows isn't characteristic of me, but otherwise it is all right. Ninety percent of the people I asked immediately recognized that it was me. One person reacted immediately: "Now there's a real convict!" And when I objected—"What do you mean? Don't you see the resemblance?"—he started mumbling apologetically, "Oh, yes, absolutely . . ." All that remained was to thank him for the compliment! [. . .]

You write: "Every time when I eat something that is a little better, I . . ." Imagine, even in Dvinsk, my comrade and I would say (and all the more so here): "We are stuffed to the gills, lying here sweating, and at home our loved ones' every bite is poisoned by the thought 'how are they doing there?'" Don't think so often and bitterly about me. Essentially, the conditions I live in are entirely satisfactory. Don't let a single thought of this kind worry you.

Don't write anywhere about Arsenii right now. On April 1 he wrote to the NKVD to ask that his case be reviewed or his article and sentence reduced in severity. On April 28 a response arrived noting that in June 1941 the Presidium of the Highest Supreme Soviet had declined his request for a pardon. Although this wasn't exactly an answer to the letter, it made the outcome of the whole thing clear. When those who have been amnestied begin departing, his fate will also be clear. Then I will write.

You should destroy *Sovremennye zapiski* [Contemporary Notes], keeping only those things of lasting value, such as Zaitsev's biography of Turgenev. But it would take time to sort through it all.[111] Send my ex libris if you have it handy.[112] Thanks for the adventure novel, which I

111. *Sovremennye zapiski* was an émigré journal printed in Paris between 1920 and 1940. It was banned in the Soviet Union, so destroying it entirely would have been the safest course of action.

112. It was common for Russians with large libraries to have personalized book plates to glue inside volumes. Formakov is requesting a copy of his.

am expecting. Don't buy Latvian books, but anything in Russian (just cheap editions, so you do not spend too much money!!!) that you can get will work. Buy them! It is very pleasant to receive newspapers in both [languages]. I look forward to them.

Since Peter's Day (June 12) I have been working as a senior work-checker–sorter in my old workshop.[113] It is easier, more prestigious, and more pleasant in all respects: you don't have to go unload train cars so much and in terms of leaving here it's more rewarding. This is all thanks to your prayers, my dears.

I kiss your mouth and eyes and each finger individually. I give Dima a hug like one man hugs another, with a hearty slap between the shoulder blades. I toss Zheniurochka high up in the air and catch her, kissing her on both cheeks. Your Senia, their papa.

[In the margins:] Lugovskoi told me that our house burned down because the flames spread from the high school, which Petr Iv[anovich] had lit on fire. He [Petr Ivanovich] is in the Dvinsk hotel right now.[114] [. . .]

♦ ♦ ♦

July 26, 1945
No. 48
Hello, my sunshine!

As you can see, I am writing on the paper you sent. I just got your parcel (Dima writes that word correctly, but our postmaster writes "parcils received" for so and so) that contained seventeen newspapers and five sheets of paper. I always shake out all the paper in search of the surprises you usually tuck in. And this time I also got lucky! The newspapers are new and interesting, and the main thing is that this means half a kilo of butter and three liters of milk! I don't need any money transfers or big packages right now. Regarding the package that you sent with the person who was headed here—and at such a terrible time when you were so sick!—it apparently has disappeared entirely. It is really too bad, not because of the material loss, but rather because of

113. There is an obvious mistake here: Peter's Day (Petrov den') would have been July 12, not June 12.

114. "Hotel" again presumably means prison here.

the nobility of spirit and the heart-warming feeling that the packages
you send always radiate. Oh, what a wife I have! And here all we have
are wh . . . both in our settlement and outside it.[115] Here even the wife
of Grishin's friend quickly became someone's lover. This is despite the
fact that she was receiving letters from her husband in the Urals and
from her children on a collective farm. Nikolskaia from Rezhitsa has
gotten all settled in now and is going about paired up with partners
who are well fed and useful, with a fat money pouch (as it is defined
here, of course!).

Let me describe my day for you. Just before 5:30, the noise in our
sector wakes me up. The two bread distributors for our brigade have
brought the bread from the bread-cutter and are distributing it. They
have already put 450 grams on the nightstand by the head of my bed. It
is covered with a napkin (a rag). Tokens for breakfast, dinner, and supper are also there (they are made of metal). At 5:30 the siren sounds:
it is wake-up call. The radio comes on at the same time. We hear the
news from Moscow, where it is 1:30 a.m. I pull my blanket over my
head and say my prayers in an order that I worked out, which has not
changed in five years, praying, most of all, my dears, for you. I get up
and pull on my pants. My feet are in sandals. I throw a pea jacket made
of the kind of material used for soldiers' coats over my T-shirt and head
to the lavatory (I don't wake in the middle of the night). When I get
back, I take a white tin pot and an aluminum bowl and hurry to get my
food before a big line forms. I get 500 grams of thick soup made with
meat broth (grain, cabbage, sometimes potatoes) and 250 grams of
oatmeal with a little pork fat [*salo*]. Through my connections (*blat*; for
the newspapers . . .), I often get double portions or a little extra. Then
I set aside a cup of soup for my dinner. Having set down my breakfast,
I wash well with soap. In the summer the wash basin is in the corridor.
I eat, crossing myself, and then I thank the three of you in my thoughts
and, looking at your photo, kiss myself on the spot where I wore my
wedding ring three times. In the same way I say "good morning" to you
after my prayers, and I do the same thing at night. Having eaten, I wash
my dishes in boiling water, put them on the table, and then read lying
down for forty-five minutes.

115. Formakov includes the first letter of a vulgar Russian word for prostitute
and then stops himself.

At 6:45 I head to work. If I have to go about a block to get food, it is two to my workshop. I turn in the night shift's work to the store-woman after having turned it over to be sorted, and then I sit down myself. (Also, there are masses of flies in the barrack during the day, and at night there are bedbugs. Today we sprayed everything with boiling water.) At 12:00 we take a break for "dinner"—200 grams of hot cereal. Sometimes I get a double portion. [I eat] half the morning's bread ration. I also read for half an hour lying down. From 1:00 to 2:00, I am always very sleepy. Our window directly faces the door of the post office. At about 3:00 I go to pick up the mail. I give it out. Those who receive something are so happy! At about 4:00 I go to the club, which is nearby, to read the *Krasnoiarskii rabochii* [Krasnoiarsk Worker]—yesterday's [edition]. It is a little like *Sovetskaia Latviia* [Soviet Latvia], but even worse and smaller. My work is broken up by breaks for fresh air, conversations with my comrades, the exchange of news (who has heard what on the radio), rumors . . . By 6:00, I start collecting [people's] work, weighing it, writing notes for the report. And then I'm done! I put the work I have checked into the storage closet and set off for "home." I take off my work shirt, wash all over (to my waist). Twice a week after that I go to the barber to get a shave. On Friday at this same time I go to the bath house. Then I get supper: 500 grams of thick cabbage soup or some other kind of soup, 250 grams of oatmeal, sometimes another 200 grams of tea with saccharine or two cucumbers or a piece of fish. And 300 grams of bread . . . After supper, if there is no film, I lie down for an hour and read. The window is open and the doors. There is enough air. Then I take a walk. On Wednesday and Friday the library is open from 8:00 to 9:00. At 9:30 I head back. Reading, letters, conversation, sometimes a game of chess. At 10:00 they sound lights out, but I generally go to sleep at 11:00. Prayers under the covers (after having washed my feet), a good night to each of you, and to sleep! "Like a balloon on a string; like a squirrel on a wheel . . ."[116] [. . .]

May God give you everything good.

I kiss you countless times. Eternally yours, Ars.

[In the margins upside-down:] For technical reasons, my address now ends in a seven and not an eight. Nothing else has changed!

116. The source of this quotation could not be identified.

[In the margins upside-down:] What do you know about Igor and B[oris] Pravdin? July 27. Just now I got the letter with the postcard and the [information about] the amnesty. Shen is also terribly pleased and sends his regards.

♦ ♦ ♦

July 30, 1945
No. 49

"You will remain always the same,
My winged genius."[117]

Dear Niushenka:

How could I not chat with you in this bright hour of late summer dusk on this bitter anniversary day! In the end, there is nothing so significant in the fact that our difficult separation, the days of which have been so monotonous, began on this day. But all sorts of memorable days oppress the human heart, because, with the establishment of anniversaries and terms, our historical existence on this crazy planet really begins. [. . .]

Since March of this year, there has been a man from Riga, a Latvian, here: Iv[an] Vlad[imirovich] Efimov, a silent fellow, who's not very friendly and who performs heavy labor. I managed to get him permission to use the library. Yesterday I offhandedly told him how hard it was for you to get to Dvinsk. "Oh," he said. "It is so far away. Or else she could just go to my father, and he would arrange for permission. But as it stands, by the time we got our letters back home, your wife's leave would have ended." In short, he promised to write his folks. His father is Vladimir Iv[anovich] Efimov (31 Daugavpilskaia, apt. 1, their own house). He works in the food trust and has good connections. In general, it would be good to remain connected: you and he [the father] could exchange information about our fate, and about packages, and so forth. I won't be able to secure permission for a package from here, and it isn't worth it anyway: it is so difficult and right now there is no point.[118] But at some point they will allow it on a general basis. You couldn't send packages from Kharkov, but now they are arriving [. . .]

117. The source of the citation is unknown.
118. A note at the bottom of the page confirms that permission for a package has again been denied.

Our small joys: beginning in August we will have Sundays off and, it seems (it hasn't been announced exactly yet), will work an hour less.[119] I am very happy about the first [development]. I really hate working on Sundays (it never suited me). And our days off also never took place on holidays.

I wonder if my second portrait will reach you. I "paid" for it with an entire soft black pencil (a gift from someone that I had been carefully saving for some time) and four views of Latvia (duplicates of the postcards you sent). I have been circling our second and last artist, so I expect that in seven days or so I will be able to get sketched again and will send it to you. Of course, I am not trying to rush you, but I haven't forgotten your promise to have a photo taken of the three of you together, and I won't forget it until I receive it. [. . .]

I encircle your proud neck with a necklace of kisses. I kiss your eyes gently, slowly, and many times. They are my guiding stars, and all the words of tenderness and the caresses that I have stored up over the past years, which have not reached you in my letters, I send you, my darling. Your own Arsenii

♦ ♦ ♦

August 16, 1945
No. 50[120]
Dear Niushenka:

You know that such a long break in communication makes me panic, but I am proud that I guessed the reason perfectly: a trip to Dv[insk]. In terms of the things, it is good if they have survived, but it's no calamity if they're gone. But for everything connected with Chernetsov, I send my respects—you have really pleased me with this! There was absolutely no need for you to send money. Since the 12th of this month I have had a new job and am working with Efimov. We are working in the fresh air, which is not at all bad for now. At least the threat of a move is gone, and for a long time. This is a result of improvements in my health: making needles is for invalids! Yes, it is amazingly wonderful that our photo albums survived!! I will tell Lugovskoi about his

119. A note at the bottom of the page indicates that he does not believe the second change is likely.

120. A postcard with a military censorship stamp and no return address.

wife. He will be so glad. He wrote to her, but in vain. Ask her to write to him at my address and through me, and money can be sent to him the same way it is sent to me . . .

On Sunday I will churn out a big letter. I also do not believe in and am not expecting any amn[esties]. So it will be three more years. And only God knows what can happen in this time. Children desperately need a father—like [they need] air. A stepfather is not the same: in my opinion, this is even worse than having no papa at all. And I know that even for the sake of the children, you wouldn't do this . . .

I share all your feelings about Dvinsk. I would have reacted the same way, but regarding our possessions (particularly the large pieces of furniture), I would just spit on these things from a high tree . . . Particularly the books . . . Our mutual love is touching (and even greater after the children?). Oh, what can you do! May Christ protect you all. I warmly kiss you all numberless times. Papa.

[In the margins:] Lugovskoi's health has improved, and he is working without a "contract."[121] Don't get mad at your relatives. Despite all that, they helped you a great deal.

♦ ♦ ♦

August 19, 1945
The Feast of the Transfiguration
No. 51

"You are my one happiness and delight,
You alone are my inexpressible light."

(Esenin)[122]

My dear Niushenka:
Yesterday I finally received the first letter you wrote after returning from Dvinsk. I sent a postcard immediately in answer. Today, despite the holiday, we went to load wood into train cars from 8:00 to 2:00. This is the heaviest (though bearable) labor here. I sat down to write

121. In other words, he has completed his sentence and is a free laborer.
122. Formakov cites Esenin's 1924 poem "Pis'mo materi" (A Letter to Mother) somewhat inaccurately. The citation is translated as it appears in Formakov's letter.

after 4:00. I didn't write to you for a long time because, first of all, my living situation, which had been stable for half a year, was turned completely upside-down beginning on August 8, and the last week was spent laying the foundation for getting myself set up again. There is a shortage of manpower here, and everyone who is more or less healthy from our workshop, and that means me too (and it is a good thing that I am still such a healthy person!), was transferred to a work detail that was moving logs from the river to the railway and the railway tie factory, logs that had been floated down the river Kan. The logs are moved from the water by three conveyers, endless jagged belts that we service. Most often I am seated and serve as the motor-man. Physically this is not a demanding activity. It is like being a driver. You have the lever of the motor in your hand, you sit in the booth, and through the open door the belt moves toward you from the river carrying logs (*balany,* as they are called here) on its teeth. As it moves, people use crowbars to pull the logs off in various places, and I stay alert so that if there is even the slightest hang-up anywhere, I can hit the brakes and avoid an accident. At the river itself, the marker Ratnek from Rezhitsa sits in a booth. In a few days she will be released because of the amnesty. She marks all the logs we pull out each day with dots: 1,300–1,500 in all. This will go on for a month. Then perhaps I will be able to go back to the workshop.

Our work team is one of the leaders, so we get better rations: they feed us up a bit. Just recently they gave us some tomatoes and melons as a prize: in the space of two weeks we had met the monthly plan for moving logs. The foreman is well disposed to me. I worked in an analogous team in the winter and spring of 1942–1943. Some of my former "co-workers" from back then are still around. There are some good things about this new job: I am in the fresh air all the time; teamwork of this kind is good for you, it's like physical training. I was pretty sedentary while making my needles! Green meadows, the blue river, distant hills overgrown with forests (350 meters high) on the other side . . . Right now I am so apathetic to all these insults to my existence that it almost seems as if you could start cutting flesh from my leg and I wouldn't protest . . . [123] Perhaps that's enough about me.

---

123. As this despairing line implies, Formakov was trying to put a positive spin on a catastrophic change in circumstances.

Through the lines of your letter, I traveled to Dvinsk and, just like you, my little swallow, walked indifferently past the houses on Varshavskaia street and mourned the dacha. So it turns out that ultimately you have quite a lot of things! And of course you must ultimately decide what to do with them. It doesn't make sense to wait for me (in respect to this). I do not see my return to the family and future life as some sort of restoration of the old: here I sit at my old desk or play the overture to *Ruslan* [*and Liudmila*] on the piano [. . .] In the future I need only one thing: the three of you around me. The apartment and its furnishings are not important. Do what you want, when you want, and how you like. Now I can sleep on a bare floor, not eat for days, mop floors, and darn stockings, wear whatever is available. (Just now I counted. There are sixteen big and small patches on my work shirt and three patches on the knees of my cotton trousers, but I wear it all as if I were King Lear or the sovereign of the beggars from the ballet *Esmeralda*—proud and independent.) The main thing is that in all this time I have accumulated a store of unused energy that, multiplied with yours, which is so lively, will give excellent results. For this reason, don't hold anything back or prepare anything "for my return." Use everything up before 1948—make sure that you and the children survive [. . .]

Offer the newspaper sets to the State Library, although that may perhaps cause complications (here I pound my fists on the table so hard that the chess-players jump).[124] The devil take it! What advice can I give you from here? Save the good books for Dima. Sell the rest if you want and however you like. The piano too—everything, everything! If we live, we can get it all back! But right now it is just a burden . . . Well, you clearly need a second room. The children are getting bigger and it is cramped for them, and that leads to more acting out. But in general I do not understand life today at all. It is like I am from Mars! And giving you advice from there is like having a shoemaker correct an artist's work.

The second half of the summer has been unusually wonderful. On August 5 I even went for a swim in the river for the first time in five years, but today I did not risk it: I had just gotten over an illness. In

---

124. The newspapers, of course, are all émigré publications and therefore politically suspect.

addition to the funds you sent, I have about 200 rubles of my own, of which I spent ninety rubles on a half kilo of butter (it has gone up in price again!). I am still waiting to get the Wallace book and the newspapers from July (sent on the 11th). Don't send anything extra: no money (not under any circumstances), no valuable books (in nice binding, moreover). A new person is running our post office and almost nothing is going missing.

I am very eager to get a list of which letters *from Papa* you received (by the dates or by the numbers) if you can, beginning in March of this year at least.[125] Thank all the people in Dvinsk who sent their regards to me. I cannot picture anything more paradoxical than Nik[olai] Iv[anovich] in the role of a village schoolteacher. That is more absurd than me as a loader! . . .

We are so indebted to Savelievich and the aunts that all the rest of this is nonsense. Forgive them, as I do, and give them what you can if you can. At one point you mentioned the idea of Dimochka enrolling in the conservatory. My dear, if this is somehow possible, do it! This will give him an outlet for his leisure time, could replace joining a youth organization, and will introduce him to the great world of music, which has given you and me such joy. But is he musically gifted, and in what area? You have a better sense of this than I do. Perhaps singing? It is so unfortunate that you were not able to make use of the pass that you received to the sanatorium. But your trip to Dvinsk, despite all the hard work and hassle, also gave you a break.

I have enough paper for now. You don't need to enclose any in your letters. But I am using my last envelope today. From now on, I will either glue them together myself or I will send a folded letter as everyone here does [. . .]

My prayers are always with you. I warmly embrace you and kiss you, my swallow, my glorious sixth-grader Dima (who again has not written to his father in ages), and my sweet daughter Zhenichka. She is before my eyes always like a flower bud. I kiss Grandmother's hand. Your Senia; your papa.

125. By "letters from Papa," Formakov means letters sent illegally.

♦ ♦ ♦

August 26, 1945
No. 52

"The unattainability of fate: to part,
To suffer, and to love."

(Igor Severianin)[126]

Happy holiday, my darling Niushenka!

The only reason why I am not writing this letter in green ink is be-cause I have decided to save the powder for another week or two until the next departure of a new group for some new location. I might sud-denly have to leave, and you can't really take an open ink bottle with you. This has all made me so nervous recently: the constant uncertainty about when exactly the fate of our settlement will be resolved. [. . .]

There has been another change in my work: I have ended up at the railway tie factory right in the breach. I roll logs to the trolleys, and then move the logs to the factory on the trolleys. Our unit contains six men. The work is purely physical; it is hard but not too much. The fresh air and a month or two of physical exertion are even very healthy for me. Our food situation has fundamentally improved in recent days. They have added 300 grams of bread a day, so I get a kilo, which is more than enough, and the hot food has become much better as well. Money has more value now. Now you can buy 300 grams of bread for eight rubles, but about two years ago, you paid thirty for it! I, by the way, never sold my bread and also never bought it (partly because I had no money). I always focused on butter. It keeps for a long time, you can add it to anything, and your body needs it. But in the last few days, after learning of your gift of 300 rubles, I decided to treat myself to something sweet, knowing that this will be even more pleas-ant for you, perhaps, than for me. I bought half a kilo of honey for forty rubles, and I have been eating it with fresh cucumbers for dessert. A luxurious life . . .

I talked with Arsenii about his wife's desire to write somewhere. He thinks this could be done (it won't make anything worse) at the very

126. Formakov misattributes the citation: it is from Konstantin Balmont's 1905 poem "Osen'" (Autumn).

beginning of October or even the end of September (in advance of the anniversary of the October Revolution).[127] It could be addressed to the Presidium of the Highest Supreme Soviet of the Soviet Union (Moscow, Kremlin) from a wife and should include her address and year of birth and Arsenii's address and also that he was sentenced to eight years by the NKVD's Special Board in Moscow in May 1941. She should provide two justifications for the request for a pardon: the crime that he was sentenced for was committed under the conditions of capitalism in fascist Latvia, and no one suffered as a result of it. His orphaned family might also be noted. It should be sent registered mail . . .

Yesterday Kostia Smirnov went to visit his mother. He promised me he would look you up in Riga and tell you in detail about our life here. Efimov has been transferred with me to my new job. As I have gotten to know him better, he has turned out to be not a bad young man. [. . .]

August 27. I was surprised to learn that I had received a package from you. Today at work a person who serves in the administration said that two weeks ago he had gotten acquainted with a lieutenant named, let's say, Latsis in a public place, who asked if he knew me (he did!) and also how he might go about getting me a package from you. Everything was explained to him . . . So you found a reliable, if slow, way to get something to me. The man who told me about this promised to phone Latsis and let him know where to leave the package. What a miracle!

August 28. The [Feast of the] Dormition. I still haven't gotten a letter from you. I will send this off and then will answer the letter with a postcard. I have run out of envelopes. I fashioned about ten "handmade" ones yesterday out of the wrappers from your parcels. I warmly hug and kiss you all. Your Senia.

[At the bottom:] I enclose some poetry.

[Upside-down in the margins:] I ran into our head bookkeeper. "Greetings from home," he said. "It turned out that you had wired money."

127. A traditional time for amnesties and pardons.

♦ ♦ ♦

September 30, 1945

No. 9

My dear Niushenka:

You should already know about the great joyful event that has cast its bright wing over us from my telegram and postcard. On the 27th, the Feast of the Exaltation of the Cross, I read the very long and, as always, interesting letter from you, which arrived with the small bouquet of heather, and then on the next day, or, more accurately, the next evening, I had just gotten back from work, and I ran into a young fellow who works at the garage. "My congratulations, Ars[enii] I[vanovich]!" "On what, Kostia?" "They've cut a half year off your sentence." My heart did not even leap with joy.[128] It was only later that my reason allowed me to perceive this as something joyful. A half year is, after all, a sixth of my remaining sentence. So now we can orient ourselves toward January 30, 1948. That means this month is almost over, and 1948 hardly counts. 1945 is almost over, moreover. So there are really two years left, double the amount of time we have been corresponding. If God would only help you get through this time!

It is only now that Moscow has sent its answer concerning our New Year's show. Moreover, far from everyone who was put forward received a reduction, and all those who did got the same reduction in their sentences.

Today (Sunday), I am unexpectedly at home, although our guys are working. The thing is that we need to send some of the technical literature in our library to the central administration [of Kraslag], and so I was left behind. I spent the day working with the books and now in the evening am writing to you.

You asked about Grivka (although perhaps now that you have transferred to a new school, this is no longer important).[129] I have one consideration in connection with this: under the regulations that are currently in place, I will not be allowed to live in a capital city or a regional center. Grivka is another thing entirely! For the children, the provinces would be a better place to live (the weather, nature, playing outdoors).

128. He had hoped for a more significant reduction and was initially disappointed.

129. A village near Daugavpils.

But there is one big qualification: you couldn't be a thorn in people's flesh there. In Riga, there are a lot of people, and you are a grain of sand, but there people could start delving into your affairs much too often. The wife of one of the other fellows from our neck of the woods has already moved from her farmstead to the hotel in Dvinsk.[130] In that sense a big city is better. It is also better in terms of how it is supplied. Anyway, this is probably off the table until next summer, so I will touch on this topic again in future letters. The most awful aspect of your current life is the lack of a second room.

In regard to Dima and the piano, your amazing desire to preserve, to the extent possible, the tone of our life in previous times is staggering. But in this case, despite my ardent love of both my son and music, I think you should change your closed-off, individualistic, family-based way of life and move in a more contemporary and communal direction (forgive me, I am weighing in on all this from afar). The country will not allow a talented young lad to go to waste, and the public musical institutes will train him. It would not be very productive to try to train him at home without an instrument. [. . .]

Regarding packages, I have no real need for them right now. If they start to allow them from Latvia, it won't be from the capital, just as they still aren't allowed from Leningrad or Moscow. People there ask those traveling for work to other cities to send packages for them. You will be able to take advantage of something like that at some point. People send all sorts of things here in packages, from suits to eyeglasses, from logarithmic rulers to aluminum pots and pans, not to mention groceries. The packages are opened and checked when the addressee goes to pick them up at our post office. You aren't allowed to send razors and knives, but everything else is handed over after a very superficial inspection (without all the cutting things into pieces and ripping things open that took place in Dv[insk]).[131] [. . .]

What you arranged to have brought to me in April still has not reached me, since I do not know the man's address or even his first name, but I do have acquaintances (the engineer Rybin at 25 Budennyi street, for example) who could get it to me. If I receive what you sent

130. In other words, she has been arrested.
131. Formakov contrasts the "superficial" inspections in camp with the more thorough procedure in the investigative prison in Dvinsk.

Portrait of Arsenii Formakov done in the Krasnoiarskii Labor Camp (Kraslag).
Pencil. Dated and signed by the artist, [Evgenii Karaulnyi]; September 1, 1945.
Hoover Institution Archive, Arsenii Ivanovich Formakov Papers, Box 2, folder 12.

somehow—and I am taking measures since I learned Medvedev's last
name—then I will immediately telegraph (if I can), but if you haven't
gotten a telegram before receiving this letter, let him know yourself
to pass on the package at the address I have provided. "If you pledge,
don't hedge!"

October 1. I did not finish packing up [the books] yesterday, so I stayed
back from work today as well . . . About our possessions again: if there
were a guarantee that I would spend the remainder of my term here,
I would ask for some other items from what we own, but, as things
stand, I am afraid to do so: even on a "good" move to a site 150 kilometers away, everything will get lost or stolen, and you torture yourself
trying to haul it all.

We are again receiving bread according to the old ration: 750–850 grams. The hot food is good: sometimes I can't even eat it all. The fall weather is especially mild this year. Today it feels like a real Indian summer day outside. I am worried that the censors won't let the crosswords through. On the 26th and 27th, our central cultural brigade premiered the show *A Bottle of Rum*, which included three of my songs. They were a hit, as was the rest of the show, which was very well staged. To thank me for the songs, the brigade's designer, Evg[enii] Karaulnyi, drew a portrait of me from the waist up, which, along with the portrait by Mochalinskii, which I already sent you, will give you the chance to imagine what I look like now: somewhere between the two arithmetically.

October 3.

> Once again I have received lavender heather
> From the hands of my beloved
> As a symbol of the happiness that
> Flashed away inexorably before we drained it.

I composed this at work yesterday. I worked without my jacket on almost all day—that is how warm it was in the sun—and I remembered how five years ago on the Feast of the Exaltation of the Cross it was just as sunny and, while I was out on my walk [in the prison yard], I heard a voice from the tower: "Ars[enii], everyone in your family is alive and well. They send their greetings." What a miracle and a joy this was! I have no idea who this unknown friend was and whether or not he said anything to you about this. Last year in November it was already 45 below here.

I am dragging my heels with this letter, because I am expecting one from you any day. But it hasn't come, and tomorrow I will hand this over to be mailed. Please do not write to Arsenii things like: "We are used to getting word from you every fifteen days." I have told you more than once that he writes every three months. Everything else is from me ("Papa"). It is a good thing that up to now no one has noticed this. By the way, on all of Arsenii's official letters, there is a round stamp that indicates local inspection. The telegrams are also from Papa.[132] Today

---

132. In other words, the telegrams are also being sent illegally.

is a day off. The next one will be the 14th, the Feast of the Protective Veil of the Virgin.

Well, finally they have delivered it: a parcel that seems to be from September 17 (the postmark is hard to read), which contains one coloring album with images of wonderful children from around the world. The band that ran around the parcel is broad, and was marked in pencil "500 rubles." It is clear to me that there was something else in there, but that something else was swiped, the devil take it! Everyone looked at the album together, but I am not sure what its purpose was supposed to be: perhaps you meant me to compose verses to each picture and then send it to Zhenichka for her birthday? [. . .]

I warmly embrace and ardently kiss you. We will see the sky yet even if it is just a plain sky with no diamonds. Your Senia [. . .]

♦ ♦ ♦

October 14, 1945
No. 10[133]
Dear Niusha:

I wish you all the best on the big holiday. After all, yesterday was the anniversary of Riga's liberation. How quickly the year has flown by! I am still working from dawn until dusk, but in even more harsh conditions. I am getting incredibly tired. I am not losing courage, but I am concerned about the lack of letters from you since the package of August 28, which was received on September 25, and the postcard from September 3, particularly since I am so eager for news: how is it at your new job, why and so forth, what did they promise you? The crosswords didn't come. The books either. Three weeks! The only thing that has made it through this "line of silence" is the album with pictures for coloring, which was clearly sent with something else, which went astray . . . They say that someone in the administration of our village post office went on leave, and for that reason things are backed up. But I got the postcard and the telegram from Lugovskaia! Her Volodia has disappeared from my field of vision. Money from her has been received for him here. In a few days I will send her a postcard. If there isn't word from me for a long time, don't worry. I have made definite arrangements

133. On a standard postcard with a military censorship stamp and no return address.

that if I am suddenly moved or there is an accident (knock on wood!), you will immediately be informed by telegram, so don't be afraid because of a long silence. I write very regularly. Yesterday I signed official paperwork that the end of my contract is January 30, 1948.[134] Well, we'll see. In a few days, when I finally get one from you, I will send a letter! I kiss you and embrace you warmly. Greetings to Dima, Zhenia, and Grandmother. Yours, Senia

♦ ♦ ♦

October 19, 1945[135]
No. 11
My sunshine, Niushenka!

The day before yesterday, I got a stack of Russian newspapers and Dimusha's letter from September 13 (!), which informed me about the mumps and about your "defeat" at the hands of electrical current. Then today I got two parcels with Latvian and one Russian newspaper. Hooray! But I am still without letters. I'll wait, I can be patient! . . . On October 16, my pal Iv[an] Vlad[imirovich] Efimov received two packages at once from Riga (from his parents and his godfather) that weighed eight kilos each. They took two weeks to get here. His parents' address is: Riga, 31 Daugavpils [street], apartment 1. His father's name is Vlad[imir] Iv[anovich]. A second brother is in the Red Army. They also wrote and asked him to send authorization, but that was not possible. Now somehow they have managed things. How? Perhaps they will tell you.

I have plenty of envelopes, paper, and even saccharine now. Everything arrived—thank you. I have been off work for two days because, for the first time here, we are conducting an Olympiad of the performing arts that involves five or six different "settlements." I read Nikitin's "Rus" (in an abridged form). All day today we listened to each other. There were some wonderful numbers, from serious jazz to gymnastics with rings. Our choir sang "Borodino." All of this brought back so many bitter memories. [. . .]

134. "Contract" is a euphemism for sentence.
135. A standard postcard with no return address and a military censorship stamp.

I am still trying to get back to my old job making needles. Everyone keeps making promises, but, alas, nothing has come of it! I kiss you countless times plus several more. Kiss the children. Give my respects to Grandmother. Yours forever, Senia. [. . .]

◆ ◆ ◆

November 16, 1945
No. 20[136]
Hello, Niushenka!

The day before yesterday two of your letters arrived: one dated September 28 on sixteen pages and one dated October 2 with a photo. Today I got another dated October 22. Apparently a backlog somewhere is at last being cleared. It is good that I did not get anxious this time. I will write you a long letter on Sunday, November 18. This urgent postcard addresses one issue: on no account should you waste money on a package (I mean your bonus). Judge for yourself: 200 rubles is an enormous amount of support for me. I can spend it when I want: even all at once on the groceries that are available in our shop. The prices in our shop are probably no higher than those in Riga. In other words, it is just not advantageous. Paying 300 or 400 additional rubles, like some old-world landlord, for a package is just madness. I start to shake just thinking about it. I thought they had found a simple (and no-cost) way around this. My advice or even orders are: I am full (right now in my current situation), 200 rubles will provide me with extras for three months (seriously!), and the kind of expenses that you were contemplating should not even be considered. Send me another 200 if you have them for New Year's. Put together a package with the things I asked you for at one time or another (plus a soap dish) and, when you can, send it through someone who is traveling beyond Latvia's borders to Pskov, Gdov, or someplace like that—God willing, with more success than the last time. You can send it using your own name or really anyone else's and mail it to my address, indicating that I am a prisoner. You finally informed me of the last name of the lieutenant [you sent things through the last time]. I had almost begun referring to him as Medvedev and could not find him. So listen to me and do as I ask. I kiss you all warmly. Your Arsenii.

136. A plain postcard with no return address and a military censorship stamp.

◆ ◆ ◆

No. 21

November 18, 1945

Thank you, my darlings!

In front of me I have three of your letters dated September 28, October 2, and October 22, and also a packet of issues of the newspaper S[ovetskaia] L[atviia] that goes up to October 31 and included envelopes, paper, and postcards, and, on a heart in a leather wallet, your picture, finally in a form that is suitable for this format. I have received all this by mail since November 14 and immediately responded with two extra postcards. Since I have written enough about myself recently, today I am answering your letters, surrounded by these "first-hand sources," which, as always, both worry and, at the same time, have an amazingly calming effect on me.

So, answering point by point:

The photo. You sat for two hours before my photo and could not find anything to write. I immediately reacted when I saw your face, suffused by coarse electric light, with the words: "Not so awful!" Yes, exactly! Not so awful, Niushenka. Give me this woman who has been worn out by life, and in three months I will take away three years of premature aging and in a year a full decade. *Absolutely not awful!!!!*

The children. [. . .] I have colored the coloring book that you sent, added verses that capture the main theme, and will mail it back to you as a gift for Zhenia for her fifth birthday. Better that it arrive early than late. As soon as you receive it, let me know, but do not give it to her before December 30. [. . .] The story "Volk-duren'" [The Wolf-Fool], which you sent with the coloring book, has gone astray, as have all three volumes of Wallace. It is really sad! It is clear that this happened here in our settlement, but there is nothing to be done about it. They would take a pauper's last bag! . . .

If you can, send me another book with drawings for children exactly like that or similar, and I will give it to one of our bosses. You had a good idea, as always, when you sent that, and although I did not guess what you had in mind, I put it to pretty good use, didn't I? [. . .]

Now, *about the package.* It is absurd to buy food in Riga and mail it here, particularly since I am sure things are cheaper here, or at least not more expensive. I forbid you to pay 300–400 rubles to get someone to pull strings [to mail the package from Riga]. Efimov came over to see the newspapers that I got from you yesterday. [. . .] We talked things over: out of the three packages that were mailed to him, he has received only two. Imagine the horror: you expend so much money and effort at once, and it all goes into a hole. And you aren't like the Efimovs. No, no. Don't even think about it. As soon as I read your thoughts about this (I must . . . I will provide . . . give me time . . . there is no informa- tion . . . I will do as the Efimovs did . . .), I even wanted to telegraph immediately: don't you dare waste money on a package! But then I abandoned this idea, because I was afraid of scaring you, and also I try to avoid using this means of communication very often.

By the way, as is clear from my list of dates, my mailman has been doing a great job. Almost nothing has gotten lost. I now also give him a newspaper every time to use for cigarettes. His services are invaluable.

I would, of course, like to receive a package from you (but not food), but they won't hand over any documents to us. Is that clear? That means that we either have to wait for postal regulations to change or find some other smart way to manage things: get the package all ready, and then entrust it to someone who is going to the RSFSR (for instance, to Pskov), and have them take it to the post office there. But perhaps I will manage something from here. [. . .]

Dima's letters go astray not because they are long but because some portion of the mail must go astray. Compared to others, I am receiving everything amazingly well.

Books. Tridtsat' dnei [Thirty Days] and *Arsen* are very popular.[137] We most enjoy reading for entertainment or good classics (like Dickens). Don't make a special effort to buy anything, but if something comes your way by chance, send it. "A person with books" enjoys recognized status in "society" and has the opportunity to trade. Thanks to your efforts, I already have a collection out of which I can operate. [. . .]

I am ashamed. You have not been to the movies in five years, and I go every week. But understand, my sweetheart, what a breath of air this is in our stuffy existence. I live like an ascetic. I do not allow myself any liberties in my daily life, the way that even Vanechka does, who even

137. *Arsen* is a five-act play by Sandro Sansiasvili that was published in 1936. *Tridtsat' dnei* was a popular serial that ran between 1925 and 1941.

drank during the holidays, or my old brigadier, who took on a young cleaning woman in his workshop and for his own enjoyment. I talk with almost no one, beyond the most essential things. It is very difficult for me at work. Food. Sleep. So how could I not be enticed by films? All the more so since on any given day I could have to leave for another place where there are all-consuming midges, a wasteland, wilderness, taiga, lit up by campfires, parasites, and no movies! Understand how it is and forgive me. After all, I can't let myself go morally.

Tomorrow Dima will be ten! I remember his first cry as if it were just now, and his red face and the bottle-green color of his eyes! And for half these years, you have carried him in your arms alone, without me. How can I not respect that; why should it surprise me that your face resembles that of the Byzantine tsaritsas on the frescoes in church: proud and sorrowful, beyond your years? [. . .]

It doesn't matter, my dear. Everything can still be brought right other than that which is irretrievable. In that you are right. I kiss you all both together and individually. Say hello to Nina and give her my thanks. Yours forever, Senia

Addendum to No. 21
November 19, [1945]
To our newborn, Niushenka!

Today I am celebrating Dimusha's tenth birthday in such a fashion that the sky itself is getting hot. Yesterday I spent my whole day off finishing Zhenichka's book *Piat' ras* [The Five Races] and wrote the main part of this letter to you. I baked five sweet biscuits for today, and then in the evening I suddenly decided to go to the doctor. This kind man immediately determined that I was ill and freed me from work for today. Today I slept almost until 1:00 p.m., and then I made six pancakes for dinner from what remained of my flour. I ate breakfast, a double portion, and then I had dinner, taking a double portion as well and also having a baked potato. We bake it in the following way: we wash it but do not peel it and put it on the burner of the stove, covering it with a clay bowl. It cooks quickly and is very tasty, and it is cleaner and more convenient than doing it in the coals.

After dinner, I read lying down. Suddenly an acquaintance came in: "Ars[enii] Iv[anovich], I have come for you. Come right now to room N." I head there. My friend from Budennyi street is there. "I have brought this for you." He hands me your letter to him dated November 1. "I had to leave the crate behind to get everything into my briefcase, but the cloth it was wrapped in and even the string is here." Then he says in my ear: "I looked at the handkerchiefs, thinking they might hold money or something. There is a cross inside one." How that made me happy! Now it is around my neck.

The handkerchiefs are scented with your perfume. [The crate contained] everything that you wrote about and even more. This evening Volodia Shen and two of the nicest of my other neighbors will receive a cookie, a candy, and an envelope each in honor of Dima's birthday.

It is hard to say what pleased me most (aside from the cross), the wallet, which I really needed, the stamps (I ran out just today, and the postman has not had any at all lately), or the ham. Thank you for everything, my dear. I am getting enough to eat, but I haven't had anything sweet in five years, and certainly not anything tasty. I am filled with respect as I remember that you dashed off with all this when you were sick with a high fever. In the evening (right now it is about 5:00), I will make potato soup with ham, and with that I will finish this cycle of bodily joys and go to bed with a cheerfully colorful perfumed handkerchief under my head. [. . .] What a day of marvels!

I turned in a petition to the infirmary, requesting to be sent to the house of rest. It just came back from the commission: they did not pass me. They remembered, the devils, that I had been in March, and you can't go more than once a year! But I think that something will work out. Today has been such a day! I will learn the resolution tomorrow. Rybin said that he had offered you his services. I am afraid that he will leave here soon, and right now there is no need. But what if Glebovskii's mother would send him a package and it were really from you to me?

Best wishes and good night! There is snow outside, the moon, a frost, the beauty of Christmas. Your Ars[enii]

♦ ♦ ♦

No. 23

[December] 4, 1945[138]

Happy birthday, my sweet Niushenka!

My greetings on your upcoming name day. My heart radiates such warmth and love that it is impossible that you do not feel at least a little of it. I kept thinking about how I might make you happy on your birthday, but I couldn't come up with anything other than a poem. But at the same time, I kept thinking back to a phrase from a letter that I received not long ago in which you talked about going to a dinner party, where you read my poems, and a woman who had heard them burst into tears, but you did not: "I do not cry, but afterwards it's painful for me." This was a revelation to me and also confirmation of what I had subconsciously expected. You have almost never written anything about the poems that I sent you—nothing at all. Even when I sent you a whole book, you didn't say a thing! And now I see it: "It's painful."

My sunshine, I know that it is hard for you to read the poems I compose! But I cannot help writing rhymes on my one, now unchanging lyrical theme: about you, about the children, and about our wonderful love. And once I have written them, then I can't stop myself from sending them . . . But this pains you, it torments you, both this whole correspondence, and also all these painful years.

In anticipation of your birthday, I was hoping to limit myself to sending just a greeting on birch bark (during the war here, when some people had no paper at all, they would write "postcards" on it and would send them through the mail) and a drawing with dried flowers, but suddenly I became so intoxicated with poetic inspiration that I was even composing in the early morning, when you stand in a crowd of workers for about ten minutes, waiting to be led out in work teams somewhere, and the sky is like black silk, the stars are bright and glowing, and your neighbor's face is a solid dark mass, and you can't make out or recognize who is in front of you. I also wrote during our brief breaks at work, when you sit down on a log that isn't covered in snow with your

138. Written on good paper with a hand-drawn illustration of several sprays of flowers on the top of the front page. Formakov dates this letter with a Roman numeral X (instead of XII) for the month, but both the number of the letter and its contents suggest it was written in December.

back to the wind and rest while others smoke. I wrote during the ten to fifteen minutes we get for dinner, lying on a bench in our warm lodge, and late at night in the barrack, when the night shift was heading out and most of the day shift was going to bed. The poems came pouring out on their own, and I jotted them down with the pencil you sent on scraps torn from an envelope and in the margins of newspapers, on the first shred of paper I found. Later on, when I saw that more and more separate poems about you were appearing, I put together a first draft in ink and carried it around with me so that I could add to it and make corrections. It gradually became clear that the main subject was you: the schoolgirl, the beloved bride, the wife, the mother, my guardian and correspondent [korrespondentka] (what a horrible word, but I cannot I cannot come up with a Russian term!), and two colors ran through everything, like a leitmotif in opera, dark blue (and light blue) with yellow, and it all focused on meetings with you—at least, I think so. Everything was bright and celebratory—nothing to pain your soul. So I decided that these verses of mine would not cause you any pain. That's right, isn't it, my darling? And you will accept them as a gift from the bottom of my heart, without tears or suffering, but in the mood of "sweet sadness" that I always feel when I look at your picture. Right now it is comfortably ensconced in a perfume-scented wallet. It reminds me of home and is so familiar! It is so good to always have it with me! But what I have around my neck on a cord is even better. Only you, my precious darling, could have come up with such a brilliant idea. There were only two—no, a little more—weeks left until Dimochka's name day, when I finally received your April package, which was so timely. [. . .]

At the request of the administration, I wrote the arrangement for our New Year's concert, which I will stage myself. First of all, this is a pretty good guarantee that I will not be moved and also a chance to start working somewhere warm and under a roof.

I am not sending you any New Year's wishes, my darling, since you already know what unbelievable (to the point of madness) dream is hidden in your heart and also in mine. I only wish that you encounter fewer hardships on your difficult path and that motherhood brings you more joy, that the children don't get sick, and that you are not tormented too much at school (by other people's children and the administration).

Today (the [Feast of] the Presentation of the Mother of God) we had a Stakhanovite shift. We sawed and chopped 120 cubic meters of wood, and, although I am not exhausted to the point of complete prostration as I was at first [when I was transferred to this type of work], still my hands are so worn out from rolling logs that, despite the wonderful fountain pen (that you sent, my angel!) and new disposable pen (also from you), my writing is still not as nice as I want it to be always, and in this letter in particular. Tomorrow we are celebrating Constitution Day, but we will work on the 9th instead.

I send my best wishes to my sweet children Dimusha and Zhenichka along with the birthday girl and hope that they will bring their mother joy with their love and obedience always, particularly on this day. Dear Anna Ananievna, I send you my best and kiss your hand with sincere emotion.

Your always devoted Senia

Your loving father

Birch-bark note from Arsenii Formakov to Anna Formakova. The inscription reads: "On the bark of a Siberian birch tree,/Which, like life, is crooked but dear,/I write you tenderly: 'To your health!/Happy birthday, my darling!' 1945." Arsenii Ivanovich Formakov Papers, Hoover Institution Archive, Box 1, folder 3.

[In the margins:] I enclose a snowdrop that is a present to you, a small collection of poems, all of which are about you, and my birch-bark greeting.[139]

[In the margins upside-down:] The miraculous way in which you managed to get the ex libris to me makes me ask: do you happen to have a copy of "Smert' poeta" [The Death of the Poet], my poem about Lermontov's death that was published in S[lovo] in, I think, the spring of 1940? I have forgotten it entirely. Everything that you have sent so far, including the crossword, I have been delighted to receive. The novels by Wallace seem to have gone astray. I think this is the mischief of one of our bosses who is a great bibliophile [. . .][140]

♦ ♦ ♦

December 5, 1945
[No.] 24[141]
My own dear Niushenka:

I send you my best wishes for your birthday and your fast-approaching name day! I really would like for a whole bouquet of small joys to surround you on these days, which I always remember very warmly. In the light of our family celebrations (Dima's, yours, Zhenichka's), 1945 is ending. For me it was entirely filled by my living connection with you and the children. It brought our remarkable country brilliant victories over the fascist aggressors in the West and the East. We can remember it fondly, moreover, because my term was reduced by six months. I hope that our entirely peaceful 1946 will be even happier and more pleasant. For the fifth time I am celebrating it [New Year's] far from you but without tears and lamentations, as befits a man.

Of course, eternal caretaker of others, you concern yourself less than anything with how best to celebrate your own holidays, and I am not there to make your days at least a little special. But never mind! We will put it on my account, and when we next meet again, I will recompense

139. The hand-made book of poems is in the Hoover Institution Archive's Arsenii Ivanovich Formakov Papers: Ars[enii] Formakov, "Vse o tebe: piatyi sbornik stikhotvorenii," 1945 (uncatalogued).

140. The word "boss" (priekšniek) appears in Latvian in the original, but spelled with Cyrillic letters.

141. Both pages of this letter feature camp censorship stamps.

you with interest and will talk you into celebrating your name day twice a year! Then we will really celebrate!

The large number of newspapers that I have accumulated are now once again in demand, little by little filling my new wallet. But please don't send *Cīņa* anymore.[142] Just the Russian [paper] is fine.

On the 9th and the 10th, there will be a rally of the leading workers from our farm. I will recite verses of welcome to them at the rally and will participate in the concert. This obviously means that I will be released from work for three days, and there will be a banquet. As Pushkin said: "Inspiration cannot be sold, but a manuscript can be."[143] [. . .]

In the book of Krylov's fables, which made its way from your large library here in such a miraculous fashion, I found a scrap of paper with a list of groceries and prices—apparently a record of what was bought at the bazaar. It was in my mother's handwriting. This is one of the small miracles that our lives are full of. And on the Liupen book, there is an inscription: "M. Formakov, 1918." It was my gift to Misha on his birthday twenty-seven years ago! I do not know why, but I am a terrible hoarder. I love every object, and it takes me the longest time to decide to get rid of even the most trifling thing. As a result, even here, despite having lost and squandered so much, I still have a full suitcase/trunk, and your canvas traveling bag is also stuffed to the brim. Moreover, everywhere I have piles of paper covered in writing. And this is despite the fact that it is in such short supply! Of course, I must confess that thanks to my close association with the affairs of the club, I have almost always had paper. But there were people (in truth, from the unfortunate tribe of smokers) who were on the hunt for scraps of paper and even [here the censor has blacked out two lines].

Soon it will be midnight. I am on duty in our tent until 1:30, and then my partner will take over. Some time ago this system was introduced for the sake of security. Otherwise if someone got up at night and went out, they never closed the hook latch on the door, even upon their return, and as a result, one morning we discovered that three pairs of felt boots and two pairs of pants had gone missing. It was a good

142. Formakov gives the newspaper's title in Cyrillic transcription.

143. Formakov cites, slightly inaccurately, a famous line from Pushkin's poem "Razgovor knigoprodavtsa s poetom" (A Conversation between a Bookseller and a Poet).

thing that the long arm of the law caught the thief with someone else's felt boot tucked under his arm when he was on the way back, and everything was brought to light, and the things were returned. If not, it would have been handled strictly: [the person they'd been issued to] would have been assessed ten times the value, just as if the things had been destroyed through negligence, and then they would not have been given any more state property to use. While I was getting a medical exam, someone stole my sweater from the vestibule of the out-patient clinic, and I barely managed to secure an order from the head of the camp that it was not to be classified as negligence and that [I was to be assessed] only twenty-five rubles, the ordinary value of the item . . .

In general, I have reread everything and see that there is little that is festive in this letter. Nonetheless, you should see everywhere between the lines my holiday smile; my face, clean-shaven and scented by Riga soap; tidily parted hair; and a clean blouse. You should hear my pleasant voice, which is the only thing that has survived intact from my youth, calling out: "Happy birthday, baby!" Best wishes, my darling! May Chr[ist] protect you! Let me kiss you tenderly and wish you a good night. Your Senia. [. . .]

♦ ♦ ♦

Kansk, December 20, 1945
No. 28
Hello, my darling Niushenka!
[Saint] Nikola is true to his reputation: today, like yesterday, it was minus 48 in the morning and minus 45 at dinnertime. There is a thick fog outside. The windows are covered with a thick layer of frost from inside. But in the barrack, for now, it is warm, and at night I still sleep completely undressed under one blanket, only pulling my short sheepskin coat over my legs just before morning. Today, by the way, after five days of persistent visits to our storeroom (armory), I managed to exchange mine. The old one was starting to rot and was a bit worn out. This one is heavier but also longer and fluffier and, in general, is well suited to minus-48-degree cold snaps. But while I was in the process of picking it out, I got so cold that I had to rub my hands for two hours before they began to feel normal again.

Since December 12, I have been in a special brigade for those who are recuperating. As I wrote to you, on the 6th a log hit me in the leg.

I am no longer limping, but my left shinbone is still sore, so I cannot sleep on my left side: it puts weight on my leg . . .

No outside work is being conducted now. I am in rehearsals for our New Year's concert and wrote the script for it—a frame for the various numbers. I play Father Frost. Olia Vrublevskaia plays the snow maiden Snegurochka. She is young and has a full face. Her mother is also here. What it must have been like for her to see Olechka take up with a "husband," particularly given our living conditions here!

I got the letters and newspapers from Lugovskaia. I will send them on to him [her husband]. He lives not far from here, but I haven't had word from him so far. I received your 400 rubles, as I received the other funds you sent, and yesterday I indulged in some luxuries: I bought a kilo of untrimmed pork at our shop for sixty-four rubles. I immersed half of it in liquid and sealed it in the tin from the meat that you had sent, and then I fried the rest yesterday and today with pieces of onion and the remains of a potato. It was astonishingly good! Completely forgotten (prehistoric) taste sensations! . . .

Four letters were brought for me. All at once. By Vania Efimov. The postcard you sent as an "addendum" on November 2 and the letter (unfortunately only four pages long! Stop limiting yourself this way!) from November 18. [. . .] Of the two remaining letters [that I received], one was for Lugovskoi from his wife (I need to forward it to him), and the other, dated November 11, was from Glebovskii for me—"How can we meet up? I have brought you a package." That letter was mailed locally from Kansk and took a month and a half to reach me, and here we are griping about issues with mail service between Kansk and Riga! [. . .] Why are you writing about two and a half more years? It is just two and then one more month, which hardly counts! [. . .]

If nothing changes, I will certainly make it through these two years, but will your strength hold out? This is what really worries me. For this reason, for all of us, I beg you: send less material support to me. You are not obliged to do all this, and, moreover, I have no great need for it now. If I sell a newspaper, that gets me a second dinner or supper. Two or three newspapers gets me 300 grams of bread . . . And I won't run out of newspapers. Thank you for everything, my dears!

I wish you a happy New Year and a merry Christmas! I give everyone big hugs and kisses. I pray that the fates have mercy on us sinners, but who can say if they will listen? I kneel and rest my head on your knees. How good it feels! Yours, Senia [. . .]

[In the margins upside-down:] You asked about the possibility of a visit. I will write about this in more detail in the spring. All the "pluses" and "minuses . . ." If we were to realize this idea, it wouldn't be any earlier than summer. Oh, my dear, will it ever really happen?

♦ ♦ ♦

Kansk, December 28, 1945
No. 31
Good afternoon, my dear Niushenka!

Our postman is sick, and in general the mail is not working very well: a few letters will get through right away, and then they'll start disappearing like Amu-Darya into the sands, and it isn't unusual for September letters to appear in December.[144] For this reason, I wait patiently by the sea for good weather, all the more so now that life has been spoiling me with small joys (albeit of local dimensions) since November 19, when I began wearing around my neck all the time the protection of your gift. The main thing is that I am still in the brigade for those who are recuperating, where I was detailed following the commission's review on December 25. Since the next review won't take place for another ten to fifteen days, I will have a wonderful winter vacation. As a result of the departure of the Lithuanian cook who helped me, a few gaps in my food supply appeared (I started getting regular portions as opposed to double), but a conversation with the head of the kitchen resolved everything, and now things are perhaps even better than they were before. The head [of the kitchen] is a very good man. Then the mass transfer from here out into the taiga that we have been expecting for some time took place. I wasn't affected—this is the most important thing. But V. Shen wasn't so lucky. I feel bad for the boy: he'll end up going under. Here people helped him . . . It seems that I am secure here for the winter, which is very important. I feel as though a huge weight has been lifted off my shoulders . . .

144. The Amu-Darya is a river in Central Asia.

Finally, the last in this series of pleasant events: I purchased a kilo of honey (seventy-seven rubles), so that I have something sweet for the holidays (using your funds, my dear), and also Vol[oldia] Lugovskoi visited. He lives not far from here in a subdivision [*podotdelenie*] of ours and managed to get away for a visit.[145] He was here from 12:00 to 8:00 and spent most of this time with me. He has full cheeks and a ruddy face and looks wonderful. I fed him supper (using an extra coupon that I got in exchange for a newspaper and then getting double portions of both the soup and the main course as a favor from someone I know). For some reason, I was very sincerely glad to see him. We had a heart-to-heart chat, which I haven't done with anyone in a long time. Just the day before, a letter for him from his wife that had been addressed to me and also her photo had arrived, as well as some newspapers that had also been addressed to me. He got everything, but from now on she should write to him directly. He has returned from the hotel and is waiting for his contract to be signed and to learn his term.[146]

By the way, he told me that many Latvians are receiving packages, and, as one letter made clear, they are being mailed with the help of Kirhenšteins.[147] Either people send a petition to him or they go and see him personally. Also, he supposedly gives permission for both one-time and periodic packages. Since I know that the idea of sending a package gives you no rest, and I would really not object to receiving some things, why don't you try going to see him? Fill out the required application and bring it with you. [. . .]

I am living right now like a real gentleman (it makes me ashamed when I think about what you have to bear). I go to bed at 12:00 and get up at 6:00. Then I eat breakfast and go back to bed until 11:00 or 12:00. I have dinner, and then I read in bed. At about 4:00 I take a walk to the post office (has anything arrived?) and then go to the club (to read the paper), to supper, and then, from 8:30 until 9:00 or 10:00 p.m., to the rehearsal for the New Year's concert that I wrote the script for (by the way, it includes "Vse khorosho" [All Is Well] and the wonderful Rezhitsa Mikado Ukhtin). Then I spend time reading and writing (or

145. In other words, in an affiliated subcamp.

146. Aesopian language: Lugovskoi was rearrested in camp and held in investigative confinement. Now he is waiting to learn his sentence.

147. The microbiologist Augusts Kirhenšteins chaired the Presidium of the Supreme Soviet of the Latvian Soviet Socialist Republic from 1940 until 1952.

drawing) until 12:00. And that is how things have been since December 6! My leg is still a little sore when I sit, but then it passes. In short, I am greeting the New Year in great shape. If only the mail system would disgorge, like a whale from its belly, more letters from you! [. . .]

New Year's Eve. I expected to receive something from home by today, but, alas! Preparations for the show prevented me from continuing this, but now that is all behind me. It went quite well. If there had been children present, I would have cried, and I wouldn't have been able to act the part of Father Frost. Ukhtin gave me a big scare. It is a big weight off my shoulders. The administration was satisfied. There was no New Year's spruce: they don't grow in the forests around here, and the trucks that might have brought one from far away were late . . .

I got back, had supper, and now I am chatting with you. Soon it will be midnight here—your 8:00 p.m. Yesterday it was 40 below, but now the weather is milder again. It is snowing a little. Efimov brought a half liter of milk back from work. He has put it on the stove to warm up and melt. It is noisy in the barrack. Everyone is here, and the noise of the dominos clanking is deafening. The radio is droning something. I am tired. I am going to get in bed and think of you and our children. I will remember earlier New Year's celebrations and your radiant face will shine before my eyes until I fall asleep. Perhaps I will see you in my dreams. Alas! I do have dreams, of course, but I never remember anything when I wake. It is as if it never happened.

January 1, 1946. So, happy New Year, my dear! One more year of life, be gone; one more year of separation passes with a click of the beads on the abacus. One of the first greetings I received was from you. Yes, my small miracles continue: a man who looked familiar came up to me on the street and passed me word from Vitia that you had written to thank him and to ask his permission, which he gave.[148] Oh, my resourceful sparrow! Oh, my dear little bird! Of course, I will get everything you send through Victor. You can even send books to his address without sending a letter along with them. Just write my last name on the books, since books do go astray. But again, I ask you not to take on extra

148. Formakov omits a key phrase. Anna Ivanovna asked for permission to continue to use Vitia as a courier.

expenses. Just send what you have on hand and what doesn't require additional expense. I raise my New Year's glass of foamy milk to you and drink to your health as well as to Dimusha's and Zhenichka's. In a few days, I will probably have to go back to work, but you are on break, so you face additional work and chores about the house. Lord! When will I be able to take some of this burden from you, so that you can sit, like a little doll, while I wash the floors and peel the potatoes, and darn stockings? . . . Greetings to Grandmother! Yours on this New Year's just as before, Senia [. . .]

1946

January 6, 1946
No. 32[1]
Happy holiday, dear Niushenka!
Greetings to our dear name day girl![2]

On this festive evening, when there is an empty place at the table, the night shift has gone to the workshop, and the day shift is getting ready for bed.[3] I sit down to talk with you, all of you, my dears, with my spirit as quiet as this holy night, so snowy and soft. You are my only purpose and meaning amid what I must endure. To the *right* of me, as I came back after getting bread, a new moon that I had never glimpsed before hung by a golden thread.[4] The fact that I had my ration in my hand and the bonus I received for November (seventy-four rubles) in my shirt pocket seemed a sign of good fortune. In general (I spit over my shoulder to ward off ill-luck!), I can honestly report about myself: today I have been recuperating for exactly a month. It looks as though I have a 99 percent chance of being sent back to the needle-making workshop.

1. A drawing of a candle and a pine bough appears by the salutation.
2. January 6 is Christmas Eve for the Eastern Orthodox, and also Saint Evgenia's Day.
3. The empty place is for the Christ child.
4. A sign of good fortune.

Hand-made Christmas card sent by Arsenii Formakov, dated December 2, 1945. The front reads: "Happy holiday!" On the back, Formakov writes: "Merry Christmas. I send you all heartfelt greetings, warm hugs, and kisses [. . .]" Arsenii Ivanovich Formakov Papers, Hoover Institution Archive, Box 1, folder 1.

I have 250 rubles in my personal account and 200 in a bond. In my nightstand I have 750 grams of butter and a little honey, and in a few days I will get a bucket or two of potatoes. I had a bath, and I am clean and shaved, and my hair has been trimmed. I am in a clean shirt and underwear. The senior inspector in the workshop is going to the house of rest, and I am supposed to start working as his assistant, and, in general, they hope to be rid of him. Tomorrow there will be a film at the club; the day after tomorrow, we are off.

Efimov came by just now. For some reason in recent weeks he has been very clingy, and I really have no one now that Shen is gone. We agreed that tomorrow we would have a feast in honor of the holiday, pooling our resources. He will bring milk and sugar. I managed to get coffee, and roasted and crushed it in a porcelain mortar. I have your sugar cubes and butter. Tomorrow evening after the film, we are going to have our feast here. I really don't want to have it by myself! And perhaps I will get something in the mail. Yesterday I sorted all the correspondence, but I didn't find anything for myself. The day before yesterday I got both Latvian and Russian newspapers from the first ten days of December. I immediately started trading: the fellows had just received money [. . .]

Since our New Year's concert, my stocks are again solidly up, to such an extent that our most important boss came up with the following idea. On Friday, he said to the female inspector of our Cultural-Educational Sector: "Tell Formakov to get ready to go to Ingash to review their mass cultural work there." As if the only thing I do is conduct supplemental reviews! The trip did not take place for technical reasons, but even the proposal was flattering.[5] I was a little afraid, though: you go (sixty kilometers by train; then two kilometers from the station), and perhaps you end up staying there forever. The conditions here are the very best . . .

Right now at the club we are preparing to stage Gogol's *Zhenit'ba* [The Marriage] (I play Iaichnitsa), and then Ukhtin is thinking about doing *Bednost' ne porok* [Poverty Is No Vice] (I would play Liubim Tortsov). Efimov got struck by logs twice today at work, but it ended fortunately. He got hit once in the cheek! The radio hasn't worked since New Year's, and it isn't clear when it will be fixed. [. . .]

Today I have been thinking a lot about Zhenichka in particular. I really know nothing about her (not even her height, despite how many times I asked Dimusha!), but what a tenderness I feel for her, so broad and warm! [. . .] I have never decorated a Christmas tree for her or shown her Father Frost. Here I put on the costume, acted the fool, gritting my teeth . . . But in the final analysis, that also was for her. I need to stay afloat and swim. If I go to the bottom, I'll never see the children [. . .]

Now that everything is in the past, I can confess that four months last year (from August until the day I was injured) were very hard for me physically. Sometimes you drag yourself along the path to the train car with a cross-tie on your shoulder, particularly one that is heavy, damp, made of larch (which is like oak). You are drenched in sweat, your heart beats as if it is about to jump out of your chest, you breathe so heavily you start to wheeze, like an overheated horse, and you begin to think: let my leg buckle. You'll fall and the cross-tie will come crashing down on you from above, and that will be the end: no more suffering,

5. Although in some camps and periods many prisoners were de-convoyed and could leave the camp for short periods of time without a guard, the right to travel beyond the immediate vicinity of the camp was a much rarer privilege accorded to valued specialists and inmates who enjoyed unusual trust. GARF, f. 9414sch, op. 1, d. 2526, ll. 22–240b.

everything will end forever! But you, your loving gaze or memories of your heroic feats, would suddenly pierce my consciousness like an electric spark, and the fainthearted thought would be chased away, and I would again be dressed in the impenetrable armor of spiritual courage, and you can do what you like with my physical self—burn it, beat it, apply pincers, crush it—my spirit is higher than this, and none of it touches me. I understand the holy martyrs and the heroes of the Revolution whom no tortures could force to descend from the heights of spirituality to the depths of physical sensation . . . But "brevity is the soul of wit." One thing is for sure: it is good that I won't be going back to moving timber and cross-ties. Needles are truly more pleasant!

January 9. Everything happened just as I said. Vania Ef[imov] and I celebrated "as a twosome," as we say here. I had sweetened coffee with cream for the first time in five years! [. . .]

I am calmly waiting for your letters, regardless of how long it takes them to arrive. Don't worry if there is a delay with mine. They move at the appointed pace. This is already the eighty-second! How good it is that at least this is possible! I give you a big hug and kiss. I kiss and bless the children. Yours always, Senia [. . .]

◆ ◆ ◆

January 11, 1946
No. 34[6]
My sunshine, Niushenka!

Just now late at night I received two more parcels from you with Russian and Latvian newspapers from November. Tomorrow morning I am moving to a new workplace, where I will be a specialist in mass cultural work (just look at me now!). I don't know if I will be there for long. I will send you a telegram if I return suddenly. I will have a new address: Ingash station, Krasnoiarsk railway, P.O. box 235/7 (just like now). My mail will be forwarded from here. We share the same accounts office.[7] In the hope of a better future, I embrace you and the children warmly and kiss you. Your loving Papa Senia. This pen is terrible, but I have packed all the good ones.

6. Hastily written on a plain postcard with a faint camp censorship stamp.
7. Therefore he will not have to wait as long for the money in his personal account to be transferred.

◆ ◆ ◆

January 27, 1946
No. 36[8]
Dear Niushenka!
My dear children!

I have again returned to Kansk after being away for two weeks. I am well rested and as fresh as is possible at my age. While I was away, I received Dimochka's letter dated December 4, the first part of which was dictated by his mother. The letter was very good and interesting, the first "real" long letter from my son. It is too bad that this happens so rarely, but I understand that boys want to live in the moment as opposed to pouring out words to a father who is as far away as the moon and who recedes farther from their memory all the time.

In terms of relations with Uncle Vitia, you must break them off immediately and never resume them again.[9] I do not need money, but I am eager for tender letters. It is very possible that the administration will acquiesce to my petition, and you, Niushenka, will get permission to send me a package. Send what you have on hand out of what I requested, but don't waste money buying anything. Tomorrow, after a big interruption, I will return to regular work. These moves delay the arrival of your letters, which is slow anyway. So far I have only experienced Dimochka's birthday with you. And so many other noteworthy days have taken place! I kiss you all, Papa

◆ ◆ ◆

February 6, 1946
No. 37[10]
My dear Niushenka!

With my transfers from brigade to brigade and my moves, for the last half year letters from you have been arriving much less well than they did at this time last year: even the newspapers (the Russian ones) have started going astray, and the Wallace books didn't arrive. In terms

---

8. On a plain postcard with a camp censorship stamp and Formakov's old return address.

9. It was not possible to ascertain why Formakov urged his wife to break off contact with Uncle Vitia.

10. Marked with a camp censorship stamp.

of your letters, it is like the cat's tearful complaint: not a single long one; just a postcard from December 24. I still haven't received a New Year's greeting . . . And the sprig that I found in your parcel conveyed entirely negative symbolism: the bare stem all by itself and then the pine needles separately. But Volodia Lugovskoi's wife is still sending things to my address. Giving him the parcel for the last time (by the way, despite the fact that some things have gone astray, I still receive many more than he does), I joked, "I will write to my wife and tell her to send my mail to your address. Perhaps I will start receiving letters more regularly."

After sober reflection, I finally came to the conclusion that perhaps the root of the evil is in our [Riga] postal branch (the local one). Letters from the main branch arrived without any problem, but in the region where you are, there are some really terrible workers. On the last parcel you sent with *Tsirk* [Circus], all the stamps remained uncanceled: they didn't put the stamp across them. Now, those are some workers!

But, in general, I thank my stars again for what makes it here . . . As you can see, I am again in Kansk, and one very kind-hearted boss told me where to write, so that you will get permission to send me a package, and for some reason it seems to me that this time it will work. *Don't send money!!!* I am really eager for a calendar and [a list of] holidays. You need to break off all communication with Uncle Vitia, period!!!

Since February 1, I am again in the needle workshop. Norms have gone up significantly since I left, but I still achieve 150 percent every day.

February 9. The Marriage was performed four times and was a success. Everyone took particular note of my Iaichnitsa. I do not know if my success in organizing mass cultural work in Ingash is the reason, but the administration has made me the head of our amateur drama circle and also the chairman of the mass culture commission, which supervises the work of all the circles. We are busy preparing for Red Army Day (a concert), after which we will stage *Poverty Is No Vice* (Ukhtin will direct; I will play Liubim Tortsov). [. . .]

Have you turned Zhenia over to the kindergarten? I am not worried about Dima's Fs. Let him sow his oats (he's that age!). He can be held back for a year: after all, he has time for it. Regarding the known evils of youth organizations, they do exist, but if you take into account the atmosphere in which the child's family life takes place, you have to admit, worrying a lot about this doesn't make sense: perhaps it will be very beneficial! Today I bought a half kilo of butter for ninety rubles, and I still have money in my account and in my wallet. They promise there will be potatoes soon. I have not been starved or even really underfed in a long time. I am again working indoors where it is warm. I spend my free time at the club . . . And, oh, if I could only hear your voice more frequently and read those beautiful, neatly written lines!

Kisses to you, my sun that never sets! Greetings to Grandmother, Aunt Mania, and Zorenka. I write a few lines just for the children below. Yours forever and ever, Senia

To my dear children:
To my splendid son Dimochka and my beloved daughter Zhenichka!

Write to me and tell me about how your life is going. Let Dima sit down at the table, and then Zhenichka can dictate to him: life's like this or that, Papa, we're not grieving, we remember you, we are listening to Mother and respect Grandmother.

A terrible war, my children, devastated our motherland, passing through like a storm. Many cities were destroyed, many families were dispersed. Our glorious Red Army dealt with the enemy. It smashed the German leadership and brought Germany to its knees. The war ended in victory. Now we need to heal all the wounds: fill in holes, repair houses, help people return to the places they call home, and rebuild their little nests. Our family was also devastated by the war. You saw fires and bombing, ran, and hid. You have your mother to thank for the fact that you are alive. Now it is hard for you all to live. Things are crowded and chaotic; sometimes you can't get certain things or can only obtain them with difficulty. My dear children, try to live now as you would have lived if there had been no war: amicably, lovingly, helping each other, not quarreling over trifles, understanding how hard things are now. Be affectionate with your mother, take care of her too rather than just letting her take care of you. Most important, do not bother her when she is resting: she, poor thing, gets very little peace. Be attentive to her. It will please me and make me happy here too if you live that way. Many kisses, and big, big hugs. Your loving papa [. . .]

[Upside-down in the margins:] Send me a Russian reader at about the fifth-grade level. Even an old one will do. I will "earn" a good deal with it.

[Upside-down in the margins:] If you are going to send a package, it would be better to insure it. The Efimovs insured theirs for 1,000 rubles.

[Upside-down in the margins:] February 21. This letter has been sitting here all this time through no fault of my own. A new one will follow. [. . .]

♦ ♦ ♦

The city of Kansk
February 15, 1946
No. 38[11]
My precious Niushenka!

Today I have a double holiday. Some letters have come at last: yours from January 6–9 and Dimochka's from the 11th with the postcard of Father Frost. I am very glad that the poems that I sent for your name day reached you and that you liked them, and that you had a Christmas tree. Thanks to the warm words that you wrote on Christmas Eve, I was able to share in the preholiday atmosphere in your room, hear the breathing of our sleeping children, who are the most precious thing in my life (even including you). I could even smell the aroma of their languid bodies and clean linen and see their sweet children's pajamas and the shoes that were left out in expectation of Father Frost's arrival. Oh, my darling! More and more often, you are putting things off until we meet and not writing, but in the bottom of my heart, I have no hope of such a meeting, at least no ordinary natural hope, but instead an entirely fantastic thought that, like the *Victoria amazonica* flower, which I have never seen, smolders and flutters, reddening, a thought about the possibility: but what if?[12] But "what if?" doesn't at all imply predictability!

11. Stamped by the camp censor.
12. Formakov probably has in mind Igor Severianin's 1908 poem "Viktoriia regiia," which compares a rare romantic meeting to the fantastic flower *Victoria amazonica* that is white upon opening but then gradually reddens.

Your news about Stas is interesting. What do you know about Petia and Iura? Efimov read me a letter from his mother. She asked if he had quarreled with me because you have not been to see them for a long time, and she can't manage to visit you. I am again getting together with him pretty frequently. We chat about places familiar to us both. I loan him books to read when I have them. Sometimes he buys milk for me and brings it.

February 19. Today, after having traveled to Ingash and back to no purpose, your parcel with Russian newspapers from the second half of December finally reached me. It also contained a piece of a Christmas tree but nothing else (that is not a reproach; it is just information).

February 20. Now finally I have gotten a letter from you (no. 3) and also all the stamps that were enclosed. It is good that you are numbering them. No. 2 is still lost somewhere. [. . .] Don't burden your friend with any undertakings. You can send me a package when you get permission. Thanks for your efforts with Kirhenšteins. Since it didn't work out, we just won't worry about it. We'll just wait. After all, we know how to do that. You're right about that! I don't need Latvian books; send Russian ones when you can. In my last letter, I asked for a fifth- or sixth-grade literary reader (or even a little older). If you can manage to get one, please send it. A friend of mine here, to whom I owe a lot, is studying Russian, and he really needs it. Up until now only a single children's coloring book has arrived, *Circus.*

On the 23rd we are having a big concert in honor of the Red Army with our own mixed-sex choir and the jazz and brass bands. I am serving as the emcee and will recite my poem "Pobeda" [Victory]. I sent it to you at one point in no. 25. It is too bad that postcard no. 29 from December 21 didn't arrive. It was written at night on the eve of your name day and was very heartfelt. At the time, I felt the inseverable connection between our souls particularly strongly and was in a sunny frame of mind. It was a really nice postcard. After all, it isn't always possible to express what cannot easily be put into words.

Since February 1, I have again been working in the needle workshop. For the past few days, I have felt a little fluish. I am taking Calcex. My temperature is normal. My upper incisors have worn down. I dream of getting crowns (out of stainless steel), but that isn't feasible right now.

Although there may be a chance on the horizon. [. . .] I kiss you warmly after giving you and the children a big hug. I enclose a postcard. Yours forever and ever, Senia. [. . .]

♦ ♦ ♦

March 3, 1946[13]
Greetings, my dears!

I ask all of you to forgive me for everything, since today, it seems, is the last Sunday before Lent. Yesterday, I was detailed to the house of rest (for two weeks), and I will spend my name day here. Last year I was on rest leave at the end of March. There are twenty of us here. It is a new, relatively comfortable building. You get a high-calorie diet. Things won't go so smoothly with my letters as they have in the past. Niushenka, don't worry: no clouds or sunshine are visible when you look at the horizon. Everything will happen as it is supposed to happen. But you need to break off all contact with my friend immediately, so that neither he nor I get into trouble.[14]

Our winter is quite something: before Candlemas it was minus 38, but then the next day we had real spring weather, which, ever since, has been appearing and disappearing, making itself felt. Of course the weather for me is no longer such an important factor since I am again working inside, where I worked for two years up until last August. I hug and kiss you all as a group and individually. I hope that with the end of the rationing system everything will become less expensive where you are, and your lives will become better and happier. Your papa, who is far away but whose heart is with you.

P.S. Sending things registered mail does not guarantee that I will receive them. Send everything regular mail: it will save money.

13. On a plain postcard with no camp censorship stamp and the return address: "The city of Kansk, Krasnoiarsk region, general delivery, I. Arsenievskii." This name recalls Formakov's favorite pseudonym, F. Arseniev.

14. Formakov hints that sending things through his usual courier is no longer safe, perhaps as the result of a crackdown. Note that more communications are traveling through the official camp mail system in this period.

◆ ◆ ◆

March 9, 1946
No. 39

> I wander in silence and darkness,
> Exhausted, in the labyrinth,
> And for a long time have not understood
> The deceptive paths that I am on.
>
> I wait tediously to see if fate
> Will tire of burying my hopes,
> And, before my death at least,
> Extend a guiding thread to me.
>
> Once again I will climb out to freedom
> To die under a clear sky,
> And, dying, gaze at nature
> With clear eyes.

(F. Sologub)[15]

My dear Niushenka:

The letters that you addressed to Ingash are at last beginning to arrive. Yesterday I received your postcard from February 3 (no. 4), a parcel with two books—*Zhizn' prodolzhaetsia* [Life Goes On] and the short stories of Grigulis in Latvian—and, most touchingly, two calendar charts. You may recall that last year I received a calendar at this exact time and also while I was in the house of rest. A (small) calendar of saints [*sviattsy*] is the only thing I still don't have, and I now have three different dates for Easter. I can't tell which [calendar] to believe.

As I already wrote, since March 2, I have been at the house of rest. There are twenty of us here. The building is new with a really big room: three windows on the left, three on the right, and a door in the center of the shorter wall. There are ten cots on the left and ten on the right.

15. Formakov cites, slightly inaccurately, Fyodor Sologub's 1896 "Tsarevnoi mudroi Ariadnoi" (By the Wise Princess Ariadne), which builds on the Greek myth of Theseus and the Minotaur and had obvious relevance to Formakov's personal situation. Like Theseus, Formakov found himself in a terrifying and confusing place of confinement and depended on a "lifeline" provided by a woman for survival.

There is a nightstand/small table by each, and there are white flannel blankets. In the corridor in the middle [of the room], there are two big tables, which are covered with white tablecloths. There are plants, pictures, a radio, two stoves, and two electric lamps. We get up at 7:15, wash ourselves in the heated corridor, take our medicine (I take fifteen drops of heart medication, adonilen, I think it is called, just because, if it's a sanatorium, then we ought to act like it). Then they serve breakfast: 300 grams of bread, a bowl of meat soup with vegetables, a piece of grain-based pudding with tripe soup or carrots, and 250 grams of milk. Then I sleep for an hour. Dinner is at 1:00: meat soup, a piece of meat (oh-ho-ho!) with stewed cabbage, and 250 grams of bread. "Why is the Cossack so well fed?" . . . For that reason, I go straight to bed until 3:00.[16] At 4:00 I go to the club to read the latest newspapers. Supper is at 7:00: porridge made with milk, salted herring, and 300 grams of bread. Then I go to rehearsal or a movie.

We had a concert on the 8th in honor of International Women's Day. I presented the program. Our jazz band performed in costumes that had been sewn just for this: white pants with cuffs and white jackets with scarlet lapels and scarlet cuffs. It was terribly stylish! . . . You act as master of ceremonies, make some witty remarks, and then head backstage, release your soul, and you just want to wail . . . For this reason, I never let it go; my soul is always in a corset. Having finished with the concert, I am starting work on a production of a new contemporary comedy *Samolet opazdyvaet na sutki* [The Plane Will Be a Day Late], which we will put on at the beginning of April.[17]

Whether to send Dima to the fourth grade is a big problem. Weigh everything carefully, my dear, and, if it is necessary, make the decision now to hold him back for a year so that he knows and doesn't wear himself out. Otherwise he will work frantically all year and then it will be cruel to hold him back. I am really sorry that all his letters from this year, except for one, seem to have gone astray.

In my free time, I always read. I have plenty of light reading material here: there is always something. You'll get a book and sometimes

16. Formakov references a popular Russian folk expression: "Why is the Cossack so well fed? Because he eats and goes straight to bed" (Otchego kazak gladok? Ottogo, chto poel, da i na bok).

17. The play was written in 1946 by Natan Rybak and Igor Savchenko.

a new magazine too. For this reason, Niushenka, I don't really need from you the kind of books you use to kill time. It's only worth sending something speci . . .[18]

P.S. Perhaps the newspapers have started to go astray because you have been inserting a "filling" in them. If this is the case, it would be better not to do that anymore! Someone may have noticed. Lugovskaia has begun, like you [. . .]

♦ ♦ ♦

March 19, 1946
No. 40
Dear Niushenka:

I do not know how regularly my letters are reaching you now, since I am not sending them the way I used to, but yours are still as rare as a thaw during a Siberian winter. The only explanation is the article in the January issue of *Sovetskaia Latviia* that I borrowed from Efimov about the disorder at Riga's post offices.[19] Nonetheless, I never received anything from you in connection with your birthdays in November and December, nor the New Year, nor, for that matter, March 15.[20]

That was my last day at the house of rest. It was as sad as it was last year. So as not to get too upset, I kept myself busy moving back to my old place. I filled my mattress with new shavings, got a shave, and visited the bath house. In the morning, when I was still in bed, Efimov ducked in to give me his best wishes. I asked him to bring a liter of milk in the evening. He promised, and we agreed to have supper together at 9:00 p.m., but neither he nor the milk ever arrived. That is a characteristic example of his swinishness. However, another comrade of mine brought a liter of milk and didn't even take money for it. He said it was a gift. I boiled a pot of potatoes, and we ate them with the milk, and I also had two cubes of sugar from the package you sent . . . Anyway, that's not the most important thing. We talked about poetry. After he left, I spent a long time lying and thinking. It was quiet. The

18. Here the letter breaks off. A page is clearly missing.

19. Here a line is blacked out in a way characteristic of the censorship system, although there is no censorship stamp on the letter. The blacked-out text begins with the phrase: "But here . . ."

20. March 15 was his birthday.

radio hasn't been working in our section for about two months. Bitter thoughts, resentment, powerlessness. And I haven't gotten word from you in so long! I accept that last fact as my due, but that does not make my bitterness any less.

On the 16th I went to work in my needle workshop. But my mood has remained foul. Moreover, it has been about two weeks since I lost the object you sent, which I used to wear around my neck.[21] I usually took it off in the evening, when I got back from work, so that the cord didn't get wet, and placed it on my little table, but this time I put it on my bed, and then, in my hurry, I forgot to put it back on. And that night I carried the blanket outside to shake it out, and I realized what I had done only the next day at dinner . . . Lost in the most ordinary way! And I also saw this month's new moon from the left side.[22]

Yesterday I watched *Bez viny vinovatye* [Guilty though Guiltless]. Ostrovskii held his own, but the theatrical elements stuck out and there was almost nothing cinematic about it.[23]

I am writing this today so that I do not forget, but I will continue the letter just as soon as I receive something else from you via Ingash. Also, concerning the details of my life: I wrote to you that when I left for there, I received, among other presents, thirty rubles! Well, after I returned, I gave them back to the person who had given them to me very insistently, not taking no for an answer (it was the person who visited me on March 15). And now someone else, for whom I translated the words to several foreign foxtrot songs, has given me a cream-colored soldier's blouse with a turned-down collar. I usually borrow a tie and a shirt to wear under my jacket for performances. Now I will just need to hunt for a tie . . . And now I must add that there has never been an instance when I have failed to find a way to repay a favor and do a good turn to someone who has helped me, although sometimes it took time. The cause of my father's death put in an appearance here, but, by taking energetic measures (including shaving everyone's head), a good result was achieved.[24]

21. Formakov means the cross.

22. An ill omen.

23. Formakov saw the 1945 Soviet film adaptation of Ostrovskii's play directed by V. M. Petrov.

24. Formakov's father died of typhus. Censorship rules barred inmates from mentioning epidemics, which explains why Formakov references the illness

Right now only the upper incisor that is next to my artificial tooth is bothering me. It is getting ground down farther and farther, but they won't let me get a crown for it. I don't want to pull it: there would be a hole . . . For now, I am tolerating it.

My compatriots here are getting optimistic letters that almost sound as though they contain citations from official sources: people are expecting their return home. Lugovskoi and I were just talking about this. I do not have any faith in such miracles. Our century is the age of materialism!

I live without making any plans on a five-year scale, just doing the minimum: trying to survive the day at hand with as few losses as possible . . . Also, I haven't written the most important thing: during the two weeks I spent recuperating, I gained three kilos without buying anything extra. In a year that would be about eighty kilos. And in ten years . . . No, joking aside, I got very well rested: they fed us well, we had milk every day, and, most important, I got an hour of sleep after breakfast and just as much after dinner. I had nothing to worry about. It was quiet. [. . .]

March 20. Today, after a break of a year, I received a letter and a greeting card from Liza and Kotik. They are planning to move to town. They work at a cooking oil factory. Taniusha is working as a technician on the shores of the Pacific Ocean and earning 900 rubles. It is touching that they remembered my name day. What do you say? Warm kisses. Your Senia [. . .]

♦ ♦ ♦

April 7, 1946
No. 43, Kansk[25]
Happy holiday!

My dearest wife Niushenka, my splendid son Dimochka, and my sweet daughter Zhenichka:

---

obliquely. After this line several words are blacked out, which may have provided additional information.

25. Decorated with a dried carnation that is pinned to the letter with hand-lettered ribbons that read: "Christ has arisen" (Khristos voskres). A sprig of pussy willow is drawn in colored pencil at the bottom of the letter. A camp censorship stamp is visible (see illustration).

С Праздником!

7.IV.46. №43
Канск.

Дорогая моя
женушка-Нюшенька,
славный сыночек Димочка,
милая доченька Женичка!

Из далекой суровой Сибири, из самой её серединки, под вой апрельских мяте-лей, когда с утра нога вязнет в снегу, а к полудню автомобили застревают в грязи и их надо выталкивать, шлю я вам от самого сердца горячий, как солнце Сахары, свой самый теплый привет и поздравления с праздни-ком Св. Пасхи. Как бы мне хотелось по-настоящему прижать каждого из вас поочередно к своему сердцу, крепко-крепко, чтоб аж косточки хрустнули, и торжественно расцеловать троекратно в честь праздни-ка воскресения из мертвых, возвращения из небытия, свершения самого немыслимого, чуда из чудес, праздника праздников! Праздник рели-гиозный совпадает с праздником природы: солнце побеждает тьму, весна изгоняет зиму, ломается лед, вскрываются реки,

Letter from Arsenii Formakov to his family dated April 7, 1946. The ribbons across the dried flowers are hand-lettered with the traditional Easter greeting: "Christ has arisen." A faint camp censorship stamp is visible on the document. Arsenii Ivanovich Formakov Papers, Hoover Institution Archive, Box 1, folder 4.

From the very heart of distant, harsh Siberia, from amid the howl of its April snowstorms, when, in the morning, your foot drowns in snow and by midday automobiles are getting stuck in the mud and you have to push them out, I send you my warmest greetings and best wishes for the holiday of H[oly] Easter, from my very heart, which burns like the sun over the Sahara. How I would like to give each and every one of you a real hug, holding you each in turn close to my heart, squeezing you so tight that your bones creaked, and then kissing you three times with great ceremony in honor of the Feast of the Resurrection of the Dead, the return from nothingness, the most unthinkable feat, the wonder of wonders, the holiday of holidays! This religious holiday coincides with a natural holiday: the sun defeats darkness, the spring chases away winter, the ice breaks up, the rivers open, and even here the starlings are whistling by their nests. In greenhouses, you can see white and red radishes that are as miniscule as grains of caviar beginning to come out, and in our porridge they sometimes give us green onions.

I am putting together a lively comedy for the 21st, *The Plane Will Be a Day Late*. Then I have the concert for the 1st of May and a Victory Day concert. I am working peacefully in my needle workshop. I have been reading Turgenev: his writing is as clear as the water in some lakes; he plans things out very carefully, his characterizations are very subtle, and nothing seems overloaded in the way that it so often does in the work of our [contemporary] novelists—as if thickness is the only thing of concern in writing a novel!

Today my mood is very sunny. I am chatting with you. I am reading a good book and listening to the radio.[26] It's good that the weather changed this morning! This morning, after our usual breakfast, Charlie from Bukovina, for whom I wrote the words to the foxtrot (he sings with our jazz band), dragged me back to his bunk and treated me to sweet coffee and cookies. Before dinner, reliable Serezha brought me my cap, which had been washed and turned. At one time, you, Niushenka, sent it to me in the Dvinsk hotel.[27] It has lived through so much over the last six years . . . Ivan Iakovlevich has promised to come by in the evening and bring the three volumes of Blok that he has obtained for just this one night. We will read them together . . .

26. Here several lines have been blacked out by the censor.
27. By "hotel" Formakov again means the Dvinsk investigative prison.

Of course, there are also unpleasant things: jibes, legs stuck out to trip you, dirty tricks on a variety of scales and various levels, but in comparison with what I have survived, nothing now gets me too upset; no one makes me lose my cool.

Physically, I am not in bad shape so far. I don't think it's likely that my heart has gotten much worse. My doctors haven't noticed this. In my coat, my felt boots, and my quilted trousers, I weigh eighty-seven kilos. I have little grey hair. I am scarcely starting to go bald. Soon I am going to start having issues with my teeth. It is good that I basically don't eat sweets, or they would have given out sooner. I've had an abscess on my left heel for five days. Tomorrow I will go to the clinic to get it drained. It is from a nail. I got new boots not long ago, and I started developing a sore spot immediately.

Judging by the last parcel, you, my darling, subscribed to *Sov[etskaia] molodezh'* [Soviet Youth] for the year. I like this paper; there is a fair amount that is useful in it. But there is no need for three newspapers, obviously, particularly since the demand for them has almost disappeared. For reading material, one is plenty for me.[28] [censorship mark] By the way, he says that Georgii Fedorov, my primary school student from long ago, is now in a high-ranking position in Dvinsk, and that in Riga one of the Zil brothers is a pretty big boss. Perhaps one of them could be useful to you? Past experience has convinced me that all my students remember me positively.

The days are flying by. I have twenty-two months left until the end of my term! Will there really be a moment when I can hide myself in your hair and cry tears of heart-breaking joy? I kiss you, hug you, and wish you a happy holiday once again. Kiss, kiss, kiss. Christ has arisen! Christ has arisen! Christ has arisen! Your Senia, your papa. [. . .]

♦ ♦ ♦

April 16, 1946
Kansk[29]
Happy house-warming, my dear ones!

Yesterday I finally received the letter that I have long been expecting from you, darling Niushenka, and it made me extremely happy even

---

28. Either the paper situation in camp has improved or pre-rolled cigarettes have appeared. Two lines are blacked out by the censor here.
29. A camp censorship stamp appears on the first page of the letter.

though it contained much that was sad and painful. First of all, your illness, although you didn't even write what it was. You were sick for a whole month, my poor sufferer, and I did not know anything about it, although I had a sense that things were not good. I am used to breaks in our correspondence, but this time I was worried . . . Thank God you overcame your illness, as you have so many other things up to now.

The joy of your recovery was followed by the joy of house-warming. A new burden fell on you, my long-sufferer, but if only it will prove worth it, if all your care will have an impact on the children's hearts and the proper environment will have a good effect on them in regards to their upbringing!

Children, obey my command: behave yourselves very well!

I can barely remember Vitebskaia street. I think there was a Russian school there, a red brick building located in a courtyard, and there you and I were almost . . . Or am I bitterly mistaken? My memory loses track of things as often as the post office. [. . .]

I have lost all hope of being able to send you permission to mail me a package, but people have firmly promised to bring one to me from the station. For this reason, when you are able, send a package as baggage on an express train to the Kansk station and then put my entire address on it. Send the baggage claim check to me in a special registered mail parcel for valuables [*tsennyi paket*] (with five seals). Insure the package.[30] Insure it for 1,000 rubles. Here it costs two rubles a day to store something until pay day. It would be better not to send food, just the things I asked for and that I can't get here.

Don't *ever* send me money again unless I ask you to. You need it more than I do. [. . .]

May G[od] keep you! I send big hugs and warm, warm kisses for you, my enduring joy, for my heir Dima, who, I hope, will always make me proud, and for the daughter I have never seen, Zhenichka. My greetings and respects to everyone who remembers me. Yours with all my heart, Seniurka

[Upside-down in the margins:] I am sorry this is hurried. The mail is being sent off today.

30. Here approximately two lines are again blacked out.

♦ ♦ ♦

May 2, 1946
Hello, my dear ones!

You can't imagine how much I miss you! My one joy is letters, and I haven't had any in God knows how long. [. . .]

Yesterday I chaired the meeting held in celebration of the holiday. Then there was a big concert of our amateur groups. Everyone, including the guests of honor, was quite satisfied. My number was the greatest success of them all. But this isn't what I need at all. The most important thing for me, now as in all my life, is a character trait that I hope to pass on to the children (and you too, Niushenka): do whatever you do as well as possible. For this reason, I always try to achieve the best possible result in whatever I take on, and, thanks to a certain amount of talent, I almost always succeed in this . . . I wrote a script for a fairy tale for a puppet theater, which was used by the city schools and which unexpectedly earned me 200 rubles. In addition, out of the 500 rubles you sent for my name day, I have only used up a hundred so far. For this reason, Niushenka, my dear friend, don't worry about me at all in this regard. I will wait for your letters to get here, and then, if something is wrong, I will send you 300 rubles. [. . .]

Since the 1st of May I have been in new quarters. They have set aside a separate section for those of us active in cultural work, in which we've created a little cabin for ourselves by screening off two trestle beds. My partner in this is the head of our club, a good and pleasant man. This is very important—to have your own little corner, where you can, at least sometimes, be completely alone . . . But this is all trifles . . . The main thing is to get to our reunion as soon as possible! [. . .]

May 4. I still haven't received anything from you, my dears. I have never been as worried as I am now . . . One after another, my acquaintances here are leaving for different places after having finished their contracts. Tomorrow the engineer who has led our jazz band is leaving. He is a very nice man of about my age, but his hair is completely grey. Engineers have it pretty good. Their specialty is in short supply, and they are always needed. I am trying not to think about what will happen when I leave here. [. . .]

Judging by the letters that have come from your area, this year has also not been easy where you are—just as it hasn't been for the country as a whole.[31] I imagine that your stores of usable goods and your strength in general (both material and spiritual) are running out. I earnestly pray to G[od] that he help you hold on. And then I will catch you up in my arms! [. . .]

If you need to write to me urgently (as an exception), you can send a simple letter or a postcard, or, if you want to send a registered letter, then use your maiden name Zakaznova and do not put our last name or initials anywhere, and address this communication to: The city of Kansk, Kr[asnoiarskii] kr[ai], 2 Pobeda street, near Zagotzerno, Maria Ivanovna Klimchuk. Her husband used to be one of us.[32] An acquaintance of mine goes to visit him. In short, I could receive such a letter "from Riga" in the space of about ten days, but of course, that is a violation of the rules. I warmly hug and kiss you, Dimochka, Zhenichka, and Grandmother. Greetings to everyone. Papa

♦ ♦ ♦

May 4, 1946
No. 47
Kansk[33]
My dearest wife:

Forgive me, sinner that I am, for not having written to you in a comparatively long time: I have been busy every evening working on the play *The Plane Will Be a Day Late,* which I directed and in which I played the role of the engineer. The premiere was held in our club after the meeting in celebration of the 1st of May. We also ran it on the 2nd, and then again, for a third time, yesterday. It was very stressful and required a lot of ingenuity to get the play up and running. And now we can claim our laurels and enjoy the fruits. The laurels were a packed auditorium and almost two and a half hours of continuous laughter from our satisfied audience, and the fruits are that on the eve of the 1st of May our administration granted me a grocery package in recognition of my exemplary efforts in amateur theatrical work

---

31. A reference to the famine of 1946–1947.

32. Formakov means that he is a former inmate.

33. A camp censorship stamp appears on the front of the letter, which may explain why Formakov, who finished writing an illegal letter the same day that he began this one, makes a great pretense of apologizing for not writing more frequently.

(sausage, canned goods, soap . . .). On Victory Day (the 9th), I will serve as the emcee for a concert, and then, after that, we will start work on an evening dedicated to Maxim Gorky. There's what's planned for the near future. [. . .]

Today we were lucky enough to be given the opportunity to sign up for the reconstruction bond. I committed fifty rubles. It is pleasant to feel as though you are almost a citizen and at least are participating in the concerns of the whole nation.

I am so hungry for news of your life in your new home. Dima must send me the blueprint of the new apartment! Also, regarding him: have him wear footcloths instead of socks. Neither my father nor I ever wore them, and, like an idiot, I wore out all my socks here before I realized that I could just wear footcloths. [. . .] It's worth it just for the darning it frees you from. In the winter, you can wear two layers or very warm ones. Of course, it isn't so comfortable in sandals or shoes, but in slippers, felt boots, or leather boots, it is wonderful. You wear one pair and wash the other.

I felt quite poorly for several days. It was the result of getting a vaccination. I had a temperature, didn't eat anything, and my heart kept skipping a beat, but not out of joy. Now I feel fine again. [. . .]

Just now I remembered for some reason how I received the flowers from you in the hotel in Dvinsk, among which there was a rosebud that stood for (the future) Zhenichka.[34] And I had a premonition that if the bud bloomed, then everything would be fine (in other words, she would be born alive and healthy). It took a lot of effort and cunning, but I managed to keep it in the water all the time and get it to bloom. Sometimes I needed the mug for coffee. Then I would move the flowers to the bowl. Breakfast would come to an end, and I would move them to the mug . . . Eventually all three flowers were dried and for a long time I kept them behind the bracket for the electric lamp, until a certain administrator found some violation of regulations in this and ordered them tossed out. [. . .]

May 6. Hooray! Today I received a long letter that you sent (no. 2 from April 8), and I am happy, although there was, of course, a great deal that was sad [in it]. If you sent the money to Ingash, then it is

---

34. "Hotel" is code for prison.

understandable that it has been delayed. Our financial sector here assures me that it will get here. Lugovskoi came by and also had a letter. His wife wrote to him that Farbtukh, who had been told that Ars[enii] Iv[anovich] had arrived, had come to visit her, hoping to find out if he had stopped by.[35] [. . .]

Send my greetings to Tatiana Georgievna. How is Petia? I warmly hug and kiss you all, my dears. Senia-Papa [. . .]

♦ ♦ ♦

May 18, 1946[36]
Dearest Niushenka:

I am writing to you again from Ingash, where I have been sent on a five- to six-day work trip with the agitational brigade. After that, I will again travel away from Kansk, heading in the other direction, for about three days probably, and then that will be it. Although the central agit brigade really wants me, the people in Kansk aren't letting me go, and probably won't let me go in the future. However, so that I wouldn't be too distressed by this, on May 8 they transferred me to a new work assignment, which is probably the best one we have in camp: in the bread-cutting department. There are three of us on staff there along with a supervisor, who is a very calm and cultured person. Two of us are on duty during the day, the third at night. We work (one of us cuts and the other weighs; I am in the second position) from 7:00 to 5:00. Sometimes we finish even earlier. I have breakfast and dinner there. I have supper "at home." Of course, I am getting plenty to eat; it couldn't be better. It is quiet, clean, and tidy. I wear a white jacket and hat. In the evening I have my club work . . . You can reach your own conclusions, and really don't worry about sending me money or packages unless things change. By the way, in Ingash they also know nothing about the 500 rubles you sent. Submit a claim at the post office before the period for doing so ends (I think it is six months).

It has been warm here since May 9. I ran into Vrubel here. The old man cried when he saw me. He can't get in touch with anyone from

35. Mikhail Vladimirovich Farbtukh (né Ivanov) was the boss of the NKVD in Daugavpils and personally signed orders of deportation during 1940 and 1941.
36. A plain postcard with a camp censorship stamp and standard addresses for both the sender and receiver.

his family. His daughter Raisa Iv[anovna] Kuleshova should be working for the main administration of the meat and milk industry. Perhaps you can locate her? The old man really asks that you try. His address is: Ingash station, Krasnoiarskaia railroad, P.O. box 235/7. Greetings to Dimochka. I hope to God that he passes his exams. Kiss him and my darling daughter Zhenichka warmly for me. My regards to Grandmother. Warm hugs and kisses to you all. Yours forever and ever, Senia

♦ ♦ ♦

Kansk, June 1, 1946
No. 50
My dear Niushenka:

Life is unpredictable. "First, it raises you high, but then it shamelessly casts you into the abyss."[37] I have revived a little in the past month and am better provided for materially than I have been at any time in the last six years. I already wrote to tell you that, in honor of the 1st of May, I received a bonus of a very nutritional nature, and then I got potatoes at the state rate (fifty kopecks a kilo), and then I was appointed to my new position in the bread-cutting sector. You yourself understand what sort of position that is! My job is to weigh people's rations. I don't even do the cutting. There are three of us on staff. If we need more help, we call for volunteers. For the most part, we also eat there together. The supervisor is extremely cultured. I am on the day shift. It is clean and quiet. The only issue is that my legs get tired: from 7:00 until 4:00, with the exception of dinnertime, you never sit down. They get tired, but they aren't swelling![38]

Well, good fortune brings more good fortune! Pretty soon our Central Cultural Brigade, which provides special services to several dozen concerns such as ours, began trying to recruit me. The people who work for it are either professionals (there is a wonderful pair of danc-

37. Formakov uses an aphorism taken from the folksong "Shumel, gorel pozhar moskovskii" (The Fire in Moscow Noisily Burned), which was based on the 1850 poem "On" (He) by Nikolai Sokolov. Both the song and Sokolov's poem describe Napoleon's invasion and the fire that consumed Moscow as Russian troops retreated following the Battle of Bordino.

38. Swollen legs are another sign of nutritional deficiency.

ers) or highly qualified amateurs. Altogether twelve to fifteen people are involved. They wanted to have me be their emcee and recite poetry, act, and, most important, serve as their applied arts poet: write *chastushki* about local issues or a topical feuilleton.[39]

A few days ago I returned with them from my trip to Ingash, where they had taken me as though I were "one of their own," although this has not been formalized. The people here only released me for the duration of the trip, which was exactly two weeks. We gave three big concerts (with three different programs). I have known all the guys [in the brigade] for a long time and I felt fine being with them. They welcomed me very warmly and shared what they had with me very generously and sincerely.

Today or tomorrow, it will all be decided: one or the other, either the bread-cutting sector or the cultural brigade. I will not be distressed either way: they are both fine options.

In Ingash, Vrubel latched onto me as if I were his relative and cried into my waistcoat. In Dvinsk, we used to say only "hello" and "goodbye" to each other, but here we are as close as relatives. He doesn't look bad, but the lack of any connection with his family saddens him. His daughter is in Riga. Now Volodia Lugovskoi tells me that this daughter visited his wife. That means she already knows . . . I tried to comfort the old man by saying that for five years I had also not had anything, but that did not console him. Shalkh is also there, and he said that all the Mikhailovs had returned to Dvinsk. Gogochka has really aged. He asked about Danka. I had nothing to tell him: people said he had died, but I also heard that about Zavoloko. [. . .]

The financial sector has at last reported that my long-awaited 500 rubles have finally been added to my account. Hooray! [. . .] If you happen upon a joke anthology of some kind, I wouldn't say no to that, but don't make a special effort. Many thanks for getting the reader. I will expect it.

39. For Gulag bosses, camp theatrical troupes were a point of prestige; in some cases productions were very elaborate. The best groups toured and performed for free laborers and local residents as well as camp inmates. See Tamara Petkevich, *Memoir of a Gulag Actress,* trans. Yasha Klots and Ross Ufberg, foreword by Joshua Rubenstein (DeKalb: Northern Illinois University Press, 2010); and Natalia Kuziakina, *Teatr na solovkakh, 1923–1937* (St. Petersburg: DB, 2009).

We traveled to Ingash by truck. High hills, lemon-yellow bellflowers in the fields (where we're from they are violet with a bright yellow core): nothing looked familiar. On the way back, we traveled by train. And this time, so many different thoughts crowded my mind that I almost burst into tears. Even the station itself, with its platform teeming with elderly women and young girls in colorful headscarves and dresses (it was the eve of the Feast of the Ascension), reminded me of our Latgale region . . . In the train car, I sat by the window. The fields and copses swam by. The sun had already set. The birch and spruce trees, the dark peasant cottages, the empty road . . . It all seemed so familiar and dear and painfully sad . . . I am not going home to my wife in Lipinishki![40]

Soon it was dark. After all, we had left at 9:00. Our bayan player started playing; our guys started singing. Then they got sick of it and stopped. I overcame my momentary weakness and took heart. Venus shone brightly in the West. I began to sing: "Gori, gori, moia zvezda" [Shine, Shine, My Star]. No one knew this song.[41] Then I sang Vertinsky's "Moia zvezda" [My Star]. I sang very softly, and I thought a great deal about you, my star! And then I closed this radio-show with the old Siberian convicts' song "Zvezda, prosti! Pora mne spat'" [Farewell, My Star! It Is Time for Me to Sleep], which somehow miraculously surfaced from somewhere deep in my memory. We had a version of it by the bass Sibiriakov on a phonograph record, and I heard it repeatedly in my youth. Well, the patterns woven by memory are fanciful, and the way that life's paths intersect is capricious! [. . .]

I have an assignment for Dima: describe your new apartment, how the building looks, what floor the apartment is on, the layout of the courtyard, and where your garden is. Thank you for the aromas: all through the newspapers and the Zweig there was a fragrance as rare in our daily life as an exotic flower.[42]

---

40. A village near Daugavpils.

41. Although composed in 1847, this Russian ballad did not become popular until World War I. Associated with the White forces in the Russian Civil War, it was banned in the Soviet Union until 1944.

42. Formakov received a book by the Austrian novelist Stefan Zweig.

June 2. At night.

> "There are many women in the world,
> But I was fated to meet one"

(The Gypsy Princess)

Today I at last saw the Russian film *Silva,* which was shot in Svedlovsk and has been making its way through the movie screens in neighboring areas.[43] I watched it and grieved. You know about what and why. "Do you remember the happiness that passed us by?" Could one really forget it? [. . .]

On June 3, I was reassigned to the cultural brigade. If there are no changes, then we will go on "tour" some time in the next ten or fifteen days.[44] For this reason, I will be writing to you from all sorts of places on the way. Our mail will [still] come here and then will be forwarded on to us. This, of course, is sad, because it will delay my receipt of your letters even more, and I am, by the way, still getting very few of them as it is.

There are twelve people in the collective now: 1) the foreman, our director, a ballet dancer and actor; 2) a ballerina and actress who was his partner even before he was arrested; 3) a dramatic actress who also declaims verse; 4) a woman who plays older women and comic character roles; 5) a singer and actress; 6) a bayan player and actor; 7) an artist, actor, and guitar player; 8) a mandolin player and actor; 9) an artist and actor; 10) a storyteller and genre actor; 11) an actor; 12) me. All very different people, but cultured. We live all together (the men, of course) in a big room with two windows (it's a little longer than our dining room and just as high-ceilinged). We all wear the same uniform: dark green flared trousers with cuffs and the same kind of shirt with a turn-down collar. We perform in our own clothes. I act as the master of ceremonies at all the shows, serve as a second director, and, finally, write for the wall-newspaper that we put out and compose skits on "local issues." Goodbye, my dear! I send warm kisses to you all. Greetings to everyone who remembers me. Yours forever, Senia [. . .]

43. Based on Formakov's favorite operetta, *The Gypsy Princess.*
44. The word "tour" is in Latvian but written in Cyrillic letters.

♦ ♦ ♦

June 10, 1946; the second day of the Feast of Trinity
No. 51[45]
Dear Niushenka:

On the Feast of Trinity, we were at the state farm for the holiday that marks the end of sowing. Although it has been raining frequently, it is remarkably warm. They welcomed us joyfully and fed us until we almost burst. We are performing on the summer stage. I am acting as the emcee with great success. I've been in the Central Cultural Brigade for a month already. Its members are freed from all [other] work and just travel around the district with concerts and shows [. . .] We get along well. Our base of operations is in Kansk, so my address remains the same, but I will write to you from the places I go. On June 8 in Kansk I got your letter from May 17—just half a sheet. I managed to make out a line that our censor had blacked out that said that my letters were getting blacked up. The thing is that I almost never write to you unofficially now, and all the official letters are marked with circular stamps. When you get something I have sent unofficially (for instance, not long ago, I sent Dimochka a book for his promotion to seventh grade, since I think he was promoted), let me know indirectly. In terms of my material well-being, everything is just going swimmingly, and, if they cut my sentence again in recognition of my good work, then everything will be truly excellent. [. . .]

On the 8th, I received the parcel with five issues of *Komsomol'skaia pravda* and pages of clean lined paper.[46] I am writing on this scrap paper because everything is in Kansk. Kisses to you and the children. Your Senia

♦ ♦ ♦

June 23, 1946
No. 55[47]
My dear splendid Niushenka:

Yesterday I had the indescribable satisfaction of receiving a snapshot of you with the children, the very thing that I had been dreaming of and

45. On a blank ledger sheet formed into a *treugol'nik,* with no camp censorship stamp.

46. *Komsomol'skaia pravda* was the newspaper of the Communist Youth League (Komsomol).

47. There is a camp censorship stamp on the letter.

longing for desperately all this time. It arrived along with the photographic portrait and the long letter from you, which I had long been expecting.

Just yesterday I managed to get out into the fresh air for the first time after my return from Ilansk and, moreover, for a whole day: the banks of a quiet tributary, along which logs move from the Kan, simple willow bushes, a glade with pink and white clover flowers, the opportunity to swim as much as you like, and to lie naked, roasting yourself as if on a brazier. Summer this year, unlike spring, is just wonderful here. This outing included supplemental pleasures such as milk, eggs, fresh cucumbers, half-sour pickles, and even wild strawberries. Really these are cultivated strawberries, but here they don't grow any larger than large wild ones . . . I did not open the book I had taken along. Although I tried to be careful, I still got sunburned.

On my way home, I was handed your letter. I had in my hands a bouquet of flowers. Indeed, I had picked them for you. The thing is that in our sector we are undergoing artistic renovations. Our artists have painted the walls and at the top have added medallions with portraits of Pushkin, Gorky, Lev Tolstoy, Ostrovsky, Chekhov, Lermontov, Tchaikovsky, and Rimsky-Korsakov. There are only nine of us, and each of us has a separate trestle bed. Mine is in the front corner under the window. Each bed has a little night table/cupboard, which is covered with a dark blue gauze napkin with open stitch work. On mine I have a frame with photos of you, the children, and me, and also a sprig of heather from home. By the frame, I always have several flowers in a mug (a white can from some tinned food). [. . .] I will put the new picture that you sent in a frame too, so that I can say good morning and good night to you, my dears.

Sometimes I miss you all so much that I just want to wail, but nature did not short-change me on strength of will, and I immediately set to work on some task, just to forget and to lose myself in work [. . .]

I am learning how to work as a norm-setter. It's quiet and cultured work. On Sunday I led a concert. Everyone is getting to like me in the role of emcee more and more. I manage it very simply and in a witty way, although more than once I have commented with irony on my fate: I never could remember jokes, but now, in my old age, I have had to start collecting them. I primarily draw them from *Krokodil* [The Crocodile].[48]

48. A Soviet satiric magazine.

I enclose some examples of the turns of phrase I use as emcee for Dima. At least the ones I use are all decent and don't indulge bad taste. Of course, neither public acclaim nor the footlights interest me in the slightest, but you need to stay in front of people's eyes. It's easier to live that way! [. . .]

It was so sweet of Mania and Grandmother to bring you flowers on our anniversary! Give Mania my best wishes on her saint's day. I remember very well that her day is coming up. Mine is on July 30.

Thank you once again so much for the snapshot and the splendid letter. Big hugs and warm kisses for you, Dimochka, and Zhenichka. Greetings to all who remember me. My respects to Grandmother. Your faithful Senia

♦ ♦ ♦

July 3, 1946
No. 54
Kansk

To my deeply respected spouse Anna-my-light Ivanovna, my esteemed son Dmitri Arsenievich, and my dearest daughter Zhenia-Zhenichka:

I send you all my respects and also my warmest wishes in connection with this most happy family occasion: the promotion of our dearest son and heir to the seventh grade in the school of learning. Today I woke up with the joyous peal of holiday bells in my heart, and on my letter, as you see, holiday flags are fluttering, because Dima really is a fine lad, and is striding from one class to the next just as Gulliver moved through the land of the Lilliputians [. . .]

I sent Dimochka the book *Udivitel'nye prevrashcheniia* [Amazing Transformations]. In a few days, I will probably be able to send another (for both of them) and a pair of carved pencil boxes (this is the most difficult undertaking).

I am working, as I have already written more than once, in the bread-cutting shop. There are three of us on staff there, not counting all manner of assistants, who are paid in kind. It's in a separate little building, or really a kiosk. It is very clean, and we also wear white tunics. [. . .]

Whenever there is a concert or something of the kind, I am removed from work detail and "redispatched" to the Central Cultural Brigade. They have not, however, transferred me to it completely yet. My nerves are as strong as cables, and others (my colleagues in the cultural bri-

Letter from Arsenii Formakov to his family dated July 3, 1946. Arsenii Ivanovich Formakov Papers, Hoover Institution Archive, Box 1, folder 4.

gade) worry while I am completely calm. The last six years have made me a fatalist.

I am very glad that you, my dearest, received a comparatively long leave. I hope to gain some benefit myself [from this] as well: at least a couple of fat letters, like those you wrote a year ago.

I have a devilish amount of money: 800–900 rubles. A few days ago, after a long lull, our camp store again began to trade actively. I bought a kilo of honey for seventy-eight rubles. Today they have butter for 130–150 rubles a kilo. I am going to try not to miss out . . . Considering that a kilo of butter lasts me a month, you can calculate that I have enough money to last me until Christmas. For this reason, until I give you the signal, for G[od's] sake, don't send anything, not even a kopeck. I really wanted to send the children fifty rubles at one point for "the pictures," but I couldn't: they won't allow it, and, in my position, I can't take the risk.[49]

My temples are getting greyer and greyer. I shave twice a week, and if I skip it, then this grey stubble appears, which is just awful. I have a lot of grey hair on my chest as well. Perhaps you haven't forgotten how shaggy I am? But despite it all—the furrows and wrinkles and the burden of years—I feel so young and energetic that, if I were just set loose in some field of activity, I would transform the world, if you, my dear, and all of you were by my side.

May the powers of heaven keep you! I embrace you warmly and kiss you ardently. Your Papa-Senia. [. . .]

♦ ♦ ♦

Kansk, July 30 (!), 1946
My dearest Niushenka:

A day doesn't pass but that I stop several times to admire the photo you sent showing the three of you together—my life's meaning and light. You move toward me so happy, unconstrained, and in such a lively way and probably are thinking of me in that moment. Everyone looks at it together and separately. People take you and Nina for my daughters. When they learned who my wife was, they begin to exclaim: Oh, she is so young! What a clean city! What short dresses! Oh, the boy looks so much like his papa! And so forth. And I stand there all "self-satisfied" like a peacock who unfurls his tail and challenges everyone to battle. Well, who's got better?

On the 27th Vrubel left for Dv[insk]. He had come here from Ingash in the morning. He had a three-year term, which was shortened by half as a result of the amnesty. He had served half of it. He really thanked me for getting him in touch with his family through you. He promised to run over to the office to see me quickly before he left, but he didn't, the bandit! True, I did not plan to do anything in particular, but still, I would have thought of something. At least he has seen me both in my daily life and on the stage, and he promised to tell you everything if he saw you. And, of course, you will certainly see him!

We spent the 26th fifty kilometers away on the banks of the Kan out in the wonderful fresh air. We were giving a concert for the men

49. A page appears to be missing here.

who float the timber down river. We swam, ate strawberries growing in fields (one ruble for a cupful), and wandered down a road that ran through meadows. I am still surprised by how amazing Siberian nature is [. . .]

This was perhaps the first time that I have been in such rich, primeval meadows. There was gigantic pink fireweed, and a honey-scented fluffy white lungwort, daisies, and lush wild carnations, and an endless abundance of [other flowers] in violet, dark blue, light blue, blue-grey, lavender, turquoise, and all sorts of other colors, mostly legumes (such as vicia).[50]

The Kan, which is fast-flowing and empty, reminded me of the Dvina beyond Kreslavka.[51] The high left bank is covered by forest, the lower right bank with bushes and individual trees.

We traveled in three trucks. It was very cheerful and pleasant. In the evening, I sat alone for a long, long time on a raft, looking at the rapidly streaming water. The sunset was almost over, the colors were fading, but the waters ran on and on with no end or beginning. That is how life is! [. . .]

I have parted ways with the Central Cultural Brigade after having been assigned to it temporarily. Although I live with them, perform, and wear their "costume," I won't go on their long-range tours. I will stay here because otherwise the local mass cultural work will suffer. That is what the administration has decided. And I have been delegated (more accurately, I delegated myself) to the rate and norm-setting bureau. For the first time in six years, I am just doing white-collar work. I do calculations, keep statistics, figure out wages, and will set norms for reports. There are four of us for the whole settlement. You can always snatch an hour to go take a nap or go to the bath house or to the post office in the afternoon. Normally I work from 7:30 to 12:00 and then from 1:00 to 6:00. When the monthly report is being prepared, we have to stay in the evening as well. All the others are splendid young men. Our office is bright with flowers and a radio. Since everyone's pay depends on the norm-setter, it is understandable that they enjoy unusual respect.

Vania Efimov recognized the street in your photo. Misha Kallistratov remembered going to school with you, how he ran into Dima on his

---

50. Legumes are a family of flowering plants.
51. Kreslavka is the Russian name for the Latvian town of Kraslava.

way to school (a fiery boy!). Volodia Lugovskoi (he's suffering from malaria, the poor guy!) lost himself in daydreams about his own wife. We meet almost every day—although not for long: after all, we are from the same region!

With all my strength, I will try to make it on the list for privileges again [for a sentence reduction], and then on July 30 of next year: *finita la tragedia!*[52] That is the earliest possible time! It is close in comparison to all the dates before, but it nonetheless seems so far: a year [away]! [. . .]

Hug and kiss our children! Greetings to all who remember me. Yours forever, Senia

July 31, 1946

♦ ♦ ♦

August 10, 1946
Dear Niushenka:

How did you spend your vacation? How are the children? How does the harvest look?

In the last week, I have received three parcels of newspapers and the postcard that Dimochka sent the night before leaving for the shore. It is good that you took the children to the beach!

Our short summer, it seems, has already come to an end. It isn't hot anyway, although I am going around all the time with bare feet in sandals. Our cultural brigade has gone on tour, and there are only two of us in the room now. Oh, how great it is! Yesterday (after thinking about how you would have sworn if you saw my hesitation) I put together a mountain of a feast. I had bought a kilo and a half of fresh potatoes (5.15 rubles). There was butter and fresh dill! I boiled them on the electric burner for dinner and for supper . . . I am getting my upper canine treated. I have a temporary filling already. The doctor seems to be saving me from having it pulled. They gave it three courses of radiation with the X-ray. I am alive and well as before. I have mastered my new job. All the best, my darling. Greetings to everyone. Your Senia

52. The popular expression Formakov uses means "this tragedy will be/is at an end."

♦ ♦ ♦

August 10, 1946[53]

Hello, son!

I just can't seem to get accustomed to the thought that you are already in the seventh grade. By the time I return, you may even be a post-secondary student! You will speak with a low voice, shave every day, and look me, your hunched old man, over from head to toe, gazing down from your exceptional height. [. . .]

Time flies with the speed of a dive-bomber. You are now at an age that is always challenging for teachers: you are leaving childhood, but still have not really become a young man. At this transitional age, children are sometimes overly quick to take offense and sometimes undisciplined. They get offended when they imagine themselves to be too adult; they act badly when they remember that they are still children. [. . .] There is one cure for this: time. In a year or two this critical period will pass. If you, my friend, note something like this in yourself, try to, as much as you can, be less hard, more sincere, and warm-hearted. Then everything will pass without any big complications. [. . .] Kisses, your papa

My darling daughter,

I got the long letter that you wrote and jumped so high from joy that I hit my head on the ceiling. Then I ran through our settlement and showed everyone: "Look at the letter that Zhenichka sent me!" Everyone lined up obediently, and I let each one see and smell the dried dog-rose that my daughter sent. And then I told everyone how you worked in the garden, and everyone is still exclaiming: "Zhenia is such a treasure!/Having such a daughter is a great pleasure!" Kisses and hugs, your loving papa

53. This letter to Dima appears on the front and back of the top half of a page. The letter to Zhenia below occupies the bottom of the page, again front and back. A hand-drawn line marks where the two letters could be cut apart. A tracing of a ship decorates Dima's half of the page.

Illustrated letter to Dmitri and Evgenia. August 10, 1946. Arsenii Ivanovich Formakov Papers, Hoover Institution Archive, Box 1, folder 1.

◆ ◆ ◆

To my daughter Zhenichka

I stretch out my hand,
Form a smile,
And say: "Well, hello!"
But my voice suddenly breaks—
Will you wriggle from
The greedy arc of my arms
Like a frightened fish?

I am much worse,
Simpler
      and older
Than the father that you imagined,
But I will warm you
      so much
That you, my fatherless orphan,
      Will start to love me at last!

September 7, 1946

◆ ◆ ◆

September 9, 1946
My dear Niushenka:

On September 5 I received the letter you wrote with an indelible pencil at the exhibit on August 20. This is a record! If only it almost always worked that way! I am waiting impatiently for the claim ticket for the baggage, which is probably here, but since there is no claim ticket, no one knows about it. Of course, for me, the nicest thing in your letter was the news that our children had a good summer—in the fresh air with no illnesses. Pray God that it will remain so! And how are you, my dearest? Of course, you didn't get any rest and haven't gotten better? Oh, when will I be able to watch over you as you watch over them? Don't you deserve this? [. . .]

Kallistratov and Efimov got packages as baggage a few days ago. Ef[imov] used to stop by every day, but now he is afraid and doesn't show up. He is afraid that maybe he'll have to treat me! A real Pliushkin and, moreover, stupid![54] Now it just seems funny to me, since I am not going hungry and even enjoy various delicacies periodically, but at one time bearing this would have been painful!

Your landlords' kindness touches me a great deal. Tell Marfa Timofeevna and Platon Varfolomeevich, whom I respect from afar, that I am sincerely thankful for everything humane and good that they do for my family. [. . .]

Well, G[od] bless you during this new winter. I am always with you in my thoughts, my dears. Countless kisses! Yours, Senia

[In the margins upside-down:] Today, in my personal account, as a fellow giving a report might say, I still have 379 rubles. There you have it!

♦ ♦ ♦

September 15, 1946
No. 61 (in between I sent unnumbered letters. I don't remember how many)[55]
Good day, dear Niushenka:

As you can see, I am writing on your paper with a new ballpoint pen and my favorite fountain pen (although the green one from your first package is still whole). I am writing to tell you that I received your long-suffering package the day before yesterday, earlier than expected, thanks to the courtesy of the post office. Nonetheless, it sat at the station for a terribly long time, so I had to pay about thirty-four rubles in storage fees. I had money ready, but when Efimov needed to redeem his, he had to run to all his acquaintances. I loaned him ten rubles, and he still hasn't paid me back. (That is just to give you a sense of his character.)

The wrapping on the package wore through on one edge, but the rest was completely intact with the exception of the tomatoes, which were horribly rotten [. . .]. In the pot things were just as in the crate (or more so). But amid a whole jumble of moldy things, I found one completely whole, firm, and juicy tomato, which still smelled of your nimble hands, fanned by the wind of the Dvina, and nourished by the golden sun of

54. Pliushkin is a character from Gogol's *Dead Souls* who hoards his goods, allowing them to decay rather than sharing them with others.
55. There is a camp censorship stamp on the letter.

the Baltics. It is amazing that only the white rusks suffered from this whole catastrophe: two-thirds of them were so completely moldy that I had to toss them out.

Yesterday, I drank coffee together with a pal who visits me more often than anyone else: white rusks, lump sugar, milk, and a conversation about literature on the eve of our day off. Then, amid conversation and to the sound of the radio, I did some sewing. When the fellows saw the marvelous footcloths you had sent, one called out: "Let's trade! I'll give you whatever you want if you give me one of those to use as a scarf." I, of course, refused to trade, but I seized on the idea, and I sewed a wonderful scarf out of two of the pieces (my knit one really started to rip after being washed, and no matter how I darn it, it just gets worse, and I even have a skein of brown yarn!). For footcloths, the remaining two pairs are plenty. The pot is wonderful. I have no words to describe how I felt about the pillow: ah, fluffiness, a cloud, a soap bubble! The medallion to wear around my neck is the best of all.[56] As soon as I found it, I put it on. You really pleased me; you pleased me so much! Everything else was just wonderful and very much needed except, perhaps, for the soap, of which I have a surplus now, and I will keep the second toothbrush in reserve. The things that I recognized from home were particularly touching. Even the brown rusks are so neatly made and tasty that I eat them as though they are special treats (although I am not short of bread). And I still have the canned goods to look forward to. Oh! In my new shirt, socks, and tie, I will cut a fine figure at the next concert. [. . .]

In terms of the future, the postman says that a general order has been issued: all post offices are now supposed to accept packages for prisoners. All the better!

It is already below freezing here in the mornings. Even for Siberia, this summer has been very short.

For a whole month, they have been treating my front right upper canine. They put in a temporary filling to test it out, but somehow it seems to be going badly, and I have to have it pulled. I am very grateful for the vitamins and the rinse. The foot powder is above and beyond.

The new leather belt is, of course, a real luxury. I accept it as a gift for putting under the Christmas tree. The blinding whiteness of the

56. It is a religious medallion, of course.

linens frightens me so much that I cannot even bring myself to wipe myself with the towel. And I thought that my linens were reasonably clean!

As you see, I am so overjoyed by this gift that I am reeling like a rabbit in a stubblefield, moving from one thing to the next.

Take care of yourself as well as the children. Greetings to all who remember me, and especially to your landlords for their kindness and attention. I kiss you a billion times. Your Ars[enii] [. . .]

◆ ◆ ◆

Sunday, September 29, 1946
No. 62
Hello, my darling!

Once again, writing a letter to you is like a visit with you: the time and the place have been selected in advance most felicitously. Now it is 9:00 in the evening. All my roommates (there are three of them now) have gone to a dance at the club. [. . .] In the kitchen, the orderly is rustling about. The radio is playing music. I had a wonderful supper of milk soup with your noodles. Yesterday they distributed sugar to us. One of my comrades brought me an apple. Volodia (he also visited me after supper) got a letter from his wife. She wrote that she had been to see you three times and that you were working a great deal and went headlong at everything just like a meteor. I liked that a lot. The children, apparently, are well raised (my compliments to you, madame!). Dima looks just like his papa except that his eyes are black. (I smile with self-satisfaction.) Niusha plans to send him to a music school to learn to play the violin. (Oh-ho! It is good that you can learn something about your family at least from bystanders!)

Joking aside, I have not been getting your letters regularly. Aside from the letter you wrote at the school exhibit, I haven't received anything in a long time. Perhaps there is some hold-up somewhere? A few days ago, several Latvians received between five and seven letters each all at once. For one of them, the earliest was from the 6th of March (sic!) and the last dated September 6, and all at once! [. . .]

In September I went twice as part of a work campaign to our farm (more than twenty-five kilometers away) to help dig potatoes as part of a voluntary Sunday workday. I ate my fill of tomatoes there (3.50 a kilo). I saw several people from Rezhitsa there—Zubov and Morozov. They've gotten on well. One is practically a senior agronomist. The other is a brigadier known for his big harvests (he got fifty hundredweights of potatoes a hectare). Well, so we had a little heart-to-heart chat. The farm is in the hollow between two steep and high hills that are covered with golden groves of birch trees. It is so beautiful! We walked back: since the morning, plenty of snow had fallen on the golden leaves and grass. Such a lovely scene would delight anyone's soul.

I am trying to stage *Fakir na chas* [Fakir for an Hour] but am not having any luck: they transported one of my actors to another location to dig potatoes, another moved to the city for good, a third learned of the tragic death of her mother and quit, a fourth fell on the way to rehearsal and broke her hand . . .[57] At any other time, I would have been climbing the walls, but now I am a rock! . . . I replaced them with new actors. I am going to have to delay the premiere. All my evenings are spent at rehearsals from 7:30 to 10:00. Today is our only day off. I wanted to let them memorize their parts. [. . .]

May G[od] protect you all. Warm kisses and big hugs. Papa Senia

♦ ♦ ♦

October 14 (!), 1946[58]
My dear Niushenka, Dimochka, and Zhenichka:

Today is a big holiday for me because, as a result of the rarest of fortunate coincidences and the kindness of a number of people, I can send a small gift to my darling children: a carved pencil box with an inscription from Papa for each of them. If it reaches you, then it should be almost in time for Dimochka's name day, and you can give Zhenichka hers at the same time just to keep him company. In terms of their dear mama, a powder compact will soon be sent to her.

I think that my children will do well in school as their mother and I did and, looking at their pencil boxes, will remember their father and wait for his return.

The flowers in the pencil boxes are for all of you, but for Mama most of all.

I haven't gotten any letters from you in a month. I just know what Zhenia Lugovskaia wrote to her husband. My kisses are on the little

---

57. A 1945 play by Vladimir Dykhovichnyi and Moris Slobodskii.
58. A plain postcard with no return address and no camp censorship stamp.

boy's head and on the bird on Zhenichka's pencil case. Warm kisses to all of you. Your papa

♦ ♦ ♦

November 8, 1946
No. 68[59]
Happy holiday, my dears![60]

We have been celebrating for three days. Yesterday in the club we had a holiday meeting with a report and a reading of the boss's orders. I am among those whose names are being sent to the center for a possible reduction in sentence. It will take at least seven months to get an answer, but if it is positive, it may lead to my immediate release in July of next year. It is terrifying and sweet to think about it.

I haven't received anything at all from you in three months (since September 3). I keep trying to reassure myself that all is well.

So, after the official part of the holiday, there was a concert of our amateur group at which I, as always, served as the master of ceremonies. I wore my striped trousers for the first time with the suspenders that you, Niushenka, sent in your package, a shirt with a red tie, and my black jacket, which had been turned for the holiday. I had a part in my hair and have the beginnings of a bald spot. I was not in make-up. I don't like wearing make-up.

The first part of the show included, along with Ukhtin's choir, the final scene of Margarita Aliger's play *Skazka o pravde* [A Story about the Truth]: the final night for Zoia (Kosmodemianskaia); her visions and apotheosis.[61] It was about thirty-five minutes long. It was very dramatic. There was a very good and diligent actress to play the part of Zoia (otherwise I wouldn't have done it). In general, it didn't turn out too badly. In the second act, our mixed-sex choir (fifty people) sang and, by the way, gave an encore of "Bul'ba" (the Belarusian song). Then our jazz band performed with soloists, and then finally there was a trio of gymnasts on the horizontal bar. You can imagine what memories

59. A camp censorship stamp appears on this letter.

60. Soviet citizens celebrated the anniversary of the October Revolution on November 7.

61. A 1945 play about a teenage partisan who was tortured and executed by the Nazis.

this evoked! . . .[62] I made some light witticisms, and then, at the request of our young people, we got permission for a dance. I left them to carry out the benches and reach an agreement with the band so that it would play more, and then I headed back to my "home," had supper, and now I am writing to you. [. . .] We still have one more day off ahead of us. Outside, it is snowing lightly. It is a quiet, festive night, like Christmas, with a full moon.

All is well with me, in terms of where I am living, money, food (sometimes the food is tasty, sometimes it isn't, but I always have enough to eat), my work in the rate- and norm-setting bureau, and also in general. Everyone knows me, respects me, is deferential, courteous . . . And only the thought of you and my daily longing for news from Riga never leave me; I worry constantly and am tormented by [thoughts about] how everything is there and what is taking place. I have already asked Volodia to write to his wife and ask her to find out what has happened to you. [. . .]

On the 19th, for Dima's birthday, I am going to have a really big feast: I have your macaroni, sprats, and sugar, and will get milk. I will reread all the letters I have received from you—there is a good-sized stack of them!—and the poems I wrote for you. I haven't copied over any of my poems from this year systematically. I didn't have anything to write them in and then, when I got the booklets from you, my darling, I didn't have time: I was in rehearsals every evening! . . . Now I will get started on putting together a new collection. The first one broke off before 1946.

It is already half past 12:00. There is no point in depositing this letter in the mailbox, so I will finish writing it tomorrow, but for now, good night, my friend Niushenka and my splendid children, my son Dimushenka and my daughter Zhenichka.

November 9. I couldn't get to sleep for a long time: there was some baritone singing on the radio: "*Yeuth* will not return . . . "[63] Then an orchestra conducted by Golovanov played [Tchaikovsky's] "1812." I've spent all day sewing, mostly stitching back on buttons that had

---

62. Formakov is presumably recalling the gymnastics exercises performed at Sokol events.

63. Formakov mocks the affected pronunciation of the singer.

Побежали Топтыжка и Маша за ёлкой, да потеряли топор по пути. Что делать?

Стали они перед ёлкою и думают...

Решили они друзей себе на помощь звать: белок и зайчат.

У них зубы острые. Подгрызли звери ёлку.

Маша и Топтыжка отвезли её в школу.

А белок и зайчат позвали в гости.

Вот они сидят на ветках, у свечек греются и кричат: «С НОВЫМ ГОДОМ!»

New Year's cartoon by Arsenii Formakov. Undated. Hand-drawn and hand-colored. The captions tell the story of Masha and the bear cub, who went to get a New Year's tree for school, but lost the axe on the way and had to get the help of the forest creatures to cut and transport the tree. Arsenii Ivanovich Formakov Papers, Hoover Institution Archive, Box 1, folder 7.

fallen off from both key and not so key places. I also went through my papers: I still haven't lost the habit of saving every scrap that has writing on it! . . . I got the manuscripts of my poems ready to be recopied into the little book. I ordered a half kilo of butter for tomorrow. I visited Efimov. Both he and others find that I have aged a great deal over the last year . . .

Well, my darling, an old fogey will be coming home to you. And my heart is working badly; I notice it all the time. At least my legs aren't swelling, and I am not having attacks. I need to go to the doctor again. I thank you, kiss you, embrace you, and bless you. Your Senia. Your Papa.

My address has changed: P.O. box LK 235/7
My respects to all who remember me!

♦ ♦ ♦

November 17, 1946
No. 70 (no. 69 is a fairy tale for Zhenia)
Dearest Niushenka:

After two months of waiting patiently, but with difficulty, I was overjoyed to receive a long letter from Dimusha. It again contained sorrows: his banged-up forehead and Zhenichka's bronchitis, but the main thing is that you are all alive and more or less all right. [. . .]

I composed a fairy tale for Zhenichka. It all started when I got my hands on an appropriate postcard. I copied it, and then I started to compose a poem on the back of the card. It expanded into an entire story. Then I made it into a little book. I worked on designing it for five full hours one evening, and it didn't turn out too badly. Now I seem to have an opportunity to send it through someone via registered mail, so I am sending it much sooner than necessary. I just hope it reaches you, and you can give it to her at the right time.

With Dimochka, things have gone badly: I can't seem to send the pencil boxes at all. There are no books. In a few days, I will try to send a chipmunk (stuffed animal) in a parcel. It has no eyes. I really should put on beads with a single wire. [. . .]

Your Senia. I kiss you tenderly and bless everyone. Greetings to everyone. Kiss the children.

1947

January 9, 1947
Dear Niushenka:

I was patient, but when all the holidays began and I still had not received a single line from you, I really began to miss you. And the weather turned very un-Christmas-like: gloomy and grey with cold Siberian winds (or, as they say here, *vebrá*). [. . .] Then, at one point right around the New Year's, Volodia came running up to me: Zhenia had sent a letter in which she wrote that she had been to see you just after the November holiday, and you had been fired from the school before November 7. She had also written some things about the children, which I already knew.

And then suddenly on the evening of the 8th [of January], I got such a marvelous gift: four photographs, the most precious thing that you could send. [. . .] All the detail in the photos is just wonderful. I have studied them more carefully than ancient Egyptian papyri are by certain Egyptologists: there we have your building (but the window isn't yours), the yard, the furniture, and the plants . . . Oh, how happy these pictures have made me! And somewhere there is a New Year's letter on its way to me. I am waiting for it eagerly!

I swear that I do not need anything right now! I also swear that if you send me money or anything else again, I will send it right back to you. By the middle of the summer, however, if everything turns out as I expect, try to set aside about 500 rubles for travel expenses and send it to me at the address I give you as soon as I ask for it. The rule is as follows: if you don't have money in your personal account, then they give you funds for the trip. If you do, then they take the cost of the ticket out of them. Well then, what's the point? . . .[1]

♦ ♦ ♦

January 19, 1947
Dear Niushenka:

For the last six days we have been experiencing a particularly sharp Epiphany cold snap: in the mornings the mercury drops below minus 50, and it is minus 51 or 52. In the afternoon it is minus 46 to minus 47. All work outdoors has come to a halt. All day long a *mga*, which is like a thick fog, hangs over us. You can't see the sun. The air is like molten steel. It feels as though it will burn your whole insides, almost like exploding gasoline, if you swallow it in more deeply. But, in general, it's nothing too dreadful! Particularly since it is warm in our office, and, thanks to you, I am pretty well equipped. The room where we live could be warmer, but at least I sleep totally undressed, without even my stockings on. But I do, of course, pull my coat over myself on top of my blanket.

Today I finished eating the Riga sprats and drank coffee with a piece of sugar between my teeth (all of it things you sent!). I am also still saving the rusks, which are like chocolates. I say this to show you how I am getting on. I have managed to make things last up to now. If I were really in need, I would have gulped everything down immediately. Does that convince you? [. . .]

I am writing in the office. It is late at night. After a long break of several days, there is electricity again. The radio is playing *The Queen of Spades* from the opera house in Novosibirsk. I have your dear photo in front of me: [where you are] on the couch. I only recently discovered how marvelous it is to have your dear faces on my desk and glance down at you tenderly from time to time [. . .]

1. The letter breaks off here.

January 20. The day of the "Epiphany Ball." Again it is 50 below. At the club they were going to try to show a film, but I didn't go. I had no desire to catch cold. This last year, I need to take particular care of myself, isn't that so, my dear ones? You have written about this too . . . Never fear, Senia won't make a mess of things. Now the main thing is for you to get through the last few months: what *bogatyrs* you've raised![2] [. . .]

Vania Efimov wants to get a spot with us and take courses to become a norm-setter. For this reason, for the first time since we have known each other, he treated me to dinner: fried potatoes with the official soup and sweetened tea with candy. I honored him with my presence, but all the same, he isn't very pleasant. But he looks wonderful! Greetings to everyone who remembers me: Nina and Boria, Aunt Mania . . . Big kisses to the children; I warmly embrace and kiss you, my one and only! Yours, Arsenii [. . .]

January 23, 1947.[3] I ask you not to get the wrong idea about the cold weather. It's just that I myself find it interesting that it can get down to such low temperatures, but people manage just fine: logs get hauled and trains still run . . . Magpies fly—although less often than usual. The sparrows have completely hidden themselves. Today one flew over after some crumbs, but he couldn't make it back. Apparently, his feet had gotten frostbitten, and he had nothing to push off with. I took him and gave him a push, and he flew . . . back home . . . to his family [. . .]

I cannot read your inspired lines about how all my things have been prepared for me, how everything waits for me, without tears welling up in my eyes. It is marvelously touching, like a fairy tale, but believe me: the only thing that I need is you, my dearest, and our splendid children who have been raised by you. The fact that you have survived these terrible years is God's great mercy on us. I kiss you all again and again. Papa Senia

2. *Bogatyrs* are the warrior heroes of Russian folk epics.

3. On a separate sheet of paper that was apparently enclosed with the preceding letter.

♦ ♦ ♦

February 9, 1947
Kansk[4]
My dearest Niushenka:

I have finally received what I was waiting for: letters are pouring forth as if from a horn of plenty—from you and from Dima, from both the old year and New Year's, letters with drawings and photos (I got everything), describing your great sorrows and also your rare tiny joys [. . .] It seems as though I can almost see with my own eyes how even your inexhaustible energy is running out, but I believe that it will last until we meet again.

You wrote about your plans to send Dima to a Latvian high school after he graduates from the seven-year school. (By the way, his New Year's grades really pleased me. His success in school makes up for a lot of the grief he has caused.) 1) Our son is Russian, and he will live in Russia. 2) Latvians will always look at him as a foreigner. Their old chauvinistic spirit won't disappear over the course of just two or three years of Soviet life. It will take decades of Soviet tutelage to rid them of this nasty trait. 3) Is there really no good Russian gymnasium near by? I wait to hear your reasoning; it is impossible to argue about a bare thesis.

My life remains the same. The weather is mild. My health is tolerable and, if compared to yours, just wonderful. [. . .]

Today is the national celebration—election day. Soon elections will take place where you are too, and you will be able to fulfill your joyous duty by voting for the candidates of the Stalinist bloc of Communists and non-Party members. My comrades who were released yesterday are so lucky! Today they are already voting!

Regarding people, not all of them are swine, as you wrote under the impression of your bitterness at life. No, far from all of them! I will go even further: if it were not for the good people I have met over the course of the past seven years, I would have never survived. And do you know who is the most marvelous person I have met? You, my sunshine! Honor and praise to you!

Thanks for all of your love and kindness, and for the children you have raised and educated especially! Yours forever, Senia [. . .]

4. Stamped by the camp censor.

♦ ♦ ♦

February 15, [1947]⁵
My dears:

Happy holiday! Yesterday I received Niusha's letter dated December 26, which was very good in tone and spirit, and, for this reason, made me very happy. Again and again: please do not think or worry about my physical needs! I take full responsibility as I say this, and also, of course, am filled with the desire to "make it." You also don't need to hunt for books. This year our library is receiving nice additions: we have things to read. The top shirt that you sent me fit perfectly. I will send you my neck measurement in centimeters just in case. Also, my tireless caretaker, do not assemble any sort of "dowry" for me in advance. Knock on wood, and so forth!⁶ And don't touch the pullover. After all, I am superstitious like Pushkin.

Your persuasive words had an immediate effect on me: do not save or set aside "all those old papers." In the next few days, I will begin to burn all the papers that have settled in boxes for no known reason. Right up to the most recent letter.⁷ I kiss you all warmly and think of you constantly. I am taking care of myself, and I urge you to do the same. Your Papa Senia [. . .]

♦ ♦ ♦

February 24, 1947
Dear Niushenka:

Forgive me for all my sins. Yesterday was Forgiveness Sunday (if the information I received is correct).⁸ On Friday the 21st, I had a real Shrovetide: I received your lavish package. It had arrived about two days earlier, but our postal department was moving to a new and very

5. A heavily damaged postcard with no return address.

6. In Russian culture, it is considered bad luck to buy baby things before the child is safely delivered. Formakov cautions his wife against preparing things in advance of his return out of a similar superstitious sensibility: sentences were often extended, and liberated inmates were more often sent into internal exile in rural areas than allowed to return home.

7. Formakov apparently destroyed all the correspondence he received from home before his release. His wife may have suggested this out of caution: some mail had arrived illegally.

8. The last Sunday before Lent. Traditionally on this day Orthodox Christians forgive each other their sins to prepare their hearts for the Great Fast.

comfortable space, and for that reason it was closed. They showed me the undamaged package with all its seals, and then they opened it, looked over everything, and began to give things to me one at a time. It all got here and got through in great shape, but they took all the foil off the nuts for the Christmas tree, and they lost their Christmassy look and aroma. Also, the two onions froze (but the garlic did well): clearly these were fruits of your garden! The mittens are wonderful. The fatback [*salo*] was stupendous; everyone marvels at it![9] I sliced it and salted it. Sausage is running 250 rubles a kilo, and I have already eaten half of it. It just so happens that I have butter, so the sandwiches are turning out really well: more than perfect![10] The cookies are a dream! The sugar is all it should be! I gave the tobacco products to various important people. The notebook is delightful! The packaging on the American vitamins is first-rate![11] People are stopping by just to see it. The two mysterious little boxes with sugary powder and a drawing of some sort of tuber are the only things that I haven't managed to decode up to now. When I have time, I will take them over to a German doctor. And the cocoa! Of course, I feel a little guilty scarfing all this down, since I sense that you yourselves could put all of it to good use. But what's done is done! For me this represents marvelous material and psychological support. It provides you with the feeling of having done your duty. I can vividly imagine how the process of packing this took place with your dexterous hands and the dexterous fingers of the children. This shows so much attention, love, and solicitous taste, characteristic of you alone.

A second parcel also arrived (with *Sovetskaia molodezh'*), and, inasmuch as events always take place all at once, during the same period I also received word from the wife of Evg[enii] Serg[eevich] Nikitin, our matchmaker. He is in the Kirovskaia oblast, and his post office box also begins with the letters LK. She is here and is working at our railway tie factory. She loads shavings onto cars. Tomorrow I also have to head out there, and, of course, I will see her. According to her, Ksenofont Kurmelev is living in our town and is a watchman at the city hospital.

9. In Russian and Ukrainian homes, thinly sliced cured fatback is often served as an appetizer. Camp inmates prized this pork product because it kept well, was calorically dense, and represented an excellent source of precious fats.

10. The phrase "more than perfect" appears in Latin.

11. "First-rate" appears in Latin.

He's living greedily and is saving up money, just as he has all his life, and won't let his daughter have new soles for her shoes.

Well, in any case, here's one fact that can be documented by witnesses: when Nikitina asked if there was a Formakov here, my comrades (in terms of place of residence and lifestyle) answered: "There is!" "Well, how is he getting on?" "Well!" they answered. That means that I haven't been lying. You have spoiled me, and now there will be no packages or money—it's taboo! And that package brought me Christmas joy, and Shrovetide pleasure, and will, of course, last all the way to my name day. That is how timely it was! It left Riga on January 30 and arrived here on February 20 (I am judging by the postmarks on the packaging).

On February 22, working under my direction, our cultural activists gave a big holiday concert that included twenty-eight numbers in honor of Soviet Army Day. I read my new ballad about four roads with some success. I enclose a sample for Dima. In it you can hear an echo of my personal mood. On the 23rd, we repeated the concert for a rally of exemplary workers. Today I am relaxing and writing. I can't manage to finish the story about the potato doll for Zhenichka, not because I don't have time, but just because I can't seem to come up with an ending that completely satisfies me. [. . .]

February 25. Today I saw Pulkheriia Konst[antinovna] Nikitina. A small elderly woman with a thick down of whitish hair all over her face.[12] She recognized me, but I did not recognize her. "How you have aged!" she said to me. [. . .] Evg[enii] Serg[eevich's] legs no longer work well, and he can barely walk even with a cane. He is working as a bookkeeper. She lives twelve kilometers outside of town. It just so happens that Kurmelev is here until March 1 in connection with work. He is married to Lebedeva and is a watchman at the city hospital. He's "living better than the director," but he's hoarding money like crazy. He has four children. She [Pulkheriia Konstantinovna] was at his place yesterday. He asked her to say hello to me and invited me to come for a visit when I am released. That will give me a place to sleep. "Pukhochka" remembered a prayer for my health, which really touched me.[13]

12. A sign of malnutrition.
13. Formakov uses a nonstandard nickname for Pulkheriia here.

Again and again, I cannot express how much love there is in my heart and how it longs to be with you. There is a piece of me in each of the three of you. When will all of this again be brought back together? I am sure it will be soon, and this certainty allows me to live and breathe. I am growing younger and am full of energy, as if never broken into pieces, because of this certainty. Hugs and kisses to you all. Yours, Senia[14]

♦ ♦ ♦

March 8, 1947[15]

What do I have the honor of wishing you the very best on? You, my treasured spouse, friend, and protector, my love and muse, who worries beyond measure, showers me with money and packages without measure, depriving herself beyond any conceivable measure for the children and for me, sinner that I am;

And you, my beloved son, Dmitri Arsenievich, whom I left a chubby, five-year-old child, and whom I find now an intelligent young man who has graduated from a seven-year school, a skier and athlete, an inveterate reader and a flourishing artist;

And you, my precious daughter Evgenia Arsenievna. Although I have never once seen you, I feel the ties of kinship in your every cell. Every curve on your little face is familiar, young lady who knows how to count to thirty and all her letters. I press all of you, my beloved trinity, so close to my heart, on this day, the last birthday I will spend apart from you, and I kiss you once, twice, three times, one hundred, two hundred, two hundred thousand times each. I feel particularly acutely now how I pine for your physical closeness. In my heart, you know, I have always been with you, as you have been with me.

Five hundred rubles arrived from you, Niushenka, just in time for this day. I was both overjoyed and terribly distressed: I cannot allow such expenditures on my account. I asked you so seriously and begged you not to do this under any circumstances unless I asked you to myself.

Volodia Lugovskoi is stuck here for two more years, poor fellow, and I had been hoping to have him bring you the presents I have had

---

14. A set of riddles for the children appears on the last two pages of this letter.

15. A hand-drawn and -colored wreath with a pink ribbon encircles the date, and Formakov includes a poem in honor of his birthday above the salutation.

set aside for so long: pencil cases for the children and a powder compact for Niushenka! Another acquaintance of mine here has suddenly become the local Zilbert and, if not in this letter then in the next, I will send you my likeness.[16] Why it looks so sad, I have no idea. I purposely thought about you and thought good, carefree, cheerful thoughts, but all the same, it turned out gloomy, judging by the negative. Since this opportunity came up unexpectedly, I wasn't able to change clothes as I should have and put on a collar and a tie and my "jacket," but I just managed to pull over my everyday blouse the green waistcoat with sleeves that you and I bought, Niushenka, during our last trip from Dvinsk to Riga.[17] Just a few days ago it was completely repaired for me and trimmed with the black edging that you sent in the package. [. . .]

March 15. Greetings from the name day boy, my dear, precious darlings![18] [. . .]

If I did not have to perform in the evening in *Na boikom meste* [In a Lively Place] and, moreover, worry about the whole production, my mood would be even better.[19] Or perhaps even worse. When you are busy and rushing about, you don't have time to descend into lyricism, and when it is a real holiday, memories really eat at your soul!

In the evening after the show. Finally, I can say, "Hooray!" The premiere was a success. The costumes and the sets turned out to be very appealing. In the auditorium, people were on the edge of their seats with attention. We started late, not at 8:00 but rather at 8:20, and then finished in two hours. Given our poor stage, this is a great accomplishment technically. Half the performers were sick with the flu, and there were quite a few blunders, but, on the whole, a real success. [. . .]

16. Zilbert ran a prominent photography salon in Latvia.

17. Formakov uses the word *spinzhak* for jacket, placing it in quotation marks. A mocking exaggeration of a lowbrow mispronunciation of the more standard *pidzhak,* which represents an English borrowing (pea jacket), *spinzhak* was associated with criminal argot. By inserting it here, Formakov underscores his own cultural alienation from the milieu that surrounds him. He still remembers the social norms of cultured society (donning formal wear for photographs) and can use *spinzhak* only in quotation marks.

18. March 15 is Saint Arsenii Day.

19. Formakov is appearing in an 1865 comedy by Alexander Ostrovsky.

After the play, I was called to the office of the woman who is our boss. The main boss was also there and asked how we all felt and then, after consulting with me, they decided to run the play again on the 16th. There will be a third performance for the best agricultural workers (March 24–26), and then a fourth one (the maximum here). We'll learn when that will take place later on. Since the 16th is a workday here, all those participating in the show have been excused from work, and they are all very pleased.

"The trick didn't work. Our Fakir was drunk."[20] For this reason, I am going to get my picture retaken by our Skakun this afternoon in the white Russian peasant shirt in which I perform in the evening. The first prints turned out to be beneath all criticism, even after every corrective coefficient was applied. [. . .]

I won't close the letter until I have the photograph. I am yours forever, now and always, and for all time.[21]

Senia, also known as Papa, who will kiss and embrace you all, my darlings, even more warmly in 1948.

March 17. I enclose two photographs. There it is: me with no embellishments. One is for you and one is for the children. I will send a third in the next letter, which is also for the children. Then they can divide them up: one for Dimochka, and the other for Zheniurka. Arsenii [. . .]

♦ ♦ ♦

It is a blessing when you find a woman
To live with till your hair turns white
In extreme old age and still, till the end of days,
Feel as in love as a raw youth.

(St[epan] Shchipachev)[22]

My darling,

Even here the weather is warming and we are waiting for the ice to break up. Today is Holy Thursday, and I've already been brought

---

20. A Russian expression taken, according to some sources, from an old review of an unsuccessful circus act involving a cobra and a fakir.

21. Here Formakov borrows liturgical phrasing: "i nyne, i prisno, i vo veki vekov."

22. From the 1946 poem "My vse mechtaem o liubvi bol'shoi" (We All Dream of a Great Love), Stepan Shchipachev, *Izbrannoe* (Moscow: Sovetskii Pisatel', 1947), 126.

several eggs for the holiday, but my soul is sorrowful with deathly despair. Perhaps this is because not long ago I received a children's greeting card for my birthday and the postcard you sent with the girl and the verses, which were *chastushka*-like but had lines that in our circumstance can cause real pain and sorrow: "There is no sweeter moment than when my darling comes." I would like to give that Time a knee in the rear, so that that moment comes a little less slowly . . .

There has also been some talk here. Iv[an] Iv[anovich] arrived home in the evening and knocked on the shutter; his wife looked out, saw who it was, and said gently: "No, Vania, go away! You can't be here!" He decided to spend the night at a neighbor's, but she summoned the police there, and they told him to leave town immediately, since he had no right to live there. But she sent packages here every month and affectionate letters saying how she was waiting for him!

Another fellow chose a city and then suddenly got a letter from his wife. He managed to secure permission to go there. He arrived and found that she has a new husband and two children. Finally, a third incident (all this has happened in the last ten days and with people I know well): a shoemaker left here a little while back. He settled in town, started earning money, and got into correspondence with his wife. Then he sent her 1,600 rubles and received in reply: "Thanks, the money was very helpful. As a matter of fact, I was preparing to get married again and threw my wedding using the funds you sent. If I can, I will repay you."

The issue isn't the acts of betrayal. Plenty of those happen everywhere, and they will continue to in the future. The issue is the totally incomprehensible lies, baseness, and deception! Of course, I have not a shadow of a doubt in this respect, but my heart does ache: how will life turn out? I clench my fists: I will get life in my grasp and make it dance to my tune! How many times has it all worked! Will it really fail this last time? Eh, my darling, will it all work out as we wish? I enclose a Japanese telegraph blank that was taken as war booty for Dima. The characters are read right to left. [. . .]

Don't send any more newspapers, and don't send money *under any circumstances*. If you have already sent the second package by mail, then there is nothing to be done. And if not, then forget about it. From every corner, people are writing that it is very hard to get groceries this spring.[23] Eat it [the food you would send] yourself, for God's sake! How can I prove to you that all this is absolutely unnecessary?

Reporting in: Yesterday I finished the second packet of glucose, the first bottle of vitamins, and the first box of them as well. I don't feel at all bad. My heart, at least, feels normal, and my other muscles have gotten so strong that I don't get up at all during the night.

For Easter, I have sugar, nuts, and cocoa (from you), candy, oatmeal, and about 700 rubles. Butter now is very rare and expensive. I will dig into it right after the holidays. I will have some pork for the holidays as well. [. . .]

April 16. Christ has arisen! Christ has arisen! Christ has arisen!

Exceptional circumstances forced me to take a break and delay sending this letter for a certain period of time. On the third day of Easter, my troupe was called to the Dzerzhinsky club in town, where we performed *In a Lively Place* for a conference of economic planners. The play was performed very energetically and was a well-deserved success. After dinner there was talk about the river being dammed up, and by the end of the day it became clear that our settlement was going to be evacuated. We were left to spend the night in the club. They gave us private rooms, and moreover, the men got the pioneers' room with a piano and a harmonium. There was a piano on stage as well, but there wasn't any sheet music, and, as you know, I can play anything from sheet music and nothing from memory. We found sheet music in the room and, although every fourth key was dropped and every third one was out of tune, I spent about three hours playing with our tenors after not playing music in so long. The guards were playing billiards nearby and didn't bother us, for which we were grateful![24] They gave us feather pillows, fed us sausage and bread . . . On the second day of Easter, planes were sent to bomb the places [where the river was] obstructed. On the third, the water level dropped, and by evening we were home, so to speak, where we found everything in perfect order. Our group and the settlement as a whole had an easy time of it through all these exceptional events. They fed us very well sometimes, and they

23. Another apparent reference to the famine of 1946–1947.
24. The word "guards" appears in Latvian, but transliterated into Cyrillic letters.

treated us better than we could have expected. Of course, the post office is backed up now.

Well, goodbye, my precious. Dimochka, be healthy and kind. Zhenichka, be obedient and give Mother a big, big kiss for me. Hugs to you all, Papa Senia

♦ ♦ ♦

> "Separation from you and bitter regrets
> Fill my heart."
>
> (from a romance)[25]

My dear Niushenka:

I long for your letters and am tormented by their absence! . . . After all, I have gotten accustomed to receiving envelopes from time to time with your wonderfully even and soothing handwriting on them or else Dima's script, as angular as a teenager who is becoming more self-assured with each passing month. I know that the letters become less frequent as the difficulties you face in your battle for survival increase, and you have never complained. "If they haven't come, then she just can't!" I never get my feelings hurt or grumble . . .

But a month passes, and I begin to curse the post office. Another passes, and I worry . . . When a third comes to a close, I am not even sure what to think. All sorts of fears and horrors pop up in my mind. And then, on June 1, my roommate dropped my mirror (the one you sent with the kitty on the back). In one corner, the mirror cracked. "That is not a good omen!" even though I didn't break it myself . . . Finally some kind people helped me. I send forward an inquiry and get an answer: everything is fine "now," as the person giving me the report put it. "Letters will come." I wait to learn what happened.

At the beginning of the summer, I returned to the building where I lived last summer. I sent you a drawing of its porch. There are flower-beds and shrubs in front of it and a table and benches where I have the marvelous opportunity to eat outdoors, and that always remind me a little of Stropy. There is an entryway with a wash basin and then two rooms. One is long and narrow, like the one that served as a storage area in our apartment on Varshavskaia. You have to go through it to

25. Formakov cites Aleksei Tolstoy's "Na nivy zheltye niskhodit tishina" (On Golden Cornfields, Silence Descends), which was set to music by Tchaikovsky.

get to the second room, which is a little like our dining room. [. . .] The left part of the [long skinny] room is painted green. We have divided it off [for ourselves] with a light partition that has a door in the middle. True, the partition does not go all the way to the ceiling. [. . .] My roommate Nikolai Ivanovich [is] the head of the club in regard to voluntary cultural work and serves as an accountant in the food-storage department in his day job. [. . .]

You can't imagine how pleasant it is, after six years of living with people continuously (no less than twenty to fifty at a time) and being constantly in the presence of others, to have the opportunity to latch the door behind oneself and . . . well, even spit at the ceiling. My roommate is a good fellow in general. Anyway, we live together in great harmony. He eats with his friends someplace else, so he often isn't here. I have a hot plate. Above the table, there is a light bulb that is covered in an orange shade with tassels (made of gauze). It was a gift that Nikolai Ivanovich received from a "lady." We always have books, magazines, and newspapers. I have the opportunity to read lying down after dinner and before I go to sleep!!! In the big room, there is a loudspeaker that plays radio broadcasts over the door, and we can hear it easily. About fifteen people live in that room. Mostly they are also active in cultural work. The walls are painted in a grey and blue-grey design and decorated with a frieze of medallions with portraits of Ostrovsky, Gorky, Pushkin, Tchaikovsky, Rimsky-Korsakov, and Chekhov! [. . .]

Lugovskoi tells me that, based on his letter from Zhenia, the photos I sent did reach you. I am very glad. So how do I look? Not too awful? Would you recognize me if you ran into me? I try not to think about getting out. Another half-year reduction as a privilege [for good behavior] may come through any day over the next one or two months, or it may not come at all, and then I will have [to wait] until January 30 unless there is something in connection with November 7.[26] Before writing to you about the possibility of another award of six months, I thought about it for a long time, but finally I did write because I wanted to inspire you to hold on through this most difficult year. Please don't be mad if fortune deceives us. I counted on it smiling upon us. It is high time for that old strumpet to start smiling!

---

26. Formakov is thinking that a special amnesty might be announced in connection with the anniversary of the October Revolution.

For a while now I have also been setting norms for the reports of our agricultural brigades and, of course, since I visit green houses and gardens, I have the chance to obtain cucumbers and radishes . . . And, when the time comes, I'll get tomatoes too. I still have some cash, and I am conserving it so that if I leave suddenly, I won't depart with empty pockets. [. . .]

June 19. Today I checked, and I still have 300 rubles in my account. Do you see how fine everything is for me? I just need to keep from getting caught up in my thoughts even for a single minute: I need to work, read, and sleep . . . But when you start thinking about things seriously, seven years are gone. I just want to get down on all fours and howl like a wolf. This is my only problem, and even you are not in any position to solve it for me. But all the same, you will be the one who has to try to heal this trauma later on with your love. And I will not remain in debt to you, because all these years were hard labor for you, but not for me. But let's not talk about that anymore . . .

June 22. I am putting on a big concert dedicated to the Great Patriotic War using a script that I wrote myself.[27] Since last year, we have had a very good summer stage from the point of view of acoustics, and on Sunday evening, when about 800 people are listening, first letting go and laughing, and then applauding wildly in appreciation, I get great satisfaction. I am satisfied by my work as artistic director and as a performer. People so need to smile for a moment, to forget, and to relax.

I warmly kiss you and give you such a big hug that your joints creak. Yours always, Senia. Your Papa [. . .]

27. In Soviet and Russian historiography, the term "Great Patriotic War" (Velikaia otechestvennaia voina) refers to the conflict between the Soviet Union and the European Axis powers, which began on June 22, 1941, when Nazi Germany invaded the Soviet Union, and ended on May 9, 1945, European Victory Day in Soviet time zones. This Russian historical term has a much narrower meaning than the English phrase "Second World War," which covers a longer time period (1939–1945) and more military conflicts.

◆ ◆ ◆

My dear Niushenka:

My dear son Dimochka:

My splendid daughter Zhenichka:

Yesterday, on the evening of July 11, I finally received your letters: one from Dima, written before Easter (sic!) on April 25, Niusha's from June 2, and Dima's from June 22 with his diploma. Whether it is the fault of your post office or our censorship office, I don't know, but that is all that has reached me from you since February 23 (besides the two telegrams, of course). I am very glad that you are relatively healthy. If you could only send Dima to camp somewhere, then everything would be just marvelous! That Zhenichka likes to twirl in front of the mirror and is a good worker makes me very, very happy. But, of course, what pleases me most of all and brings me the greatest pride is Dima's diploma. Great job, son! You have taken a big and very important step. You are on the road to an independent life, but never forget that all this was only possible thanks to your mother's care. Children, in the last few months of my absence, don't exploit her too much; all children are egoists and think only of themselves. Think about your mother at least some of the time. How is she sleeping? How is she eating? Should you be helping her with anything? Don't ask: "Is there anything I need to do, Mama?" Don't wait for her to give you instructions every time. You should feel in your own hearts: "That is what I need to do for Mama." And then do it! This will be the best kind of help.

My affairs still have not been clarified at all. Since two weeks ago, I have been able to leave the settlement on my own and go where I want before 8:00 in the evening. This is called being "guard-less" [beskonvoinyi] here. Of course, it was very pleasant to go around the city on my own, wherever I wanted, and to give two kopecks to the beggar asking for alms "for Christ's sake." Since I only had coppers in my hat, I didn't feel guilty about giving such a little mite. The main thing, of course, is the ability to go down to the river channel [protok] when you want to and take a swim. I do this very frequently, since this is a particularly hot summer.

It doesn't seem as though anything will come of the privilege [early release] I was hoping for, since the higher-ups have decided to introduce time off for good work [zachety]. For each day you work here, you will earn a day and a half or two days off your sentence. And that is for everyone! For this reason, no one is getting the old kind of privilege any more. They have announced the [new system of] time off for good work, but they haven't said when it will start. We still don't know.[28] My job is supposed to get me fifteen days off for every month, so if the system is introduced on July 1 (and it won't be later, since the order was read at the end of June), then I will get one and a half months for the third quarter of this year. That will move my release date to mid-December. October and November will also yield a month, so I may even "fly out" in the first half of November. If they start counting time off from an earlier date (they say perhaps it will be from April on), then I may already be free . . .

But so far the instruction hasn't been published, so I just have to sit and stew and, most important, leave you, to whom my heart flies, in the dark, and I have no idea when all of me will be able to fly to you . . .

It is very hard to get train tickets (to get to Moscow directly). If you can get to Krasnoiarsk on a commuter train, then you can get a plane ticket from there to Moscow. That costs 815 rubles, and the trip only takes a day. If you go in a train carrying both freight and passengers, it will take two weeks, and you'll end up spending even more on food. In other words, there are so many possible combinations that I have already shut my ears to all advice and decided: when the hour comes, I will choose the best thing that turns up.

I am drying rusks and saving up funds. The ticket will be purchased for me using state funds . . . Oh, if only it would happen soon . . .

After a long interval, today we will once again watch a film here: *Nebesnyi tikhokhod* [Slowpoke of the Skies].[29] By the way, it was shot in Latvia, so I will see places back home.

Volodia Lugovskoi has also made a "career" for himself. A few days ago, he got the right to move about without a guard, and they transferred him to work in town at the main administration. That is good in every respect.

---

28. For more on this reform, which helped improve the morale of prisoners and encouraged them to meet or exceed production targets, see Simon Ertz, "Trading Effort for Freedom: Workday Credits in the Stalinist Camp System," *Comparative Economic Studies* 47, no. 2 (2005): 476–91.

29. A 1945 Soviet musical comedy directed by Semen Timoshenko.

In a few weeks, our photographer, Lenia Subbotin, will head to Latvia by way of Moscow. He may stop by to talk with you. You can ask him about everything. He is a nice boy, but, of course, you should conduct yourself as you would with a stranger. Aside from me, anyone from here is a stranger. He [Lenia] is our guitar player and was the first person to show me around town. I am very thankful to him for the photographs, although I repaid him long ago. He has chosen Kemeri as his destination.[30]

I didn't see anything in Dima's letter about the hundred rubles that I sent him. Did they really go missing? That is vexing!

The final conclusion regarding my situation "as of today": I still have two to three months left. I will inform you immediately by telegram [when I am released]. Then it will take me three to four weeks to get to you . . . That will be the hardest part of all!

Why don't people have wings?

I will sell all my extra possessions. I will keep my fur coat, my suit, and my leather boots. I will monetize everything, because "greasing the palms" of the railway workers is absolutely necessary if you don't want to wait weeks to get on a train. They'll provide me with plenty of bread for the trip, and, really, I think I could get by without eating anything. I just want to go and to get to you, my dears!

I still have plenty of strength and energy, and in two or three years I will again manage to win a position for myself in life. After all, I have managed to get myself set up even here. I arrived starving and at first slept on the floor, underfoot. Now everyone pays me the honor of using my patronymic in addressing me. Last Sunday I wasn't paying attention to where I was going, and I stepped in a pothole and turned my ankle, spraining it. I spent two days in bed and then walked with a cane for three more. Literally, every other person [I saw] expressed sympathy and asked about it . . . Eventually it became more torturous than the limping. I kept making my explanation shorter and shorter, until at last I found the simplest and most flabbergasting version: "Gout!" By the time the person who had asked had come to his senses, I was far away![31]

30. A Latvian spa town forty-four kilometers from Riga.

31. The notion that a prisoner like Formakov might have gout astounds, because of the disease's association with opulent diets and lifestyles.

In terms of Dima, "all roads are open to the young here."[32] He described that very well at the time of his graduation. I think that Niusha's idea to send him to electrical school is the most correct and realistic . . . And if it doesn't work out, then we will see!

Out of the work for the puppet theater, I sent *Petrushka v zooparke* [Petrushka at the Zoo]. Did you get it?

Monday, July 14. The night is warm and quiet after a night and day of rain. On the radio, a cello is playing an old, melodic waltz. The scent of tobacco, that source of evening fragrance, fills the air. My soul is more quiet, bright, and calm than I can ever recall it being. I believe in our star and in the bright future of our motherland and our children. Yes, we will meet again in a few months, and I will do everything I can to make up for everything that I have missed during these years. I will give you, Niushenka, my darling, at least a little joy, affection, and attention. You will have someone to trust and to rely upon. And Dima will again have a father, a true friend, someone to help him, and a person to talk with man to man. And fatherless Zhenichka will have every opportunity to rumple and squeeze her very own real-life, big, living papa as much as she likes. [. . .] My heart just flies and flies to you! Your Papa Senia. Greetings to all who remember me. Here I have drawn fireworks! [. . .]

♦ ♦ ♦

July 21, [1947][33]
My good little dears!

Soon it will be the seventh anniversary of the day we parted, but I am as close to you and love you as much as I did then or perhaps even more, since all the trials I have endured have revealed all of you to me in a new light, and particularly you, my dear Niushenka, our mother-hero.

It is growing colder here. For me, nothing has changed, and there is no new information. I am very upset that Dima seems not to have received the hundred rubles that I sent him as a gift for his graduation

32. Formakov cites "Pesne o rodine" (Song of the Motherland), a 1936 Soviet patriotic song by Vasilii Lebedev-Kumach and Isaak Dunaevskii.
33. A plain postcard with no return address, no censorship stamp, and a 1947 postmark.

and transition to a new school! There are some real scoundrels in the world! And such a reliable fellow agreed to mail it! . . . In any case, my dear boy, I owe it to you, and you will receive it at the first opportunity . . . Would pharmacy school perhaps be better than electrical school? While discussing your future path, Dima, Vol[odia] Lugovskoi and I really fixed on pharmacy. He is an electrician but would have preferred the former. Be happy and healthy, your Papa Senia

♦ ♦ ♦

July 24, 1947[34]
My precious dears:
   Two days ago I received two letters from you dated July 6, one from Dima with a description and plan of the room and one from Zhenia with the portraits. Wonderful! In a few days I will write you a letter. I really need to know: in the telegram I sent asking for information when I hadn't heard from you in three months, was there a phrase about sending Dima a hundred rubles or was there not? If the person who sent the telegram omitted that phrase, then he didn't send the money. Today I will probably send that gift to Dima. I am sorry it is late, but it is not my fault. I aimed to get it there a month early! In our correspondence, it would be better if you didn't talk about money but instead about my gift to Dima in connection with school. Kisses to you all, Papa

♦ ♦ ♦

July 28, 1947
My dear, precious darlings:
   Several days ago, I was walking back from town on a street that runs parallel to the train tracks, and a tiny little boy called out to me. Here people call them "punks" [patsany].[35] He came up about to my knee or perhaps just a little bit higher. He had a clean face and a clear gaze. "Uncle, ah, uncle! Are you headed to the station?" "No, dearie. The station is

   34. A plain postcard with no return address and no censorship stamp.
   35. The word patsan entered popular usage in the 1920s and was used in both ordinary Russian slang and the special dialect employed by the career criminals who exerted a dominant influence on the cultural environment in Soviet labor camps. Formakov might reasonably have assumed that his wife would not know it. See P. Ia. Chernykh, Istoriko-etimologicheskii slovar' sovremennogo russkogo iazyka (Moscow: Russkii Iazyk, 1993).

back there. Why do you want to know?" "Take me to the station. I know the way from there myself." It turns out that the lad needs to take a trip. His older brother is out at the [family] plot. "Is he big?" (I ask about his age). "That high!" (he indicates a spot a little higher than his own head, meaning his height). They'll come back together from there. Their mother works in a labor colony.[36] Their father died in the war. They have many brothers and sisters. My conversation partner was named Vovka. He was five . . . So I explained to him what a station was (where the trains stand; where they stop) and how you travel (the cars and wagons move along the rails). Then he got caught up in trying to catch a butterfly among the saltbushes by the side of the road. It flew off, and so be it. I say: "It would rather fly free than beat against your fist!" "Yes," he says, and starts beaming. "Are both the butterflies and the birds God's?" "Yes, they are," I tell him, and, hoping to distinguish myself, start to tell him that there are white butterflies with black spots that lay their eggs on the underside of cabbage leaves. For that reason, they are called "Cabbage Whites." Caterpillars come out of the eggs, which eat the leaves. "I know, I know," says Vovka, very satisfied at his own cleverness. "They are white like a head of cabbage." "Exactly," I say, happy that he is so clever. And, without any hesitation, he continues: "And there are also red butterflies. They put their caterpillars on carrots!"

I was quite struck by the steely logic of his childish mind. I couldn't think of any way to sway him from this position, so I gave up. Soon our paths parted. He saw his garden plot, and I needed to turn and move along the railway tracks. "Thanks, uncle!" he cried out to me in farewell. "Thank you for the company!"

Despite all the years I spent talking with children, I really put my foot in it! Even now, I can't help smiling when I imagine Vovka showing off his newfound knowledge later on: white butterflies lay their eggs on cabbage, and red ones lay theirs on carrots. The older folks listen in amazement: what idiot enlightened their Vovka?

It's evening now, about 10:00. It's raining heavily. All day it was humid. I went out to the garden plots. I got a pair of tomatoes and about ten cucumbers and, most important, a bunch of radishes!

---

36. As distinct from a labor camp, a labor colony was a minimally restrictive site for forced labor that was reserved for juveniles and those convicted of petty offenses.

Volodia was just here. He also just received a letter from his wife and immediately came over to share the news, particularly since there were lines about me—that An[atolii] Iv[anovich] is eagerly expected; his suit has been pressed and a pullover is being knitted for him.

My darling Niushenka! I really don't need anything at all. I will come in whatever pants and shirt I have and am prepared to wear them for the rest of my life. I can sleep on the floor with a brick under my head . . . And Volodka agrees with me on this: after everything that we have been through, the most important thing for us, and, really, the only thing we care about, is you, our precious darlings. We don't want to be separated from you: that is our only dream, source of happiness, blessing, and hope! And you are still so busy with homemaking cares and taking care of us all. Take care of yourself. Eat better. Even Dimusha complains that you give them all the best things. For them, it will never be enough . . . And if you end up losing all strength, who will be the first to suffer? Why, the children will!

Dimusha, your mother has given you a wonderful book! By the way, the author, Furmanov, has the same name as you do—Dmitri. He is from somewhere near Moscow—Ivanovo, I think. "Chapai" is a wonderful character and Furmanov's depiction of him is very vivid, although the novel is weak in its literary style in some respects.[37] [. . .] But the main thing, of course, is not that but rather the vivid exposition and the heartfelt patriotism of this remarkable personality, a popular hero who died like Ermak and fought like Pugachev and Razin.[38] Incidentally, it is also very good that Furmanov does not efface some of the negative sides of his hero. This only makes him dearer and more attractive to readers!

Zhenichka, thank you for the marvelous drawings. I particularly liked my own portrait and all the flowers.

37. The novel in question, Furmanov's *Chapaev* (1923), served as one of the "models" that inspired the style of Socialist Realism. Formakov uses a shortened nickname for the work's eponymous hero. On model novels and the Socialist Realist tradition, see Katerina Clark, *The Soviet Novel: History as Ritual,* 3rd ed. (Bloomington: Indiana University Press, 2000).

38. Ermak led the Russian conquest of Siberia in the sixteenth century. Stenka Razin and Emelian Pugachev were leaders of seventeenth- and eighteenth-century popular rebellions.

The instructions for the law about time off for good work have not been released yet, and this is starting to strain even my steely nerves. I am hoping for October.

I apologize for the strain I am placing on your nerves, but, believe me, as soon as everything is entirely clear, I will telegraph immediately.

I have personally wired Dima a hundred rubles for graduating from the seven-year school. It will arrive addressed to his mother, however. I think that he will guess that he should treat his mother, Zhenia, and Grandmother to something like ice cream. Your Papa-Senia, who loves, misses, believes, and hopes.

I hug and kiss all of you, whom I yearn to be with in both body and spirit, so that I can pull you into my arms and just stand, rooted to the spot.[39]

♦ ♦ ♦

Sunday, August 3, [1947]
My dear, splendid Niushenka:
Respected Dmitri Arsenievich:
Dear Zhenichka:

Last night something very joyful happened: I got your letter of July 16, which contained a completely unexpected and wonderful photograph of my splendid children. It excited and touched me very deeply (to tears—I am not ashamed to admit it), as the very first pictures did. It is too bad, of course, that Mama is absent [from the picture]. That is terribly bad on her part, all the more so since she had her hair styled in a wave.

That wave got me so excited that I did not sleep all night. My Niushenka, who has always denied herself everything, in advance of my anticipated arrival, made the decision to take such a step! There is so much love in this for me, sinful and inadequate though I am! Such expectations—and again disappointment. But I swear to God, I am doing everything I can here to slip out even a day earlier. You have no conception! Tomorrow or the day after tomorrow we will learn the details of our time earned for good behavior at last, and only then will my [release] date be clear. I will telegraph you about it so that you are not tormented

39. This last line curls in a coil at the bottom of Formakov's letter.

Dmitri and Evgenia Formakov. [1947]. Arsenii Ivanovich Formakov Papers, Hoover Institution Archive, Box 3.

by uncertainty anymore, although I myself have been tormented no less, believe me!

My answers to [the questions in] Niushenka's letter:

1. What advice can I give you about the children? I am completely unacquainted with current life, how it is organized, the options and requirements that exist, and even with the sch[ool] system. In my opinion, one thing is clear: whatever you do, whichever choice concerning schools you make for Dima and Zhenia, it is not forever or irreversible. If I come back and we see that things aren't going well, then we will transfer them and change things. Perhaps you should let Zhenia stay home for another year. What would be so bad about that?

Decide for yourself: unconditionally and without looking to me!

2. No chaise longues and furniture! After all, one enormous problem still faces me: moving back to Riga to live. People say that's almost impossible.[40] Particularly right away. Keep that in mind!

3. I am completely crushed by the new money from you. After all, I asked you, begged you, and swore an oath. I am not sending it back

40. As noted in the Introduction, Gulag releasees were often required to remain in internal exile in areas far from their homes indefinitely. Gaining permission to return to a capital city such as Riga was particularly challenging.

immediately because I do not have it: it is in my personal account, and, in general, we are forbidden to make such transfers.[41]

4. Don't assemble a package under any circumstances. Don't take advantage of my powerlessness! What can I swear on to convince you that I am not living badly and, in any case, am living better than you?

You are such a tease! I send you these frightening drawings of myself and awful photos. And you managed to wriggle out of getting your picture taken along with the children!

But for me this would be an indescribable joy, the joy of joys! Although they have your dark eyes, I still see myself in them. All respect and praise is due to you for raising such wonderful young people [. . .]!

Hugs and kisses. Excuse the handwriting. I was rushing. Your Papa Senia

♦ ♦ ♦

August 4, [1947]
My marvelous dears!

I just can't stop looking at your picture. I even started a poem [about it]. I haven't written anything in so long! But until I can put the finishing touches on it (and poetry is, more than anything else, an exemplary ordering of thoughts and the words that express them), I want to jot down my thoughts. First of all, in the photo I see Mama. The two spheres of her eyes, black like beads, and shining like cherries, look out on Papa, sadly and tenderly. Mama's bow is atop Zhenia's head. I first saw Niushenka with exactly such a bow, when she was a schoolgirl, and the sight of Zhenia with this kind of bow takes me back to long ago in the past. I also see Mama in the tidiness of her children, in their outfits, including the three bows on Zhenia's chest (my sense is that Grandmother deserves some of the credit for this too), in their smoothly combed hair, in how refined and cultured they look on the outside, in the awareness that I see in their gaze, which is, of course, primarily the result of Mama's efforts to raise and educate you in such a difficult period and such a supremely difficult situation: without me, without a home (it burned down!), without anything and out of nothing . . . Our mama, children, is made out of the same sort of material as saints were in ancient times.

---

41. The word "forbidden" appears in Latvian.

Then, excuse me, but I also see myself in the photograph: in your broad, large, and sloping foreheads, in Dima's chin, in the way he holds his lips, and also, I think, in Zhenia's nose. Yes, my sly girl! You have my nose.

Then I track your growth on my wall. Wonderful. What is going on? If I am stuck here for much longer, Dima will pass me in height! What is the meaning of this? I really must hurry home! . . . At their current height, Zhenichka comes right up to my belt buckle, and Dima reaches to my collarbone. It is terrific, just terrific!

Now, after this relatively lengthy introduction, allow me to move on to my main topic.

Let's start with Zhenichka as the youngest. It is good that she closed her mouth: there is no reason to show off missing teeth. Also, it almost seems as follows: I have closed my mouth and am silent. Papa, you wouldn't hear me anyway, but when you come, I will spin you a long tale! I will talk and talk, and you will listen . . . Her eyes are cunning, but I can tell that she is affectionate and no small mischief-maker! (But that is no surprise! She is 120 centimeters tall!) She came out very well [in the picture]. She looks vivacious and very dear to me. And her hair is so blond! Is that right? Or is it just the light reflecting?

Now about my son. His face is so amazingly changeable. There is 1) the one I remember; 2) the way he looks where he is together with Zhenia, and she is in her little pants; 3) where he is laughing in the garden; 4) at the zoo; and now a fifth version. In each, something new obscures the familiar. His hair seems so very fine. That means his temperament is mild. His ears are big, like a musician's. In the way he holds his lips, there is something very "adult." His neck is very thin. Is that a pen flashing in his pocket? The picture was very well shot. It almost seems as if he is about to speak. What is his voice like? Do I still remember it?

Lord, how many thoughts and emotions! Thank you. I send my respects in recognition of this gift. It will carry me to the end of my sorrows! I show it to everyone and am so proud. Today I showed it to our boss. She has a fifteen-year-old daughter, who just barely managed to graduate from a seven-year school this year. Some people have stopped by just to see it! Also, about Dima's future: where does he want to go? Make the decision on your own. I approve it in advance.

Next week I will try to send you a package with two engraved pencil cases for the children and a powder compact for you: the present that

I have had set aside for so long. Don't focus on its modesty; it is from my heart.

Kisses, lots of kisses. Your Papa Seniura, who loves you ardently always. [. . .]

♦ ♦ ♦

Wednesday, August 20, 1947
My dears,

How are you? The last few months have been particularly hard for me to bear. There is a reason why people here say that the last half year is worse even than the first, but "there are happy moments too" [by-vaiut i veselye minutki]. I will tell you about our concert that we took on tour. There are three state farms in our circuit, and they have been asking us for awhile to bring a concert. But that isn't easy: 1) you need a vehicle, 2) you need guards, and there are no extra sharpshooters or vehicles.[42] It often happens that there is an automobile, but there is no one to go with us, or there are sharpshooters, but there isn't a vehicle. On Saturday the 16th, everything was in order, but we left at 7:30 instead of at 6:00. There were sixteen of us. We were all let off work at 3:00 p.m. We all shaved, got our costumes and instruments together. We fit into a ZIS truck quite comfortably (three carpenters traveled there with us). Our boss sat up with the driver. We took a trunk with our wardrobe with us, and also curtains and decorative side-panels, which were made of wood because canvas was in short supply [. . .] It was grey and cold. The roads to town and through the town were a network of back-to-back ruts and potholes, but, as soon as we crossed the river Kan and started to climb the hill, the highway turned out to be quite tolerable. For the first half of our journey, we were surrounded by fields and meadows, with villages only rarely appearing from behind the trees. The road uphill was terraced as opposed to a spiral, and at each new level, off to the west, a vista opened up allowing us to see an expanse of fifty kilometers. Down in the hollow, the city was lost amid the smoke streaming from factory smokestacks, on the horizon the Kan shimmered like a series of separate lakes, and the sunset's golden fringe dressed up the grey tones of the picture.

---

42. Even if some of the individual performers were de-convoyed, as Formakov was in this period, regulations required that guards accompany the group.

Suddenly someone shouted: "Watch your heads!" It turned out that there was a swing-beam barrier across the road in the village, and it was set so low that if you were standing and didn't bend your neck, it would hit you right in the head. Then we caught up to a gas-generator truck (which uses firewood for fuel) on which several men, including Volodia Lugovskoi, had left for Resheta station at 3:00 in the afternoon. It was impossible to pass them. They remained right in front of the nose of our truck, torturing us shamelessly. A battle ensued right out of a movie: we start pushing it, and it pulls away a bit, but then something happens to it, and it stops at the very edge of the road, and we let out a roar of triumph at having defeated the Indians. Moreover, our trumpet player Mitia plays something very inflammatory on his trumpet. Those we have defeated start yelling and waving their hats.

Here I need to make a lyric digression: for several months they have been trying to get Volodia to go on some sort of special work assignment to our central repair shop, but he kept putting it off. Finally, on Thursday evening he came to see me to say goodbye. We kissed each other goodbye "until we meet again in Riga!" I gave him four cucumbers to take with him on the trip in case he got thirsty. True, he didn't actually leave until Saturday, just before us, with two other repairmen. And then on Tuesday I got a note that he had sent from there. Things aren't so good for him there so far. As is always the case in a new place, everything appears in the blackest possible shade, particularly after Kansk. At his request, I am sending a postcard to his wife today with his address. She shouldn't worry. [. . .] Just in case, here is his new address: Resheta station, Krasnoiarsk railway, P.O. box LK 235–5.

Once we reached Ilansk (about twenty-five kilometers away), we turned off at a right angle, and that is when it really started: ruts and potholes, a wooden bridge every kilometer, all broken down with no on-ramp or off-ramp. In other words, if we had wanted to shake things up a bit for ourselves on this trip, then we sure got that to the fullest extent. Taiga all around, a forest that has been pretty well cut through [. . .], and then we go twenty more kilometers.

At 11:00 at night we see the lights of the state farm. A signal blast from the trumpet brought them all out of the barracks and into the courtyard: they were really eager for our arrival. They bring out bouquets of flowers, start kissing the girls they knew (we have two with us: a singer and an actress). We go into the club. First we sit in the dark, but then they twist in the light bulbs. Then we have supper at tables decorated with bouquets of asters: potatoes fried in strips with cured fatback, tomatoes, pickles, cowberries, fresh peas, and a half liter of milk apiece. They also give us about 200 grams of bread. Then they told us to go to bed in the barrack, but some well-wishers whispered that they were full of lice, so we decided to sleep in the club. Only our girls went off with their female friends. They brought us some cots, blankets, and bedding. We went to bed at about 2:00. Some slept on wood couches (I did), others on stools that were set in a row, and some on tables. At 9:00 in the morning, the first ones to wake began moving the furniture the others were sleeping on, and they all fell on the floor. Big laughs from everyone. We washed ourselves in the bath house and went to breakfast. The food was good and plentiful all the time.

Then I go to the office of the director of the state farm. A livestock specialist and the head guard are there. They give me material on the best and worst people in the state farm. In such situations, I feel as though I am a journalist again and am conducting an interview. Then everyone leaves, and I rework the material I have been given right there. I leave, accompanied by the sixty-seven-year-old man who is the director's orderly. He is a wonderful hay-stacker. He's about Dima's height. A thick grey beard fans out over his whole chest. And he is courting a nineteen-year-old . . .[43]

The weather is rainy, so everyone has been let off of work. Otherwise they work with no days off from 6:00 [in the morning] until 8:00 in the evening. They get up at 5:00. We gave two concerts: at 2:00 and at 9:00. After our program, there is a dance. Three-quarters of the population of the state farm is women. For this reason, our young men start to form acquaintances and begin courting very quickly. All the free laborers and their wives and children also came [to the concerts].[44] They applauded wildly and threw bouquets of flowers to all the performers . . .[45]

43. Younger suitors were in short supply because of wartime casualties.

44. Formakov initially used the modifier "from the surrounding area" to describe the free laborers, but then crossed it out.

45. Formakov depicts the audience of free laborers as less restrained in their response to prisoner performance than other sources suggest. As Alan Barenberg notes, camp theater shows "had the potential to disrupt social hierarchies and spa-

I'll describe the opening of the evening concert for you. The curtain opens to the strains of the old foxtrot "Oh, Mona," to which we have added new lyrics with the chorus "Ah, how d'ye do!" instead of "Oh, Mona!" All the jazz musicians are in white trousers and white smoking jackets with scarlet lapels and scarlet edging on their cuffs. Each one has a white aster in his buttonhole. An energetic, cheerful tune. After a few bars, our soloist Volodia Zadoenko (a baritone in the style of Leshchenko) comes out and sings: "So we have come to you—ah, how d'ye do!—our ensemble and I too."[46] (Everyone gets up and sings, "Ah, how d'ye do!") "We flew as fast as we could—ah, how d'ye do" (each time this chorus is sung by a new jazz musician). "On the way, we got stinking drunk—ah, how d'ye do! In our ensemble, we've got—ah, how d'ye do!" (Here each person gets up and introduces himself: Mitia, Misha, Leonid! And all three together sing: "Ah, how d'ye do!") Then Zadoenko continues: "On the way our car—ah, how d'ye do!—did a terrible salto" (the trumpet player demonstrates and then plays one)—ah, how d'ye do![47] "And we almost died of our wounds—ah, how d'ye do! [. . .] Our whole show is led—ah, how d'ye do!—by the man who's coming out." (I join in through a megaphone from behind the curtain—"ah-ah-ah"—and then head out onto the stage, and, having held the fermata for as long as possible, finish with "how d'ye do!") Laughter, happy animation, applause, flowers. Then I read a few tonic couplets about my impressions, noting all the state farm's best workers. I congratulate them on their achievements in the name of our whole group of cultural activists and wish them . . . There's a flourish, and the program starts. I introduce the numbers, sometimes cracking jokes to lift the general mood. I always used to do this when I taught during long explanations. In our program, we have [numbers featuring] a female singer and two male singers, a reciter of verse, and me, and also two short sketches (about ten minutes each).

---

tial divisions" and, as a result, were often a "source of anxiety" for both nonprisoner audience members and the inmates who entertained them. *Gulag Town, Company Town: Forced Labor and Its Legacy in Vorkuta,* The Yale–Hoover Series on Stalin, Stalinism, and the Cold War (New Haven: Yale University Press, 2014), 82–83.

46. Petr Konstantinovich Leshchenko (1898–1954) was a popular singer of the period.

47. In both Russian and English, the word "salto" can refer to either a somersault or a musical passage that progresses by skips or leaps.

The accompaniment is sometimes the whole jazz band and sometimes just the violin, the guitars, and the drum ... We have "Nochen'ka" [The Night], Glinka's "Zhavoronok" [Lark], a song from *Slowpoke of the Skies,* a Ukrainian tango that's a duet, and the foxtrot "Diadia Vania" [Uncle Vania] ...

It all goes well, but it is hard for the singers to sing, given how they have stuffed themselves ... After the concert, the director gets up on stage, shakes my hand, and thanks us for everything. I thank him for the welcome we received, the lads manage to finagle some tobacco for themselves for the road, and that is it. They wake us at 4:00 in the morning, and, with farewell good wishes, we're on the road in half an hour. We're back home again by 7:30. We sleep until dinner, and then, after dinner, we head back to work. That is how we sometimes travel.

Today (August 22) I ate the new potatoes back at my place for the first time. I cooked them myself on the hot plate, sprinkled dill on them, and ate them with yogurt. For good cultural work, I get half a liter of milk every day (for a ruble). That's how it is here! ... Papa [...]

♦ ♦ ♦

August 26, [1947][48]
Dear Niushenka:

Today I am finally sending the presents that I have had set aside for almost a year for you, the children, and Grandmother. They will come addressed from A. I. Kapustinskii, residing at 17 Gorky street in Kansk, Krasnoiarsk region. Yours always, Senia

♦ ♦ ♦

August 30, 1947[49]
My darling child Zhenichka!

This letter is just for you. I haven't written to you alone in a long time. I have gotten so wound up in my work, as tight as this spiral.[50]

48. A plain postcard with no return address, no censorship stamps, and a 1947 postmark.

49. The date appears in green and does not match the ink used in the body of Formakov's letter. The name Zhenichka in the salutation is highlighted in the same green tone.

50. Here Formakov draws a tight spiral. This whole letter is heavily illustrated in colored pencil.

I need to work in the office and also put on shows. I set a stool at the front of the stage and command my actors just as Suvorov did the guards. I also have to dash to the vegetable garden two kilometers away, so that I can return with my briefcase stuffed full of, say, tomatoes, and make quick trips to the city three kilometers away to drop a letter to you into a mailbox.[51] I need to cook something supplementary for myself on the electric hot plate and talk to about twenty people a day, who come to me either on business or for no particular reason; I run down to our shop to buy a half liter of milk, though the line isn't very long. What about getting the newspaper and reading it? Running to the bath house and taking a shower? Turning in my laundry to be mended? Listening to the orchestra's rehearsal, calming down the female vocalist, who isn't allowed to sing anything new, and also the male vocalist and an actor? And despite all this, it is important to never let yourself get out of sorts, to be polite and amiable with everyone and particularly with those who depend on you or who are lower in terms of their development or position (for instance, I am a norm-setter, but he is a simple laborer) . . .

On August 28, right on the Feast of the Assumption, the temperature dropped below freezing for the first time and got to 3 below. That means farewell to Siberian summer and hello to Father Frost! The potato leaves all turned black, and the cucumbers froze from the roots up. Nonetheless, our marvelous gardeners managed to produce masses of tomatoes, cucumbers, and even watermelons and yellow melons (by setting them out early in greenhouses). Yesterday I received a third of a watermelon as a present and was terribly sorry that I couldn't treat you to some of it. [. . .]

It has been raining all day today. I am sitting at the table and writing. There is a vase with a bunch of scarlet asters and a mirror, into which I glance, on the table. A cricket sings behind the stove [. . .] My neighbor is eating a salad and talking to himself: "More than anything else, I love vitamin C, cured fatback, butter, [meat?], and eggs."

I have my whole portrait gallery right here on the table. I brought it over and am admiring it. I haven't looked it all over in awhile. There's

51. Because he can now move about without a guard, it is easier for Formakov to circumvent camp censorship: he can just discreetly drop letters into ordinary mailboxes. This, in fact, is how many prisoners with this coveted status sent mail home.

my daughter Zhenichka at one and a half with cheeks just like tomatoes! Zhenichka, give Mama, Dima, and Grandmother my kisses. I kiss
and hug you as many times as there are kilometers between us. There
you go, my darling daughter!

◆ ◆ ◆

My dear Niushenka,

The day before yesterday, I finally made it to the Kurmelevs'. As
I recall, Nikitina even gave me the address and said that they were
living well, but that he himself was pretty miserly. In the summer, I
stopped by once on a Sunday, but there was no one there. This time,
I was lucky. They have a one-room cottage with one window and a
stove in the middle. There is a pig pen right next to it and a cow shed.
Petrovna was loading the stove, and I asked permission to come in
from the courtyard. When I came in, she recognized me immediately.
That means I don't look too awful! I couldn't recognize her at all. She
seemed glad to see me and insisted on offering me something to eat
(coffee with bread and butter). There was an icon in the corner, household dishes, some kind of sugar bowl from the dawn of time . . . It all
evoked homey comforts to such an extent that I spent the rest of the day
wandering around in bewilderment (I was there at about 11:00 in the
morning).

Then Natasha came. She was exactly like she was in Dvinsk. Only
then she was sixteen. For five years she had been out of school, but
then last year she started going again. Now she's in the tenth grade.
She works in the hospital and is something like a nurse's aide. The boy
wasn't at home. The two oldest were already in Latvia, but she hasn't
been allowed to go back yet. She is interested in going back with me
and is trying to get permission. She's hopeful that she will get it.

The most awful thing is that several months ago her husband was
arrested again and got another ten-year sentence in connection with
the decree of June 4.[52] An irrepressible money-grubber, he stole some
grain from a nearby warehouse that he was supposed to be guarding

---

52. The decree of June 4, 1947, dramatically lengthened sentences for petty
workplace thefts. Individuals caught misappropriating even insignificant sums and
items of state property could receive sentences of seven to ten years at hard labor. For a description of the implementation of this decree, see *Istorii stalinskogo
gulaga,* 7 vols. (Moscow: Rosspen, 2004), 1: 568–70.

and then deposited the money in a bank account that his family didn't know about. He "piled up" 28,000 rubles! His wife still hasn't learned where he is. She cries and reproaches him . . . At the same time she told me that the oldest daughter of Evgenii Sergeevich Nikit[in] (from his first marriage), Zoia, is serving a five-year sentence right here . . . When I get out, you can send money to their address if you need to . . . It has gotten easier to get train tickets from here, so that is good news!

Yesterday my friend finally sent a package with gifts to his family. A year ago, when he had some money saved up, he ordered some pencil boxes from a woodcarver for his children. He packed them up, wrapping them carefully in cardboard, as though they were books, so that he could send them in a parcel. He asked someone to take them to the post office, but they wouldn't accept them. Then, when he had the chance, he obtained a powder compact made of "*kap*," a burl from a larch. Although, one after another, people left for Latvia, no one would take them. Finally, he was allowed to move about without a guard. He decided to arrange it all himself. He carried the things beyond the gates (where the search takes place) in three separate trips, got a wooden crate at the post office, had it remade, and then he got some scraps of fabric, and he sewed it up himself.[53] He had someone else carry the crate to work, and then he put everything into it, adding a little elephant for Grandmother, and carried it to the post office. He was late. He left everything with strangers. The next time he went back and filled out the form. "Have the contents been inspected?" So he headed over there. Then he got to the window, but they wouldn't take it. The seams weren't right. It needed to be sewn up from the inside and using a sewing machine. The third time he brought a cover that had been sewn on a machine, but they had put a patch on it, so again it was rejected. The fourth time, the cord came apart when they were wrapping it around. Finally everything was right. Even then he was afraid: the new cover had been made without the crate being present—it was always left in town overnight—and when he was writing the address, he didn't allow enough room: he ended up having to use the second side. But once you've started something, you should finish it . . . He handed it in and

53. Clearly here Formakov is describing his own actions in the third person out of caution: he violated multiple camp disciplinary rules in mailing the package. Soviet postal regulations required that wooden crates be sewn up in sheets of fabric.

breathed a sigh of relief. After all, in addition to everything else, an errand like this requires a window of about three hours of free time (the town is four or five kilometers away), and you need to keep from being seen . . . But now it is done! We won't take such risks anymore.

In the morning it is below freezing. Tomorrow there is a concert in Moscow for the tenth Olympiad of Amateur Performance, and who knows what the results of that will be.

Big hugs and warm kisses to Dima, Zhenia, Grandmother, and, of course, you, my darling. Yours, Senia

September 6 [1947]

♦ ♦ ♦

Thursday, October 9, 1947
Hello, my dearest Niushenka!

It is 11:00 in the morning. On the radio they just announced that wet snow is falling on Moscow and that it is just 2 degrees above freezing, but here we have had wonderful warm sunny weather for days, with not a single cloud.

I received your long, sad letter. I see your whole life and thoughts perfectly clearly. I have only one thing to say: hold on, my darling, hold on just a little more. I know that my arrival will not make anything better initially and will just make things harder financially, but spiritually this will be an unending source of new strength and renewal for both of us.

I give you my word that within a year your life will be completely tolerable. Until then, I am willing to sleep on the floor and subsist on potato peels. I will wash the floors for you, peel the potatoes, haul water, chop wood, and trim your fingernails . . . And you will support me until I can get back on my feet (just think, I will be your dependent!).

Now, about my sentence, time off is calculated quarterly, beginning from the 1st of August. Right now everything is still being worked out, and the time off won't be clear until at least the 25th. If my work is rated "excellent," then I will receive the maximum for August and September, one day off for each day worked. In other words, my sentence will be reduced by two months. Since my sentence will end on January 30, it [my release date] should be about November 30. I won't get anything for October or November, since that quarter won't have ended. I have done everything I can and very much hope to leave on the strength of my work by the beginning of December. How I would like to be there for Dima's name day!

Well, there is no sense crying about it! I will be there for Zhenia's birthday and name day, and for yours as well. Lord, will this really all come to pass?

In any case, as soon as I know the new end [of my sentence] exactly and officially, I will telegraph. When I get out, I will also telegraph. And then I will head home through Moscow.

How are the airmail letters reaching you? I just started using this service recently, particularly since I have so many stamps. [. . .]

I am not going to spend money buying you gifts: the main thing is to get home myself. I will be the gift, and I hope it isn't a bad one, although grey-haired, a bit aged, and wrinkled.

Warm kisses and hugs to all of you. Yours always, Senia [. . .]

♦ ♦ ♦

Monday, October 27, 1947
My dears,

I haven't heard from you in an eternity: no letters, no packages, and no money. The second and third are not important, particularly since I have been so insistent that you not send packages and I don't even know if you sent money—perhaps you didn't. You wrote about the package, however, as though it were a fact . . . I am desperate for your letters. I write to you regularly every week, and always by airmail, but then I don't know how well they are reaching you.

Please write to me, my dearest, at the same address that I gave you for the money, sending a letter with all your news: Kansk, Krasnoiarsk region, the city hospital, Agafia Petrovna Kurmelev, for Arsenii Ivanovich. I visit them daily.

My plans now are as follows:

I will get out of here by the end of November and will head to Krasnoiarsk on a commuter train (it leaves here in the evening and arrives in the morning; fifty rubles). A plane ticket from Krasnoiarsk to Riga costs 1,120 rubles. You change planes in Moscow. It takes eighteen hours to fly to Moscow and then two and a half to get from

Moscow to Riga. When I think that I am less than a full day of flying away from you, I am overcome by excitement. Lord, is it possible? Less than twenty-four hours will pass, and I will be with my family? [. . .]

Someone who was in Riga recently says that underwear and other small items of clothing are less expensive there than here. I want to sell all my good things. You know what I have here. Write and tell me what I should bring and what I can sell.

I will get about 300 [rubles] for my trip, and I am promised 400 or 500 in recognition of my good work, and then let's assume that you'll send 500. That's enough for the ticket. I already have 500 saved up. If I sell things, that will yield some more (the hot plate, potatoes, lunch coupons . . .). That will cover my travel expenses and immediate needs upon arrival. Thus, everything works out well. I just have to wait a little longer. Lord, will it really happen? I have trouble believing it!

Beginning on November 1, some changes are expected in the country's economy. Perhaps a devaluation of the ruble? That would really confuse my financial calculations . . .[54] Well, it doesn't matter. I will figure things out.

There still is no snow.

I pray for your health, peace, serenity, and happiness and that you, Niushenka, steer the boat safely into harbor. Papa Senia, who always remembers you and who, in his thoughts, is always kissing you and holding you in his arms.

P.S. My lead actor is sick. I have work up to my ears.

---

54. Formakov's comments suggest that even in labor camps rumors swirled in advance of the December 1947 currency reform, despite the Soviet government's efforts to keep plans under wraps. The reform required Soviet citizens to exchange old rubles for new at rates that ranged from one-to-one (for money in savings accounts containing less than 3,000 rubles) to ten-to-one (for cash). Designed to remove vast amounts of money from circulation, decrease demand for goods, and stem inflation, the reform was seen as a precondition for ending the ration card system. Elena Zubova, *Russia after the War: Hopes, Illusions, and Disappointments, 1945–1947*, trans. and ed. Hugh Ragsdale, The New Russian History (Armonk, NY: M. E. Sharpe, 1998), 51–55.

◆ ◆ ◆

Kansk, November 22, 1947[55]
My good, dear family,
My priceless friend Niushenka,
My dear son Dimusha,
My dear daughter Zhenichka,
Incomparable Anna Ananievna,

I write to you in the absolute certainty that this is the *last* letter that I will send you from here. This is a moment to celebrate. If you had told me it would come on June 19, 1941, when I learned of my eight-year sentence and it seemed so unbelievable that I could only laugh, I would not have believed you, but this day has come thanks to God's mercy.

When I telegraphed about the money, I wrote that I would get out on December 6, and that this date had been officially announced to me after the time off my sentence for August and September had been calculated. As far as October goes, I also will get a minimum of thirteen days off my sentence for it, but the commission in charge of calculating time off won't manage to get this calculated in time, so there is almost no hope that my release date will move up any more . . .

As soon as I get out, I will telegraph. Then I will spend about two days selling my things here. In the evening I will get on the commuter train, and then by morning I will be in Krasnoiarsk. There I will board either a plane or an express train. Concerning the plane, yesterday I heard that until the 11th, all air travel is halted. This is unpleasant, and the rush of people after the interruption in service will be terrible. We have a representative there, and one of his comrades from here is going to recommend me to him. If he can't get me on the plane, then he will arrange a ticket for me on the express train. It takes five days to get to Moscow. There I will spend a day on the "transfer," as Professor Iupatov used to say. And then finally, I will be with you. [. . .]

My mood is, as they say here, "suitcase-like" [*chemodannoe*]. That means that all my thoughts are of my departure. The camp boss is

55. Formakov clearly wanted to make this folio letter seem special. It is written on better-quality paper than Formakov usually used, the handwriting is painstakingly neat, and there is a decorative flourish drawn in pen below the salutation. A small bouquet of pressed flowers is inserted at the fold. On the back side of the letter, he doodled a flower and an airplane in flight.

allowing me to stop going to work beginning on December 1, and even now I only make periodic appearances at the office. I am training my successor and also keeping things up to date . . . All that is nonsense. The main thing is [leaving] as soon as possible, just as soon as possible! Kisses, hugs, and my blessing. Yours forever, Senia

1950–1955

Formakov was greeted joyfully when he returned home to his wife and children in Riga in December 1947 and quickly reintegrated himself into family life. For a time, the whole family must have hoped that he had put his troubles behind him. He found work as an economist at a forestry trust and began doing small translations and writing poetry with an eye to reviving his literary career. On September 8, 1949, this brief idyll came to an end. Formakov was arrested on the suspicion that he had written an anonymous anti-Soviet poem that had arrived by mail at his place of employment, despite the fact that he had himself, acting in his capacity as secret-police informant, reported the receipt of the document to the authorities. Following an interrogation attended by V. N. Kozin, deputy minister of state security of the Latvian Soviet Socialist Republic, Formakov signed a statement addressed to A. A. Novik, the minister of state security, in which he "confessed" to writing the anti-Soviet document, supposedly as part of a scheme to bolster his previously weak record as an informer.[1] Taken back to solitary confinement, Formakov tried to slit his wrists with a concealed razor. In subsequent interrogations, he repeatedly repudiated his confession, noting that the session with Kozin had left him distraught and confused and that he had been led to believe he would be pardoned if he signed a formal confession.[2]

1. State Archives of Latvia, f. 1986, op. 2, d. P-1545, ch. 2, ll. 13, 48.
2. Ibid., ll. 48–49.

Aside from this doubtful confession and a handwriting analysis report that was later overturned, no evidence linked Formakov to the anti-Soviet verse, and his investigators ultimately declared that the original charges "could not be fully substantiated."[3] Nonetheless, Formakov was sentenced to a new ten-year term at hard labor for anti-Soviet agitation and propaganda, both for his activities prior to the Soviet takeover of Latvia in June 1940—in other words, for the same "crimes" that had led to his first sentence—and because anti-Soviet material, including copies of his two prewar novels, was found in his apartment during the 1949 search. Formakov served his second sentence at Ozerlag in Taishet, in the Irkutsk region of Siberia, and at Kamyshlag in Omsk, both special camps that allowed inmates very limited correspondence privileges. Inmates could write home just twice a year through the official camp mail system, contingent, of course, on good behavior; they were also much more carefully isolated than those held in regular camps and had fewer opportunities to dispatch illegal letters.

As a result, very few letters survive from Formakov's second term, and many of those that do were written to Formakov by family members as opposed to by him. Although Formakov's beloved wife, Niushenka, formally divorced him during his second term in response to pressure at work, she continued to write to him, posing as her mother (Anna Ananievna Zakaznova) or her sister (Maria Ruta) in order to minimize the risk of discovery. She also sent packages, again under various aliases. Formakov's children also wrote periodically. A sampling of the letters from Formakov's second term that survive in the Hoover Institution Archive is translated here. They provide examples of the kind of letters that were mailed to inmates in labor camps in the late Stalin period and document the continued efforts of the Formakov family to maintain ties despite very real political and social pressures and a horrible domestic tragedy: the death by drowning of Dmitri in 1951. The letters also hint at the changes that followed Stalin's death in March 1953: isolation provisions and limits on correspondence were relaxed even in special camps, which in July 1954 were eliminated as a category when a three-tiered camp regime system (light, general, and strict) was introduced.[4] As the political winds changed and the camp system began to disgorge waves of inmates who met the requirements of amnesty decrees or whose sentences had been overturned by reviewing commissions, families like the Formakovs began to hope: release and rehabilitation both suddenly seemed possible.[5]

3. Ibid., l. 51.

4. Steven A. Barnes, *Death and Redemption: The Gulag and the Shaping of Soviet Society* (Princeton, NJ: Princeton University Press, 2011), 232–33.

5. Ibid., 204–209, 232–53; Miriam Dobson, *Khrushchev's Cold Summer: Gulag Returnees, Crime, and the Fate of Reform after Stalin* (Ithaca, NY: Cornell University Press, 2009).

◆ ◆ ◆

October 14, 1950

Hello, my dearest, deeply beloved papa!

This is the second draft of this letter to you: Mama rejected the first one. I will write everything over from the beginning.

After consulting with Mama, I decided to apply to the Mechanization Department of the Latvian Agricultural Academy. I had to pass six exams: two in literature, one oral and the other written; two in math, one oral and the other written; and also exams in physics and chemistry. The math exams were particularly hard. The teacher was very strict, and our class was very poorly prepared in mathematics. [. . .]

In general, studying is interesting, although a little hard. [. . .] I spend a lot of time doing sketches. For instance, I redid the first sketch six (six!) times. I often have to work until 1:00 a.m. This Sunday I have to do two sketches, recopy several lectures on "description" (that is what we call descriptive geometry), and complete a homework assignment for higher mathematics.

I have joined the union for workers in higher education and academia. I plan to give a lecture at the auto club for the Volunteer Association to Aid the Red Army (DOSARM). Not long ago, at the request of the City Komsomol Committee, I reviewed the work of the political school at the directorate of the Latvian Railway.[6]

Mother bought me textbooks, drawing instrument set no. 14 (there are fourteen instruments in it), a logarithmic ruler, a drawing board, two triangles, a fountain pen, and some standard notebooks. Uncle Iura taught me how to use the logarithmic ruler. I get a stipend of 220 rubles. However, 200 rubles were taken out of it in the first month to cover the tuition for the first semester. In the future, I will get fifty rubles in cash each month from my stipend. Thirty of them will go to covering the cost of transportation [to and from school]. I can do whatever I like with the rest (Mama praises me for carefully managing money).

In general, our mama is a true gem: she never goes anywhere and works extremely hard to provide us with everything we need, often for-

6. The All-Union Leninist Young Communist League, or Komsomol, was a political organization for young people ages fourteen to twenty-eight.

getting about herself. She really loves us and takes care of us. We also love her a great deal. She often cries, but I don't let her do that. [. . .]

Mama treats me like an adult and often asks for my advice. Sometimes she yells at me, but that is quite rare.

We all really love you, our dear, beloved papa. We think about you a lot, remembering the days you spent with us. We will never, ever forget you. [. . .]

I am hunting through some bookstores for some vaudeville collections for you. I have two, and I will send them to you in a package.

Big, big warm hugs and kisses to you. Yours always, Dima, who loves you.

◆ ◆ ◆

Riga, April 1, 1951
Hello, dear Papa!

I send you my best wishes for the upcoming holiday of May 1. I wish you all the best. Everything here is the same. As always, Mama doesn't feel very well. Zhenia continues to do very well in school, and Grandmother is also living about as she was: she spends a day at home and then a day with us. I am continuing my studies.

Right now in Riga they are shooting a new movie: *Podzhigateli voiny* [Instigators of War], which is based on Shpanov's novel *Podzhigateli* [The Instigators] (the only book that I can't seem to get).[7] Riga has returned to 1942–1945. Detachments of SS march through the streets with burning torches, gendarmes fly by on motorcycles, Fascist flags hang from the houses, and the signs are in German. Then the police cordon off the area, the big arc lights and cameras are brought out, the extras appear, and shooting begins. The first scenes that I saw being shot by this group took place by the ministry building across from Gunpowder Tower. Some smoke was emitted, and then three SS men, who were swaying and drunk as lords, appeared out of it (of course, they were pretending). They were bellowing out a song as the cameras rolled. [. . .] So, if you get the movie *Instigators of War* there, you will recognize Riga in the crowd scenes.

7. The film, which was directed by Leo Arnshtam, came under political criticism and its release was delayed until 1957. It ultimately appeared under the title *A History Lesson* (Urok istorii). Ol'ga Dombrovskaia, "Neizvestnaia kinorabota Dmitriia Shostakovicha," *Kino zapiski* 87 (2008): 77–81; http://www.kinozapiski.ru/data/home/articles/attache/77.pdf.

Anna Formakova with her children Dmitri and Evgenia. The inscription on the back reads: "To Arsenii Ivanovich Formakov. The picture was taken June 10, 1951." Arsenii Ivanovich Formakov Papers, Hoover Institution Archive, Box 3.

My academic affairs are unchanged. In the next few days, I plan to take my chemistry final early. Our examination period will be interrupted by military camp, although, it is true, there are rumors that there won't be any camp at all this year. But if it is going to take place, I want to take all my exams and tests before the camp, so that I can just focus on my practical training afterwards. After my practical training, I intend to go with a friend and work as a vehicle-loader to earn enough for a suit and some boots. I also want to buy some skate blades for the skating boots that I have, and then next winter I will be able to skate. I will also have a suit for formal occasions now: Grandmother is remaking your black pants and red and black jacket for me. [. . .]

This winter in Riga was the longest and coldest in thirty or forty years, [. . .] but now it is already spring outside. Everything is melting, and the air is warm and moist. [. . .] As soon as the roads dry, I will begin practical training and will start learning to drive a Pobeda.[8] They have just started putting out a new six-cylinder car called a ZIL. It is something between a Pobeda and a ZIS-11. It costs more than 20,000 and is not just a car: it's a sight to behold! They just haven't appeared in Riga yet, but soon we will have these running on our streets too.

I think that is everything. Big hugs and kisses. Yours, Dima

8. Pobeda (Victory) was an automobile model.

♦ ♦ ♦

January 2, 1952

"Hi, son! Well, turn around and give us a look!"

I would give a great deal to be able to pat you on the shoulder, my splendid Dimusha, ask Taras Bulba's question, look you over from all sides, and then test your strength.[9] Who will prove stronger, I wonder? I am constantly anxious about your health, about the cause and nature of your ailment, and—forgive me!—as old people are wont to do, I pray all the time that you will be healed.[10] That is all I can do. I want to think that you are healthy once again and enterprising, that your mother cannot praise your affection and obedience enough, that your studies haven't suffered too terribly, that you have obtained spiritual equilibrium and no conflicts torment your soul. Vladimir Lenin taught us to "study and keep on studying." The most difficult of all disciplines is to learn to live, to combine the duty that you owe to your family and state with personal needs and desires. It takes years to master this discipline and sometimes people do not absorb its subtleties until the end of their days. "Do not do unto others what you would not wish done unto you!"[11]

I haven't heard anything about you in quite some time. I do not know how your spring exams went, how your summer was, or where you have been since fall.

I could not wish you a happy sixteenth birthday. Let me do that now and hug you and give you a kiss on each cheek.

You are my pride, my hope, the justification and meaning in all these years that I have lived through! With your wealth of natural gifts, you

9. Formakov paraphrases the opening of Gogol's *Taras Bulba:* Gogol's title character, a colorful Cossack chief, greets his two sons upon their return from finishing their education in Kiev, asks about their strange city clothes, and tests their strength by getting into a fist-fight with them. Although Dima died in summer 1951, Formakov's family withheld this news for months, telling him, as this letter makes clear, that Dima had fallen ill and could not write.

10. Note the apologetic tone Formakov uses when mentioning prayer to his son, a Komsomol member. The religious practice would have seemed backwards from a "modern" Soviet point of view and contrasts with the Lenin citation that immediately follows.

11. Formakov cites a Confucian saying that corresponds closely to the Golden Rule.

Camp cultural brigade. 1953–1954. Irkutsk oblast, Shitkinskii region, post office branch Novochunka, P.O. box 215/037. Formakov is on the far right in a dark suit. An asterisk, presumably added by a family member, is over his head. Arsenii Ivanovich Formakov Papers, Hoover Institution Archive, Box 3.

can become an important figure in your native country, as long as you don't, like a negligent gardener, bury them in the ground where they can be of no use to anyone. [. . .]

I couldn't give you or Zhenichka anything for your name days other than words, which seem in my heart inexpressibly passionate, but, when they are poured out on paper, die like a goldfish tossed up on a river bank. [. . .]

Be healthy in spirit and body, and if you can, don't forget the father who loves you so much. Papa

♦ ♦ ♦

Dear Niushenka:[12]

Aside from when I learned of Dima's death, the first letter that you sent me about it, which I just received recently, was the hardest thing I

12. This letter is undated but must have been written in 1952.

have experienced in all these years. You are 100 percent correct when you say that it isn't possible to write about this; we can and should only weep together. But everything else in the letter evokes in me, along with great sorrow (did you really think I wouldn't understand you, my dearest?), the most decided objections. I too cannot write or even think or remember. My face becomes distorted, and so as to avoid howling like a beast, I bite my hand to the point of pain! . . .

But regarding our attitude to what has happened, in my opinion there are only two possible points of view: 1) the person is dead and has disintegrated into constituent elements; he is gone and has dissipated into space; the parts of his body have been carried away by underground streams all around and into the depths, and the emanations of his soul are everywhere, perhaps even here and now with me or in me; 2) "his soul rests in peace" and on the Judgment Day, he will rise just as he was, and he will embrace us as our son in the hour of the Great Reunion, never to be parted again.

It is cruel and incomprehensible and arouses the fury of dissatisfaction, but it is a fact: he exists no longer in the form in which we loved him. And transferring our great love for him to a gravestone, a mound of earth, under which a year ago the material shell that once held his immortal soul was buried, would mean slipping into paganism, exchanging his eternal existence in our mighty memories for stones and flowers and grains of sand. I will tell you straight out that I am not drawn to his grave, because my Dima is with me and in me and *alive as long as I am.*

You, my dearest, in moments of great despair and the maternal grief that knows no comparison, trying somehow to keep your sanity amid the madness of what happened, transferred your great love for your son to the symbolic site of his burial, and the cemetery becomes for you your favorite place to rest with your tears and with the memories that are tormenting you. "We spend every free moment there," Zhenichka writes. Now I will turn to her: "Our happiness is buried there," you write on the photo.[13] *All* of our happiness? And is it really *there*? Think, my darling! We, and first of all you (more than I), have the happiness of having a daughter. What sort of adolescence is this for her: between

13. Formakov's wife wrote this on the photo she sent of her son's grave. Arsenii Ivanovich Formakov Papers, Hoover Institution Archive, Box 3.

the constant requiems and walks to the cemetery? What a summer for a girl! She writes with such triumph about how she managed to drag you to the zoo on May 2. Where else have you been since then, and how many times? Your anchor of salvation and refuge is not a grave. That is just a symbol of our ties with the one who has gone ahead of us to the heavenly abode. Our tie to life is our daughter, our one and only. Dimusha will not help you raise her. Alas! This means that the tasks that he did not manage to complete also fall on you. You are raising our daughter for yourself, for me, and also for Dima. The best flower in his memory will be a ribbon on her braid as opposed to a pot of hydrangeas. He lives, he is with us, he is in us and in her who is now our one and only. In his unforgettable name, I call out to you: turn your attention away from the past and from death's captivity and toward the future of our second child. To life!

She is desperate to play the piano. You could take her sometime this summer to school and show her the notes and finger positions. Let her get at least a little closer to her dream. I think you even still have some sheet music. Let her work with it herself. I spent half a year trying to teach myself the piano. I wrote out mi, so, la, and so forth in pencil. I plugged away with some sheet music . . .

Forgive me for this somber letter. The night is at an end, and I still need to write to Zhenichka. In the name of our eternal love, understand what I have to say only in the best possible sense. I did not mean to offend you. Don't you know that? Be healthy. Yours, Arsenii, Senia

♦ ♦ ♦

Riga, November 17, 1953
Dear Arsenii Ivanovich:

Just today I received the postcard that noted the change in your address. I am happy for the change in your life. It is just unfortunate that you did not receive the two packages that I sent before you left. [. . .] The first contained potatoes that we had grown ourselves, and the second contained onion, garlic, condensed milk, fish oil, vitamins, and good fur mittens. It will be too bad if the second doesn't reach you, and, if it goes astray for long, it will freeze. Can't you make inquiries?

Last week Zhenia sent a long letter to your old address. That's too bad too. The letter was very detailed, but tomorrow I will make her remember it and write it again. I haven't written to you all this time. After everything that happened, my heart hardened and did not open even for letters to you. My life goes on as it has without any big changes. Work, my cares, minor squabbles, tiredness, more tiredness . . . I haven't cried in a long time . . . I cried out all my sorrow in the first year, and now the suffering of other human beings no longer touches me. [. . .]

My vacation is very long this year, from June 10 to August 20. I spent it in Riga. My only real entertainment was a trip to Mezhapark and once to the sea.[14] I spent the rest of the time looking for firewood, painting the furniture (what remains of the old bedroom set), working in the garden, caring for the grave, on kitchen talk (who said what, how they looked—Grandmother takes it all very seriously), cooking—I have gotten so fed up with it all that I could scream. The end result of this kind of vacation is a complete nervous breakdown, disgusting stomach issues, zero acidity, desperate pain. [. . .] But, in general, I don't lose courage [. . .].

I do not murmur [against my fate]. The day after tomorrow he turns eighteen. I will buy flowers for his portrait, and I will turn down the lamp. I will not hold back . . . [. . .]

I have written you a very disjointed letter, but if you have the opportunity to write to me more frequently, then do so. Maybe my letters will become better. It is just such a torment to receive an answer only once a year and to know that perhaps your letter wasn't received . . . I send a warm embrace and wish you health and strength of spirit. Greetings to you from your near and dear. Yours, A. A. Zakaznova[15]

---

14. Mezhapark is a garden suburb of Riga that was a favorite place for outings.

15. Only six letters that are clearly from Anna Ivanovna (Niushenka) to Formakov survive in the Hoover Institution collection. All date to 1953–1955, after the Formakovs' legal divorce. In drafting them, Anna Ivanovna used formal pronouns, sometimes used third-person pronouns to speak about herself, and, in all except one case, signed them either ambiguously (A. Zakaznova) or with the name of her mother (A. A. Zakaznova) or her sister (Maria Ruta). A seventh letter, dated January 2, 1954, is written in very different handwriting but, judging by its contents, also may be from her: perhaps it was dictated to a relative. Only three of Anna Ivanovna's letters, which are dominated by family news and details of daily life, are included here. Arsenii Ivanovich Formakov Papers, Hoover Institution Archive, Box 1, folder 8.

♦ ♦ ♦

Riga, June 27, 1954[16]

Dear Arsenii Ivanovich:

I send you greetings and my heartfelt gratitude for the money sent to us on two occasions. There was no need for you to deprive yourself. As long as I am working, we have what we need for our daily bread, but your money was a support. In compensation, I will send you a package this week, but for now please accept this report on how we are getting on. On the Friday before Trinity, I sent Grandmother off for a two-week vacation in Dvinsk. She has gotten very worn out recently: she was both taking my place in terms of housework and also sewing [. . .] Moreover, she and Marfa haven't been getting along, and she takes that all to heart. It was important that she have some fun, and then Grunia sent a letter, asking her to come and stay and sending money for the trip.

Everything worked out very well. It was Trinity [weekend], and the train fare was taken care of. I baked handheld pies to send with her on the trip. There was a huge crowd at the station. We ran into some acquaintances from Dvinsk and settled Grandmother in with them. The people from Dvinsk were heading back home to perform a Service of Entreaty [*litiia*] on the Trinity Saturday of Remembrance at the graves of their relations. They took spading forks and flowers. This meeting brought up many memories from the distant past and my childhood. How strong this tradition of remembering the departed is among our Dvinsk Old Believers! Many went directly to the cemetery when the train got in and then returned to Riga that same day.

Grandmother's departure just happened to coincide with the twentieth anniversary of the death of Pelageia Kuzminichna, and I also really wanted Grandmother to conduct a Service of Entreaty on her grave and remember Dimochka along with [his other] grandmother and grandfather.[17] For this reason, I sent her on Friday. It has been ten years since I left Dvinsk, and no one has prayed at these graves. On Saturday morning, it was raining when I went to Dimusha's grave. In accordance with the old tradition, I also gave alms to beggars. It was

16. The last page of this letter bears a very clear censorship stamp.
17. Pelageia Kuzminichna was Formakov's mother.

raining lightly, and there were very few people. My soul felt at peace, as if I had done something good. Grandmother was there, and I was here. Tomorrow Grandmother will tell me how it all went (she is coming home in the morning).

I have been on vacation since June 16, but I had to go back for three days: I did some additional work on the 18th, the 21st, and the 22nd. The director was going away to study in Moscow, and some paperwork needed to be finished, but there was no one around to type it up, so I had to do it. I had not done any typing for fourteen years, but it didn't matter. I did as well as those who do it regularly. It turns out that old skills don't die (Pavlov's dynamic stereotype). During the period leading up to my vacation, I worked a great deal. [. . .] I am really tired after this year.

How am I going to spend my vacation, you ask? As usual, in Riga. Our relatives had all hoped to get a dacha together by the seashore this year, but despite all our efforts, nothing came of it. I don't want to go to a house of rest. They say the food is no good and it is loud, but that isn't why I don't want to go. I just don't want to go anywhere at all. I am not good at sitting around and doing nothing. Sometimes it is not bad to sit and look at the sky without thinking about anything or saying anything. This year it has been particularly hard to shift gears and get into vacation mode: from great haste to no need for haste at all.

This year, the spring was very dry, hot, and dusty. The first rain came only on the Saturday before the Feast of Trinity, and I rushed to our garden plot on Monday: Zhenia weeded and I hilled the potatoes. Now, just before Ligo, the rains have started, and it is a little cooler. For some reason, this year I feel the city more than ever before: it feels stuffy to me, the noise annoys me, you can't sit in the room—that's how noisy our street has gotten. On Moskovskaia street you have the trams, and under our windows you have cars. It is enough to drive you mad. It is as though they are driving on your head: the whole building shakes; our windows shake. I have been tolerating it for eight years, but in the ninth it became intolerable. In general, I am thinking of exchanging our apartment. [. . .] It is hard to exchange [space in] an apartment held in common for a private one.[18] If I don't succeed now, I will try

18. In the Soviet Union, multiple families often shared a single "communal" apartment in which the kitchen, bathroom, toilet, and hall were held in common

again next year. I have no desire to leave this neighborhood: there is the school and the cemetery, and Grandmother's chapel—it is all close at hand. [. . .]

Zhenia and Olga Ivanovna sent a letter about her papa to Voroshilov.[19] And then yesterday, when we got your letter dated June 12, she told me, "Papa is coming home. Mama will put on her suit, Papa will put on his brown suit, I will buy them white lilies, and they will head to the registry office (ZAGS)."[20] The dear child can still dream, but I don't believe anyone or anything anymore. The longer I live, the more disillusioned I am with people. I have seen nothing good from them and expect nothing from them. [. . .]

Dear Arsenii Ivanovich, this year I cannot visit you.[21] Our material resources are low, and I am trying to stretch them. I am probably a bad manager: we are always short on funds. This year has been dedicated to getting out of debt and out of hock. My salary is 1,037 rubles. After all the withholding, my take-home pay is 850 rubles. That is not a lot for three people. True, *sometimes* Grandmother earns a bit. We pool our resources, but there are a lot of little expenses, and life isn't cheap. We will use your funds as follows: the hundred rubles that you sent for Zhenia's name day will pay to have a sweater knit for her. Three hundred rubles paid for the material for a new coat—she must have it by winter. She has outgrown everything. A hundred rubles went to getting a dress made. (It has been remade three times and now is ending its existence. The sleeves have been cut off, and now it is being used as a summer dress.) Sixty rubles went to an apron. One hundred and twenty rubles went to me for a black work smock (I wore mine for three years both as mourning clothes and at work, and it is falling apart and can now only be worn at home or in the garden). The rest of the

---

and each family had only a room or two of private living space. Such living space was less valuable than private apartments, so residents of communal apartments like the Formakovs could not easily exchange their rooms for something better.

19. The letter Zhenia sent Kliment Voroshilov, the chairman of the Presidium of the Supreme Soviet, on June 22, 1954, requesting clemency for her father, survives in Formakov's criminal case file: State Archives of Latvia, f. 1986, op. 1, d. P-1545, ch. 2, l. 127.

20. Soviet families went to registry offices to marry.

21. There is no evidence that any of Formakov's relations visited him during either of his camp sentences.

money will go to Zhenia for school shoes. This year we need to fit ourselves out a bit, because we have started to get pretty tattered despite all my efforts to dress us well, and also to be careful with our clothing and neat. So now I can't even think about train fare. I will deal with our debt and get us properly dressed. I want to sell my "dowry" bedspread and get myself some new teeth put in. All this time we have managed to hang on because there was something to sell. Everything was gone, and then, over the last three years, we got into debt. This year I will get us out of it. My pay will go up next year: I will be working with the more advanced grades and will be getting extra pay for serving as a homeroom teacher and checking their notebooks. That will help us get out from under. My current position as deputy has really helped me. It cleaned my reputation up significantly. I gave Zhenia my little watch. She liked it a lot.

I have written such a long letter. Don't think that I have become completely illiterate in my old age just because I am not indenting.[22] That is just to economize. I send you a photograph that we took ourselves. We plan to have pictures taken by a professional, and I will send them when we do. I wish you health and good spirits. Yours, A. Zakaznova

♦ ♦ ♦

Riga, September 26[, 1955][23]
Dear Arsenii Ivanovich:

Ananievna rarely writes to you and your daughter is always busy, so I will have to bring you up to date today. Our life races along very, very quickly, but is rather grey, with no great sorrows but also very little joy. Grandmother has really begun to go downhill: she is having trouble with her vision, her kidneys, and her bladder. In part, it's her daughter's fault for not taking her to the clinic, but she needs to force her: Grandmother is stubborn, after all, and doesn't listen to good advice. I tell her not to use so much salt, and that she shouldn't eat spicy food, but she does what she wants, and then, in the end, she declines. [. . .]

Zhenia is studying a great deal now and spends so much time at her lessons that she does not have enough time for walks. She has even

22. The original letter is tightly written, with few indents.
23. There are camp censorship stamps on this letter.

Arsenii Ivanovich Formakov. The inscription on the back reads: "To dearest Niusha, my constant friend in life. From Senia, who will always be in her debt. July 1, 1955." Arsenii Ivanovich Formakov Papers, Hoover Institution Archive, Box 3.

gotten pale. She is trying to get all As. Things don't come as easily for her as they did for Dimusha, but she gets through on her stubbornness and determination. [. . .]

Niusha's life has not really changed. Now she has twenty-three lessons at school instead of the usual twenty-six to twenty-seven. Three of her classes were cut. It is too bad: she would have earned a lot, and then also, the director doesn't hesitate to reproach her for the fact that she is supposed to be doing the work of a position and a half but is four lessons short of this. [. . .]

I saw Arkadii's wife. His illness worries her. Many people are getting better already, but it still isn't clear when he will get out of bed. She really misses him. [. . .][24]

Greetings to you from all those at home. I press your hand warmly and wish you all the best. M. Ruta

24. During this period, Formakov wrote to his wife using the name "Arkadii." By illness, Formakov's wife means his imprisonment. Many inmates were being released from the Gulag by this time. She wonders when her husband will at last be free.

♦ ♦ ♦

To: Moscow, The Lenin Pedagogical Institute
Correspondence Department for Speech Pathology
For Anna Formakova[25]

From: Omsk 6/282 23 22 2300

Arkadii has been completely rehabilitated.[26] Leaving Friday train 97 car 11. Meet at Kazan station. Senia

25. The postmark on the back is too faint to be legible, but this telegram clearly dates from July 1955, when Formakov was finally released from his second camp term. A note in pencil on the back notes that "Arkadii = Arsenii Formakov, for secrecy." Note that in this telegram Formakov uses his wife's married name "Formakova," even as he continues to reference himself as "Arkadii."

26. In fact, perhaps due to a paperwork error introduced in the rush to review sentences in the early post-Stalin period, Formakov was only rehabilitated from his 1949 charges. His 1955 release papers reference only his 1949 sentence and note that he has "no prior convictions." During the late 1950s and the 1960s, Formakov repeatedly appealed for rehabilitation from his first sentence, but without success. Arsenii Ivanovich Formakov Papers, Hoover Institution Archive, Box 2, folder 12; State Archives of Latvia, f. 1986, op. 1, d. P-1545, ch. 1, ll. 46–174.

Appendix
Letters from Aleksandr Solzhenitsyn

Available sources provide only limited information about Formakov's life following his release from his second labor camp sentence in 1955. Again greeted joyfully by his family, Formakov remarried his beloved Niushenka and devoted himself to Evgenia, the daughter he referred to as his "one and only." He translated Latvian literature into Russian and wrote radio plays and a memoir that focused on his contacts with the poet Igor Severianin, ultimately earning membership in the Latvian branch of the Union of Soviet Writers. He also quietly shared copies of poems that he wrote while serving his two labor camp sentences in Siberia with old friends such as the modernist poet Boris Pravdin, provided testimony on his labor camp experiences to Aleksandr Solzhenitsyn, who was gathering material for *The Gulag Archipelago,* and wrote a lightly fictionalized camp memoir that remained unpublished. Frustrated that his 1940 conviction remained standing, limiting both his pension and his ability to publish, Formakov petitioned unsuccessfully for full rehabilitation in 1964, protesting that it was unfair to retroactively apply Soviet laws on anti-Soviet agitation and propaganda to acts committed in Latvia during the bourgeois period and vigorously defending both his work with Sokol and his journalistic activities as fundamentally apolitical. Formakov's service as a secret-police informant is never mentioned in the documentation in Formakov's criminal case file that is associated with this appeal; available sources do not allow us to determine whether or not he continued to make reports after 1949.[1]

1. State Archives of Latvia, f. 1986, op. 2, d. P-1545, ch. 1, ll. 46–174.

The letters that Solzhenitsyn sent to Formakov between 1963 and 1965 suggest a warm relationship devoid of any suspicion. They are included here both because of their importance in documenting Formakov's contacts with Solzhenitsyn and his contributions as a witness to *The Gulag Archipelago,* and because of their obvious historical value for understanding one of the most productive and important periods in Solzhenitsyn's life. When Solzhenitsyn began writing to Formakov in January 1963, *One Day in the Life of Ivan Denisovich* had just appeared in the literary journal *Novyi mir* (New World) to widespread acclaim, and he was regularly traveling through the Soviet Union to meet with labor camp survivors and collect information for *The Gulag Archipelago.* By the end of their correspondence, Nikita Khrushchev had been forced from power, the tides had turned against destalinization, and Solzhenitsyn found himself under increasing political pressure and unable to publish in the Soviet Union. The brief thaw that had allowed works exposing the horrors of the Stalinist gulag to appear legally in the Soviet Union had come to an end.

♦ ♦ ♦

January 14, 1963
Dear Arsenii Ivanovich:

I was very glad to receive your letter of January 4, although it brought unpleasant news about your health. I imagine what you had to bear when they gave you the wrong blood type (even a slight incompatibility elicits a violent reaction, as I saw more often than I care to recall in the cancer institute in Tashkent, where many people, including myself, received transfusions). With all my heart, I hope that you get better soon!

It seems that we have had a misunderstanding. I thought that K—k already told you about me the first time, and you just didn't want to answer me.[2] For that reason, when I visited your house, I didn't press my address on you, because that would have obliged you to answer.[3]

2. Possibly Konstantin Iosifovich Kravchenok. On Solzhenitsyn's Latvian acquaintances, see Boris Ravdin, "A. I. Solzhenitsyn i Latviia: Nametki k perechniu znakomykh i neznakomykh imen: 1944–1974," *Rizhskii al'manakh* 5, no. 10 (2014): 206–30. This article includes the first Russian-language publication of Solzhenitsyn's letters to Formakov.

3. Presumably this visit took place during Solzhenitsyn's stay in Riga in summer 1962. Nadezhda Feldman-Kravchenok, "Po ozeru Seliger s A. I. Solzhenitsynym," *Daugava,* no. 4 (1996); http://www.russkije.lv/ru/journalism/read/feldman-kravchenko-ozero-pub/.

Anyway, in the summer there was already a high probability that my novella would appear, and I reckoned that you would be able to find me if you wanted to.[4] That is indeed what happened. But let's not, Arsenii Ivanovich, remember things that did not fully ripen or that were perhaps left too long on the vine and that, in any case, are not suitable for publication. What I have in hand is a novella and two short stories, and perhaps a play, which one theater wants to try to stage.[5]

Of course, correspondence is no substitute for meeting in person. I plan to visit the Baltic region this spring and will find a couple of days for Riga, it seems. Write to me about your summer plans closer to spring. Then I will be very interested in acquainting myself with your work.[6]

By the way, the Estonians are translating my novella. It seems unlikely that the Latvians will get a similar idea, but if they did—you don't translate into Latvian, do you? So I couldn't assist you in any case, correct? . . . It is too bad.

I hope your health improves and wish you good fortune, my long-suffering fellow! I send a warm embrace!

My wife and I send our regards to you and your spouse. Yours, A. Solzh. [. . .]

♦ ♦ ♦

February 26, 1963
Dear Arsenii Ivanovich:

This is the kind of correspondent I am now! I was leafing through a mound of letters and suddenly saw that I had not replied to you (your letter arrived just before I left for Moscow, and I always return from there worn out, and it takes me a long time to get back to normal).

---

4. The work that Solzhenitsyn had anticipated was *One Day in the Life of Ivan Denisovich,* which appeared in the November 1962 issue of *Novyi mir.* Former inmates from all over the Soviet Union wrote to Solzhenitsyn following its publication. G. A. Tiurina, ed., *"Dorogoi Ivan Denisovich . . .": Pis'ma chitatelei, 1962–1964* (Moscow: Russkii Put', 2012).

5. The Sovremennik Theater in Moscow was interested in staging Solzhenitsyn's play *Olen' i shalashovka* (The Love Girl and the Innocent). A. Solzhenitsyn, *The Oak and the Calf: A Memoir* (New York: Harper Colophon Books, 1979), 52–64.

6. Perhaps a reference to Formakov's fictionalized camp memoir, "Byloe."

I am so vexed: what lapse led me to write Johann instead of Ianis?[7] People from the Baltics had already written to me about this, and I had slapped my forehead [in dismay]. The fact that I wasn't writing for publication played a role, and I just wasn't careful enough about such details. Then, when I was preparing the manuscript for publication, I had so many other concerns.

In the same way, working from memory, I changed the real last name of the Latvian "Pul's" to "Kil'gas." There was such a last name in our camp, and I thought it was Latvian.

It is very vexing and not fixable (it is off traversing the world in every translation)!

If *Iv*[*an*] *Den*[*isovich*] is translated in Latvia, I absolutely must correct this! . . .

I understand that "shmoniat'" (to frisk; to search) is formed incorrectly, but people said this too, and it sounds even more repellent. That is why I picked it.

I enclose a picture that is a bit more successful than the one that was in *Lit*[*eraturnaia*] *Rossiia* [Literary Russia].

Have you already gotten a look at my stories?

Thanks so much for the warm invitation. I did not notice the batting factory, but I liked your courtyard a lot.

I don't know, but perhaps I will end up passing through Riga at the end of April or the beginning of May. I will certainly visit you in that case!

Most of all, I wish you perfect health and then progress on your books!

Warmest wishes to you and Anna Ivanovna from Natalia Alekseevna and me. Yours, A.S.

---

7. Formakov apparently commented on the non-Latvian name of Johann Kilgas, a Latvian character in *One Day in the Life of Ivan Denisovich*. In later editions of the novella, Solzhenitsyn corrected the character's name to Ian Kil'digs, which better accorded with Latvian norms. Ravdin, "A. I. Solzhenitsyn i Latviia," 216–18; Solzhenitsyn, *One Day in the Life of Ivan Denisovich*, trans. Ralph Parker (New York: Signet Classics, 1998), 42–58.

◆ ◆ ◆

April 9, 1963

Dear Arsenii Ivanovich:

As always, I answer belatedly. Do I need to beg your forgiveness for this each time?

Of your two poems, we liked the second "Askety my" [We Are Ascetics]—a great deal. It is exceptional in its terseness, its stern spirituality, and its integrity. "Druz'iam" [To My Friends], it would seem to me, lacks this integrity.

Thank you also for the photo.

I am very glad that you liked my stories. One poet, whom I love a great deal and who publishes very little (he is a [former] prisoner too), also saw a link between "Matrena" and Turgenev: he called Matrena "Kalinych in a skirt" and also said that the atmosphere was similar to "Zhivye moshchi" [Living Relic].[8]

The fact that "Matrenin dvor" [Matrena's Home] is being abused so widely right now (in *Sovetskaia Kuban'*, Babaevskii was even in a fury) does not really distress me, since no one is accusing me of writing something that wasn't true.[9] In the two articles that he wrote for *Izvestiia* on March 30 and April 4 (the attentive reader will note a connection between the articles), Poltoratskii not only failed to refute [what I wrote] but even confirmed to a readership of several million that it was all true, even in 1963.[10]

Regarding individual words:

Kleshnit' = to grab with pincers

Podel'chivyi = easily done (it is widely used)

Nabrovyi = with beetling brows

I prefer to use such short words in place of expressions.

---

8. Here Solzhenitsyn discusses reactions to his short story "Matrenin dvor" (Matrena's Home). Kalinych is one of the central characters in the first sketch from Turgenev's *Zapiski okhotnika* (A Hunter's Sketches). "Zhivye moshchi" (Living Relic) is another sketch from the same collection.

9. S. Babaevskii, "Partiia i literatura," *Sovetskaia Kuban'*, March 19, 1963.

10. Most likely, Solzhenitsyn references Viktor Poltoratskii, "Matrenin dvor i ego okrestnosti," *Izvestiia*, March 30, 1963; "Ne stydno li?" *Izvestiia*, April 7, 1963. The truth that Poltoratskii confirms is the spiritual and material poverty of collective farm life.

I heard *soldiaga* myself in 1941.

It's *oslonias' obo chto* [to lean up against]—in contrast to: *otslonit'sia* or *prislonit'sia k chemu* [to pull away from; to lean toward].

Why deprive verbs of simple prefixes? . . .[11]

My plans, Arsenii Ivanovich, are changing. Instead of heading to the Baltics, I am now going across the Oka. I will cut myself off with its flooding and want to spend a month, up to the end of May, on the edge of the forest. Nat[alia] Aleks[eevna] and I plan to spend June in Leningrad, and then in July we will race about the Baltics a bit. At that time, we will visit Riga and you. Will you and Anna Ivanovna be in Riga at that time?

I hope that by that time you can muster perfect health and make progress in your work!

Natalia Alekseevna and I send you, Anna Ivanovna, and your daughter our very best and most cordial wishes! Warmest regards. Yours, A. Solzh.

♦ ♦ ♦

June 26, 196[3?]

Dear Arsenii Ivanovich:

We send our congratulations to your newlyweds and wish them a happy life![12] And we also wish the same to you, the parents. This letter should reach you just before the wedding celebration takes place.

I did not write to you because life was very hectic for me—for two weeks I was caught in the whirl of Moscow. Now I am in Leningrad where it is calmer, but I am at work in reading rooms from morning until evening.

---

11. Solzhenitsyn employed nonstandard vocabulary in his work (archaic word forms, lexical items associated with specific dialects, etc.), with the aim of combating what he saw as the impoverishment of the Russian language. The words he explains here appear in the story "Sluchai na stantsii Kochetovka" (The Incident at Kochetovka Station). A. Solzhenitsyn, "Ne obychai degtem shchi belit' na to smetana," *Literaturnaia gazeta*, November 4, 1965; A. Solzhenitsyn, *Russkii slovar' iazykovogo rasshireniia*, 3rd ed. (Moscow: Russkii Put', 2000); Vera V. Carpovich, *Solzhenitsyn's Peculiar Vocabulary: Russian-English Glossary* (New York: Technical Dictionaries, 1976).

12. Formakov's daughter Zhenia was getting married.

We plan to arrive in Riga on the 14th or 15th of July. We have been offered an apartment on Suvorov street.[13] The street itself is horrible, but if the apartment turns out to be entirely *vacant,* that would be more convenient, since we won't be in anyone's way. We are also keeping your invitation in mind.

Really, we won't be in Riga very long. We also need to make two radial trips to quiet places in the countryside and live there a while. We need to leave no later than the 25th.

I wholeheartedly affirm your right to use a typewriter when drafting letters. After all, bad handwriting always creates a lot of bother for the reader.

Excuse me for how brief this is. I am always rushing.

And so, N.A. and I send our very best wishes to you all. We hope to see you soon!

Yours, A.I.

♦ ♦ ♦

October 10, 1963
Dear Anna Ivanovna and Arsenii Ivanovich:

You, of course, understand that it is not forgetfulness or carelessness that has prevented me from writing to you earlier, but the tempo of life and the multitude of things that need to be done, which distract me. N.A. and I still have the warmest, most heartfelt memories of our visit with you, and we are just sorry that we saw you so little and were in such a rush. Your mutual harmony and accord, which you do not find in every family, left us with particularly positive memories.

After leaving Riga, we hurriedly set off on a bicycle trip: from Riazan to Iasnaia Poliana, Kulikovo field, and the river Ranova.[14] The trip was a great success and left vivid impressions.

And then, from the end of August until very recently, I again stayed in the forest across the Oka, working.

13. Solzhenitsyn stayed with the Naumov family on Suvorov street for several days in this period. For an interview with V. Naumov describing this visit, see Ravdin, "A. I. Solzhenitsyn i Latviia," 214.

14. For a description of this trip, see Michael Scammell, *Solzhenitsyn: A Biography* (New York: W. W. Norton, 1984), 477–78.

Now I am getting ready to head to Rostov na Donu (N[atalia] A[lekseevna] is already teaching and can't go).

In January and February I plan to be in Leningrad.

So, that is how my life is going . . . I continue to get a lot of letters, and newspapers print scathing articles. Issue no. 10 of *Oktiabr'* [October] was thuggish in its indecency, but, inasmuch as it is all lies, I don't take it to heart.[15] I am more sensitive to certain letters from friends who say that particularly the first part of "Dlia pol'zy dela" [For the Good of the Cause] seems rushed and lacks polish, which is true.

I don't know when I will again be able to publish in *Novyi mir.*[16]

How are you? How is your health? And your work? How has the young couple gotten settled in and how are they doing?

Our warmest and most sincere wishes to you! Yours, N.A. and A.I.

P.S. I am writing the address out by hand just so that Ars[enii] Iv[anovich] doesn't feel as though I am trying to "prick his conscience" with a typed address. Use a typewriter! I have no objections!

♦ ♦ ♦

December 27, 1964
Dear Arsenii Ivanovich:

For some reason, I have not received word from you in a long time, but this is probably my fault: I probably did not answer you in a timely fashion. I very much hope that this is the only reason, and that there isn't anything wrong.

Natalia Alekseevna and I sincerely wish you and Anna Ivanovna a happy New Year, health, good fortune, peace in your hearts, and no dark clouds outside.

We continue to live as before, except for the fact, perhaps, that we have purchased a Moskvich and have learned to drive it (I don't know if I wrote to you about that). That is a source of pleasure and, more

15. Solzhenitsyn is referring to V. Chalmaev's critical review of "Matrenin dvor" and "Dlia pol'zy dela": "'Sviatye' i 'Besy,'" *Oktiabr'*, no. 10 (1963): 215–17.

16. By October 1963 the brief period of liberalization that followed the Twenty-Second Party Congress was coming to an end. Solzhenitsyn struggled to get work into print, and his relationship with the editors at *Novyi mir* was souring. Solzhenitsyn, *The Oak and the Calf,* 64–67; Scammell, *Solzhenitsyn,* 464–79.

important, makes it easier to get about. Last summer we went to Belorussia. We settled ourselves in near a pretty lake in the forest, set up a tent, made a table in the woods, and just lived like that (it is great that you can carry a good deal of equipment and groceries in the car). I worked really well there.

There is no way to explain my literary affairs briefly. In general, it seems unlikely that I will be able to publish anything in *Novyi mir* in 1965, but it is possible that a Moscow theater will put on my play.[17]

We very much would like to hear about you. Please don't be angry and write back.

How are your young people?

Are your musical shows being broadcast, Arsenii Ivanovich?[18]

I send my warmest regards! Yours, A. Solzh.

♦ ♦ ♦

March 31, 1965

Dear Arsenii Ivanovich:

I am not sure how soon I would have answered your January letter, but an opportunity has arisen to travel to Riga (by Moskvich) in the second half of May. If that takes place, then I can for now evade the fateful questions that you posed to me.[19]

I heard that Vania will fulfill his service obligation a year earlier than you expected.[20] Does that mean the young couple's separation will be shorter?

We will write more when the details of our visit to Riga are clearer.

I apologize for sending such a brief note for now.

N[atalia] A[lekseevna] and I wish Anna Ivanovna and you good health, the very best health, and vitality!

Also, for now don't say anything about our visit to *any* of our mutual acquaintances, all right?

17. Probably a reference to efforts to stage *Svecha na vetru* (A Candle in the Wind). Scammell, *Solzhenitsyn*, 506.

18. A reference to the radio plays about classical music and composers that Formakov was writing in this period.

19. In "Po ozeru Seliger s A. I. Solzhenitsyn," Feldman-Kravchenok recalls Solzhenitsyn's 1965 visit to Riga and confirms that he met Formakov.

20. Vania is Formakov's son-in-law.

I also have one question that is far from idle: could we park our car in your courtyard, by which I mean could we do so without eliciting any complaints from the neighbors, and would it be safe during the day without anyone watching it? (At night we would sleep in it.) We would be talking about two days or so. Warmest regards. Yours, A.S.

Index

Page numbers in *italics* indicate illustrations